T0287895

Jane Addams and the Practice of Democracy

Jane Addams and the Practice of Democracy

Edited by
MARILYN FISCHER,
CAROL NACKENOFF,
AND WENDY CHMIELEWSKI

UNIVERSITY OF ILLINOIS PRESS
Urbana and Chicago

∞ This book is printed on acid-free paper.

Library of Congress Cataloging-in-Publication Data
Jane Addams and the practice of democracy / edited by
Marilyn Fischer, Carol Nackenoff, and Wendy Chmielewski.
p. cm.
Chapters based on presentations at two conferences held in 2002.
Includes bibliographical references and index.
ISBN 978-0-252-03406-0 (cloth : alk. paper) —
ISBN 978-0-252-07612-1 pbk. : alk. paper)
1. Addams, Jane, 1860–1935—Congresses. 2. Women social
workers—United States—Biography—Congresses.
3. Women social reformers—United States—Biography—
Congresses. 4. Democracy—Congresses. 5. Civil society—
Congresses.
I. Fischer, Marilyn. II. Nackenoff, Carol.
III. Chmielewski, Wendy E.
HV28.A35J36 2009
361.92—dc22 [B] 2008032920

Contents

Acknowledgments

Jane Addams (1860–1935), an extraordinary activist and thinker in many ways ahead of her time, has been speaking to many of us. Two interdisciplinary conferences in 2002 brought together a wide range of scholars who have been drawn to Addams. The symposium "Rediscovering Jane Addams" was held at Swarthmore College on February 1–2, 2002, with twenty presenters and discussants. The second conference, "Exploring Jane Addams," was held at the University of Dayton on November 8–9, 2002, with twenty-seven presenters. The chapters in this volume grew out of these conferences.

We would like to thank the William J. Cooper Foundation, the D'Olier Foundation, and the William I. Hull Fund for their generous support of the Swarthmore symposium. This event also received support from the Swarthmore College Peace Collection, the Departments of Political Science and History, the Women's Studies Program, the Office of the President, and the Forum for Free Speech. Without the superb and tireless assistance of Michelle Ciarlo-Hayes, this symposium would not have been possible. We also thank the late Judy Lord, administrative assistant for the Cooper Foundation, for all her assistance. The University of Dayton conference was the twenty-ninth annual Richard R. Baker Philosophy Colloquium. We are grateful for additional financial support for this colloquium from the Departments of Philosophy, History, and Sociology/Anthropology/Social Work, and from the American Studies Program and the School of Education at the University of Dayton. We also thank Linda McKinley, the Philosophy Department administrative assistant, who devoted much time and skill to organizing the conference, and Cindy King, who prepared this manuscript for publication with a keen eye and great care. We thank Joan Catapano, associate director and editor in chief of the University of Illinois Press, who has been interested in this project from its inception and attended both conferences. We also thank the anonymous reviewers from the University of Illinois Press for their assistance in making *Jane Addams and the Practice of Democracy* a better book.

Marilyn Fischer
Carol Nackenoff
Wendy Chmielewski

Introduction

In 2006, the General Assembly of the State of Illinois designated December 10 Jane Addams Day, "a day to remember her and teach about her great accomplishments, compassion, and social conscience."[1] In the past few decades, interest in Jane Addams has grown among scholars, activists, and the general public. In addition to remembering her "accomplishments, compassion, and social conscience," scholars today are exploring her intellect and her powers as a theorist of democracy. Bringing recent scholarly methodologies and resources to their work, these scholars are finding startlingly fresh resources in Addams's life and thought, applicable to contemporary challenges of war and peace, social and economic inequalities, and the responsibilities of citizenship.

By focusing on Addams as a theorist and an intellectual, this volume contributes to this new scholarship. Addams's life, actions, and writings defy simple disciplinary classification, as does human experience itself. Thus, it is appropriate that this volume be multidisciplinary in character. New scholarship on Addams may be found in many disciplines ranging from the social sciences, such as sociology and political science, to fields in the humanities, including history, philosophy, and literature. Research on Addams also fits comfortably in inherently cross-disciplinary fields such as women and gender studies, peace studies, international relations theory, queer theory, and performance theory.

Addams's primary commitment was to the theory and practice of democracy. Classical political and economic liberalism, with their stress on the autonomous individual, did not take social interdependencies adequately into account, and so were ill-suited, Addams believed, for a rapidly industrializing, urban society. She was particularly concerned that new immigrants be able to contribute their cultural inheritance and experiential knowledge to the practice of democracy. Addams's lifelong project of constructing a theory and practice of social democracy, grounded in concrete experience and built through sympathetic understanding, is one that still vigorously engages scholars and social policy makers.

Emphasizing the centrality of lived experience for theorizing, Addams was an important precursor of a later generation of scholars who have emphasized the situatedness and contingency of knowledge. Like John Dewey, G. H. Mead, and other classical American pragmatists with whom she worked, Addams defined experience in terms of people's concrete, day-by-day interactions, immersed in their social and physical environment. For Addams, theories were ways of interpreting and navigating experience. The worth of these theories is tested by how well they illuminate that experience. Addams believed the goal and final test for all theories is their contribution to the practice of democracy. Emerging from particular histories, forging particular futures, persons and environment continually influence and change each other. Because each individual's situations and experiences differ, Addams believed that each person's understanding of and contribution to knowledge also differs.

In her writings, her activism with Hull-House, the Women's International League for Peace and Freedom (WILPF), and countless voluntary organizations, Addams gave central focus to the experiences of women and resisted identification with traditional gender roles. There was a complementary transformation by the women residents of Hull-House, where they created a practical and philosophical community. Addams focused closely on the concerns and perspectives of poor and immigrant women and men who had little political power or voice in an industrializing democracy. She insisted that the voices and experiences of those whose knowledge had been discounted by dominant paradigms and political institutions be added to create the kind of civic citizenship and democracy she envisioned. To achieve all this became "women's business," and in the process helped transform social policy.

Transforming gender expectations was only one of the ways in which Addams questioned conventions. She and her colleagues also reconfigured conceptions of citizenship and the role of the state. Many progressive scholars today are suspicious about state involvement because of the way it has sometimes been used coercively to inscribe norms and conventions in social policy, based on a view that ignores the very cultural diversity Addams found so valuable. Turning back to Addams can offer our generation new visions of the state, the role of citizens in transforming the state, and hope for the role that a transformed state can play as a vehicle for supporting different forms of human attachment and obligation.[2]

For many of the authors in *Jane Addams and the Practice of Democracy,* Addams's life and work provide this progressive model. The authors presented here engage Addams in transhistorical conversations using the intellectual developments and methodological shifts in their own disciplines that have given Addams's concerns and approaches new currency. Addams models for us how to transcend traditional disciplinary boundaries and how to make daily experience, and the human care it requires, central to our theorizing.

Addams was born in 1860 in the small midwestern town of Cedarville, Illinois. She entered a world of increasing industrialization and urbanization, innovations in communication and transportation, growing imperialism, and class, racial, and ethnic tensions. She crafted and refined her theory and practice of democracy first at Hull-House in Chicago and ultimately through her work on the international stage. Addams lived until 1935, long enough to see both the shifts in U.S. social policy of the New Deal and the rise of dictatorships in Germany, Italy, and the Soviet Union, as well as the prospect of a second world war.

Biographies of Addams first began to appear soon after her death in 1935. James Weber Linn, Addams's nephew, wrote the first full biography, published some months after Addams's death.[3] Twenty years later artist and peace activist Violet Oakley produced *Cathedral of Compassion,* a biographical play, commissioned by the Women's International League for Peace and Freedom, to highlight Addams's internationalist contributions.[4] In 1965 Christopher Lasch published *The Social Thought of Jane Addams,* an edited volume of excerpts from Addams's writings. Lasch bemoaned the popular idealization of Addams as a sort of American saint and clearly stated that his goal was to place Addams in the historical context of American political and intellectual reform. Lasch identified Addams as a superb writer, an activist, accomplished organizer, and as a theorist and intellectual of originality and daring.[5] By including a range of her writings on immigration, urbanization, democracy and education, social reform, and peace in his book, Lasch attempted to convey the breadth and depth of Addams's ideas on the transformation of American democracy. John C. Farrell's 1967 work, *Beloved Lady : a History of Jane Addams's Ideas on Reform and Peace,* though far more biographical in structure than Lasch's book, also attempted a broad survey of Addams's ideas on social policy and peace based on her writings.[6] In this work, Farrell relied primarily upon Addams's published writings.

In 1973 Allen F. Davis's *American Heroine: The Life and Legend of Jane Addams* was published.[7] This was the first, and remains, the most complete scholarly treatment of Addams's life. Davis presents Addams's entire career chronologically, including significant consideration of her engagement with internationalism and peace work during her final twenty years. His book makes good use of Addams's correspondence and other primary sources. This work is a valuable, though dated, source of information about, and presentation of, Addams's role in American history. In his preface, Davis acknowledges the influence of "the American studies, symbol-and-myth school of historiography."[8] He is most interested in the relation between the legend of Jane Addams that evolved during her lifetime and the actual facts of her life, including her own contributions to the creation of that legend. Accordingly, Davis gives a great deal of attention to the publicity that surrounded Addams and Hull-House. He is also particularly interested in the ways in which Addams's personality shaped her achievements. For Davis, Addams epitomizes her era, and while acknowledging Addams's skills as a shrewd administrator, he presents her primarily as a popularizer of others' ideas and as a compromiser, not as an original thinker.[9]

Another study in this same period influenced scholarly perceptions of Addams's place in the American political tradition. At a time when challenges were being posed to the contention that there was a liberal consensus in America that embraced a kind of uniformity of thought, Daniel Levine's 1971 *Jane Addams and the Liberal Tradition* locates Addams and fellow progressive reformers within liberalism, but not as part of the rational, Lockean, individualistic tradition.[10] Addams and her fellow progressives pressed for rapid social and political change; their social reform agenda represented a transition between the era of laissez-faire American liberalism and the semi-welfare state of the New Deal era. In this work that is partly chronological and partly thematic, Levine sees Addams not as an original thinker but rather as someone who played a vital role of persuader in rousing a new conscience. She was a crucial leader in convincing Americans that new urban dwellers and factory workers should be included in the scope of those who "matter" in the social system.

Though not an extensive, nor a biographical, piece on Addams, Blanche Wiesen Cook's article, "Female Support Networks and Political Activism: Lillian Wald, Crystal Eastman, Emma Goldman," made an important contribution in changing perceptions of Addams and other women in social reform. Cook explored how the emotional and sexual choices of these reforming women, and the loving, supportive networks they developed in social settlements and in reform politics, were crucial to their reform work and their creation of new ideas about democracy. Using the new and developing historiography of women's history and early queer history, Cook attacked earlier interpretations of Addams, citing historian William O'Neill's dismissal of Addams's intellectual contributions because of her choice not to marry. Cook's 1977 article was a crucial and formative step in the feminist study of Addams and her period.[11]

Jean Bethke Elshtain's 2002 biographical project, *Jane Addams and the Dream of American Democracy,* helped bring Addams to the attention of a wider audience and was the first work to consider feminist scholarship in evaluating Addams's life. Elshtain's early work on women in social and political thought, *Public Man, Private Woman,* had made a mark among feminist scholars.[12] Elshtain both challenged the limits placed upon women by their relegation to the private sphere and offered a critique of rationalistic values of the public sphere based on her appreciation of particularized and concrete values nurtured in the private sphere. Much would be lost to ethics and politics, she contended, if women simply attempted to emulate men and abandoned care of the private sphere and its values. This concern carried over into Elshtain's treatment of Addams and helped explain her attraction to Addams as a biographical subject. Elshtain formed a personal bond with Addams in thinking that women have special resources to bring to bear in the world of politics and international relations.[13] She also appreciated that Addams had a strong sense of the duties and responsibilities binding members of the political community, and did not simply embrace an agenda based on individual rights.

Yet Elshtain's work revealed sharp differences among feminist scholars, both in terms of how to think about the moral resources of women and how to write women's experiences into studies of political development. Elshtain insisted that Addams saw women's difference in essentialist terms, based in the corporeality and fecundity of the female body. An embodied Jane Addams for Elshtain is a timeless woman bringing near-primordial knowledge to bear on contemporary problems. This is in stark contrast to the recent feminist scholars who, in examining embodied subjects, have maintained that gender, home, family, and nurture are constantly being redefined. Examination of sexuality with a range of same-gender relationships has yielded new understandings of how Addams and her colleagues interacted with culture, polity, and society. Along with postmodernists and poststructuralists, many feminists now assert the situatedness and contingency of knowledge. Even though Addams clearly adopted the language of maternalism during the years this language became central to the suffrage struggle, recent scholars have been arguing against essentialist understandings of Addams's feminism.[14]

Elshtain both depoliticized and deradicalized the historical Jane Addams and redeployed her for particular contemporary political purposes. At times Elshtain used Addams as a mere backdrop for reflections on her own political preoccupations, presenting Addams as the advocate of the nuclear family, of private philanthropy, and of antistatist solutions to modern social problems.[15] As one critic noted, "Addams' public support for the New Deal after 1933—including for the National Recovery Administration, Social Security, public works and public housing—goes altogether unmentioned." This critic goes on to note that Elshtain depicted Addams as a rather self-sufficient and autonomous figure despite the fact that she "moved so constantly, even dependently, within circles of action and association with other progressive women."[16]

Two recent biographies by Victoria Brown (2004) and Louise W. Knight (2005) challenge Davis's and Levine's images of Addams, presenting her instead as a powerful intellect, an original theorist, and a creative literary figure.[17] They use explicitly feminist criteria in evaluating Addams's life and contributions, and are attentive to specific challenges Addams faced as a woman. These biographies are especially noteworthy for breaking decisively from monographs on Addams that contained little if any original research. Drawing heavily on Addams's letters and papers available through the *Jane Addams Papers* and benefiting from the last thirty years of social historical research, these biographies are richly focused on the unfolding story of Addams's life. They are attentive to immigration and labor issues and draw upon decades of women's history, placing Addams solidly within the national debates over women's lives and the conflicts they faced as private and public actors in the Gilded Age and Progressive Era. These biographies move carefully through Addams's childhood and young adulthood and cover approximately the first half of her life.

Victoria Brown is among those recent historians who, influenced by feminist scholarship, postmodern theory, and by a burgeoning literature on representation, recognize pitfalls in overreliance on authors' own intentions and perceptions. *The Education of Jane Addams* challenges the accuracy of Addams's account of her life presented in *Twenty Years at Hull- House,* bringing into question Elshtain's heavy reliance on that resource. Instead, Brown utilizes a far broader array of resources and provides an in-depth reading of them. Her biography walks the reader through Addams's formative years, her time at Rockford Seminary, and the eight years following, before founding Hull-House. Brown argues that rather than being a "snare of preparation," as Addams claimed, that time enabled her to grow intellectually and emotionally away from her aloofness and her assumptions of masculine heroism, toward an appreciation of female support networks and cross-class mutuality. Brown gives special attention to Addams's quest for a spirituality different from that offered by organized religion or the Social Gospel movement of the time.

Louise W. Knight, in *Citizen: Jane Addams and the Struggle for Democracy*, gives close analyses of Addams's writings and speeches in light of the books she read, and shows how Addams used these resources to test and interpret her own direct, personal experiences. Using this method, Knight demonstrates Addams' stepwise movement from her father's individualistic, absolutist ethics and paternalistic duty of benevolence to a pragmatist, cooperative understanding of social democracy. Through her examination of Addams's speeches, Knight also gives new scrutiny to Addams's rhetorical skills.

Knight's and Brown's biographies demonstrate how Addams's conception of social democracy was tough, sophisticated, and hard-won, emotionally, intellectually, and experientially. They show clearly that Addams should not be described as a compromiser, but that in her commitment to process and to the theory of cooperation, she demonstrated both mutuality and the utmost respect for the dignity of all parties.

Katherine Joslin has offered a literary biography in *Jane Addams: A Writer's Life* (2004).[18] Working through Addams's lifetime of writings, Joslin analyzes Addams's literary styles in relation to the work of other writers of the time. She is thus able to demonstrate how Addams rejected academic writing, crafting her own more lyrical, imaginative style. Addams experimented with a range of literary genres, from naturalism to modernism, and used great skill in blending voices dialogically, interweaving her own with those of her immigrant neighbors. Joslin sees Addams as an author whose writings crossed disciplinary boundaries and as a figure who herself crossed boundaries of gender, race, ethnicity, and class.[19]

Recent scholars have benefited greatly from the wider accessibility of primary source material on Addams. The University of Illinois Press has reissued the majority of Addams's own books, with new introductory essays by leading scholars in history, philosophy, literature, and political science. Marilyn Fischer and Judy Whipps edited a four-volume collection entitled *Jane Addams's Writings on Peace*.[20] Jean Bethke Elshtain's *The Jane Addams Reader* appeared in 2002.[21]

Primary materials are also available on microfilm and the Internet. Several of Addams's books can be found on the World Wide Web.[22] Mary Lynn McCree Bryan and an editorial team assembled the eighty-two–reel microfilm collection, *The Jane Addams Papers,* and published an essential guide to it, *The Jane Addams Papers: A Comprehensive Guide.*[23] Bryan and coeditor Barbara Bair published the first print volume from this project, *The Selected Papers of Jane Addams, 1860–81.*[24] Now available on the World Wide Web are finding aids for manuscript collections about Addams, her colleagues, Hull-House, and the Women's International League for Peace and Freedom from the Swarthmore College Peace Collection and the Jane Addams Memorial Collection of the University of Illinois at Chicago Library.[25]

Using a rich array of available resources and contemporary methodologies from many disciplines, this volume's authors give a fresh appraisal of Addams as a theorist and practitioner of democracy. Section I contains essays on Addams's experiential methodology, explaining and illustrating how she used experience to generate and test theory. Essays in Section II examine how Addams used experiences, particularly those of women, the poor, and immigrants, to develop new visions of democratic citizenship for American politics. Essays in Section III consider the linkages between these new visions and Addams's understanding of social justice, internationalism, and peace.

Section I: Addams's Experiential Method

Addams came to "learn from life itself." She had to work her way to pragmatism and to her own conception of social democracy. Over time, Addams developed the sensibilities that enabled her to appreciate the rich minutiae of daily experience, and to reflect on how these perceptions could shape and test theory. The first essay in this section gives an account of how the young Addams used religious questioning to attain these sensibilities. The second shows how a mature Addams exercised these capacities on a most difficult challenge, that of justifying her pacifism during World War I.

In "The Sermon of the Deed: Jane Addams's Spiritual Evolution," historian Victoria Bissell Brown traces Addams's engagement with religious questions from her childhood until she founded Hull-House at age twenty-nine. Two youthful aspirations guided her search for "the sermon of the deed": her desire to contribute to the common good in the public arena, and her longing for spiritual meaning. Gendered expectations of that time and Protestant orthodoxy complicated the quest for Addams and other young college women of her generation. "Public duty" was commonly understood as masculine and heroic; women were expected to seek private fulfillment in lives of selfless devotion to family. Addams's ambition, intellectual acumen, and gendered experiences made both of these categories a poor fit.

Brown argues that Addams's spiritual journey was a necessary prerequisite to her ability to conceive of Hull-House as founded on reciprocal, democratic, social relations. Beginning with Addams's childhood under the tutelage of her nondoctrinaire father, Brown follows Addams's spiritual struggles at the very doctrinaire Rockford Female Seminary, and her dialogue in the years before Hull-House with liberal Christian texts and with her Christian friend, Ellen Gates Starr. Ultimately, Addams found a transcendent justification for her public deeds by embracing the most difficult faith of all, one based on unconditional love for all human beings.

Philosopher Charlene Haddock Seigfried places Addams's experiential method in the context of American pragmatism in her essay, "The Courage of One's Convictions or the Conviction of One's Courage? Jane Addams's Principled Compromises." Comparing Addams with William James and John Dewey, Seigfried shows that the three philosophers shared a belief that truths and values arise in specific contexts of experience and are to be assessed in terms of the meanings and consequences they hold for those affected. Seigfried also specifies occasions when Addams's experiences with women and with people of varied ethnic and class backgrounds led her to more astute insights than those of her male pragmatist counterparts, insights also noted by scholars of feminist ethics today. Set in this context, we can see how Addams's well-known penchant for compromise did not indicate a lack of commitment to principles or a lack of moral courage, but was a way of enacting and expanding her pragmatist methodology by including diverse voices as partners in cooperative, consensual decision making.

Addams's commitment to the experiential method was severely tested during World War I as she refused to alter her pacifist opposition to the war. She felt abandoned by most other pragmatists, including Dewey, who supported the war effort. Addams worried that her continued adherence to pacifism was mere dogmatism, rigidly clinging to a theory disconnected from the lessons of experience. Seigfried explains how Addams's defense of pacifism followed the same pragmatist method she had used throughout her life, and thus was nondogmatic. Addams's theory of pacifism, well grounded in experience, was not a retreat into moral absolutism.

Section II: Jane Addams and the Practice of Democratic Citizenship

At a time when many of her contemporaries sought to expunge foreign cultures and traditions under the guise of Americanization, Addams spoke strongly for what Americans could learn from these cultures and traditions, and sought to preserve the dignity of all people and the worth of Old World crafts, skills, and histories. She believed her immigrant neighbors had much to teach other Americans about caring and providing for members of their communities. Addams found in many immigrant practices a kind of social solidarity and nascent social ethic that she wished to see developed and modeled in the larger society. She believed that these immigrant practices would enrich democratic society.

Addams attended carefully to the context of people's experiences, and tried, to the extent possible, to view the actions of the poor and immigrants through their own eyes. She opposed efforts to act "for" immigrants or the poor and contended that cooperation meant that one should not "give up the consciousness of one's own identity and achievements."[26] Addams's vision was one of collaboration and genuine reciprocity. She demanded of citizens a broader engagement with the world outside their own families and narrow social circles, so that they could learn from others and collaborate in achieving commonly developed goals. For Addams, political and social progress required cross-class conversation, engagement, and collaboration.

Biographer Louise W. Knight, in "Jane Addams's Theory of Cooperation," traces how Addams adapted the theory of cooperation through such experiential testing. During the nineteenth century in Britain and the United States, theories of cooperation were widely seen as possible alternatives to competitive economic liberalism and social Darwinism. Many socialists, labor organizers, and social reformers such as Robert Owen and Beatrice and Sidney Webb saw cooperative economic production and cooperative social action as preferred paths to social and economic reform. Knight writes that for Addams, "to cooperate meant to choose to work on mutual interests with others rather than work alone on one's own project, to enter into every conversation with an open mind, and to ask how she could help."[27] Knight explores how Addams, her fellow Hull-House residents, and their neighbors designed and carried out much of their work in a cooperative manner. The Hull-House Coal Cooperative, a cooperative residence for young working women called the Jane Club, and the Hull-House Residents Council were just a few of many examples. Addams endeavored to extend cooperative practices beyond Hull-House to her efforts for social reform in Chicago, including work with the Juvenile Protective Association, the Civic Federation of Chicago, and the Garbage Disposal Reform Committee. Through these activities, Addams enacted, advocated, and explored the limits of cooperation as a method for social reform. Addams continued throughout her life to use the language of cooperation in her writings; Knight's essay recovers this aspect of Addams's theory of practical civic reform.

In Addams's era, science and professionalism were invoked in municipal reform efforts to root out the corruption of patronage politics. For the majority of Addams's contemporaries, reform meant sanitizing politics and professionalizing government, education, and social service delivery. Public administration scholar Camilla Stivers examines Addams's unique and profound contribution to American civic philosophy and institution building. She finds that the early-twentieth-century movement toward professionalization of public service privileged managerial efficiency and technical expertise, and that neutral, apolitical administration relegated ordinary citizens to increasingly passive, peripheral roles. In "A Civic Machinery for Democratic Expression: Jane Addams on Public Administration," Stivers explores how Addams's long experience living in Chicago's nineteenth ward gave her a powerful basis for evaluating the theory and practice of Progressive Era municipal reform measures. Addams knew what her neighbors could contribute to city governance and how such participation was essential to democratic expression. Stivers argues that Addams recognized how the movement to clean up corruption, depoliticize government, and eliminate political machines could distance citizens from government and treat them as customers, clients, and beneficiaries, rather than as engaged citizens. Because administrators do not only implement laws or policies but also make judgments about conflicting public values, Stivers recalls us to the fact that Addams knew that effective decision making in public administration needed to include the moral perceptions and experiences of ordinary people.

Historian Karen Pastorello offers a concrete case study of how Addams's activism and her interactions with specific persons and situations contributed to her theories of social democracy and social change. In "'The Transfigured Few': Jane Addams, Bessie Abramowitz Hillman, and Immigrant Women Workers in Chicago, 1905–1915," Pastorello argues that Addams and Hull-House residents attempted to overcome their own class and ethnic prejudices, while collaborating with working-class women on crucial issues of labor and factory conditions. Addams mentored a number of working-class women and helped them learn how to work with political officials, become effective leaders in the wider political arena, and advance their own interests. Pastorello tells the story of how Bessie Abramowitz (Hillman) became a key figure in developing the meaning of industrial democracy for women. Abramowitz, a Russian Jewish immigrant working in a Chicago garment factory, first came to Hull-House for English classes. She began organizing garment workers to protest wage cuts, and sought help at Hull-House. Addams gave the workers a space at Hull-House to meet and provided funding. This eventually enabled Abramowitz to lead a strike of 38,000 garment workers, and afterward to found the Amalgamated Clothing Workers of America. Pastorello charts the friendship that developed between Hillman and Addams, and examines how Hull-House residents and working women learned from, and taught, each other. This case study is one historical example of how Addams developed her theory of social change through activism and cross-class collaboration, characterized by mutuality, solidarity, and reciprocity.

Political scientist Carol Nackenoff argues that narratives that assemble American values and experiences in different ways and toward different ends are crucial to the dynamic of political change and institutional development. In "New Politics for New Selves: Jane Addams's Legacy for Democratic Citizenship in the Twenty-First Century," Nackenoff urges that scholars who seek to reinvigorate civic engagement, and to enlarge the public sphere by bringing human needs and interdependence into politics, draw upon Addams in crafting a usable past and a potent narrative for the future. For Addams, citizenship was a practice. She believed citizens needed to work together in order to learn to respect and dignify each other's differences; she deemed such respect essential to democratic politics. Nackenoff also points out that Addams theorized from experienced connections and relationships, offering a new image of selves that were interdependent and not simply autonomous.

The imagery of civic housekeeping that Addams and many feminists of this era used transformed notions of the home, moving bourgeois women out of the home and into public spaces and public debates. Yet some political scientists have argued that this type of feminist appeal was actually harmful and conservative in its impact. Their critique of maternalism as a political theory and strategy may help explain why some feminist ethic-of-care theorists have hesitated to claim Addams as their predecessor. In this essay, Nackenoff demonstrates an important connection between Addams's political vision and the current scholarship on care. Both seek to reintroduce moral arguments into liberal politics, give needs new currency, and render politically visible and valuable the work frequently performed by women, often women of color and the poor. Careful to note the ways in which Addams cannot be easily reappropriated, Nackenoff considers what kind of lessons Addams can offer for those creating current visions of citizenship and progressive political projects.

Finally, in "Toward a Queer Social Welfare Studies: Unsettling Jane Addams," Shannon Jackson draws on her grounding in literature and literary theory, poststructuralism, performance studies, American cultures, rhetoric, and queer theory to remove disciplinary boundaries in her study of Jane Addams and Hull-House. Drawing on data written and unwritten, Jackson explores how the Hull-House ethic of radical locality—with work, living, and leisure taking place in the spaces it sought to change—unsettled space as well as oppositions of male/female and public/private. For its residents, Hull-House was home, experimental society, and neighborhood community center. Domesticity, as practiced in the settlement house, was never a private affair. This domesticity extended beyond the walls of Hull-House, combining publicly and politically with the image of municipal housekeeping outside in the streets of Chicago. At the same time, it was reworked within the walls of the settlement house itself. The public domesticity of Hull-House revisited has political implications for feminism, sexuality, family politics, and social welfare.

Jackson directly engages the portrait of Addams that Jean Bethke Elshtain presents in her 2002 book, *Jane Addams and the Dream of American Democracy: A Life.*[28] In doing so, Jackson draws upon intersections of Addams's life and career to reflect upon current debates in gender studies. Addams, who was not a biological mother and lived in a nontraditional household that Elshtain says would be frivolous to call a family, had, in Jackson's view, only a partial alignment with maternalist rhetoric. Jackson argues that Elshtain's conception and valuation of the private reify private-public divisions and traditional conceptions of the feminine. Furthermore, Hull-House played a role in the formation of a more diffuse, macro-oriented system of public welfare, about which Addams was equivocal. To Elshtain's categorical assertion that such "institutional" formations eroded the family, Jackson points out that private relationships were disrupted by outside forces in the rapidly industrializing city of the late nineteenth and early twentieth centuries. Jackson reasons that social welfare policy tended to "normalize" and reinscribe traditional familial relations. She suggests that everyday Hull-House performances of home, family, kinship, and domesticity "unsettled" conventional gender essentialism and the relationship between kinship and obligations of care. These performances offer a way to transform the state and generate different, "queered" legacies of feminism for politics.

Section III: Democratic Cosmopolitanism and Peace

A number of authors in this volume have also reappropriated Addams for the arena of peace and internationalism. From experiencing and ameliorating life in Chicago, Addams moved to a larger social vision of broad-based, participatory social democracy whose scope extended from the national to the international. Addams envisioned a world in which peace and justice would both inform notions of democratic, participatory citizenship, and would be extended to all people. To achieve such a world Addams believed that women, the poor, and all those previously underrepresented needed an expanded voice in their governments and international policies.

From 1914 onward, Addams devoted much of her time to international peace efforts, helping to found the Woman's Peace Party and the Women's International League for Peace and Freedom. Addams stressed that war is not solely a masculine domain and illustrated the many ways in which it affected women and children. In her many writings on peace and international understanding, and through her own activism, Addams articulated theories on those effects and on women's responsibilities to work for peace. For these efforts and her work at Hull-House, Addams was awarded the Nobel Peace Prize in 1931.

Authors in this section seek to articulate a democratic cosmopolitan ethic for our time and look to the potential of new transborder and transboundary relations. Addams was fond of Mazzini's metaphor of concentric circles when she thought about world social citizenship. She insisted that "the duties of family, nation, and humanity are but concentric circles of one obligation"; each circle surrounds and completes the inner ones.[29] This imagery helped Addams herself understand "how relations in daily life could anchor multileveled democratic social ethics and politics, could combine diversity and transnationalism, and could deepen the participatory aspects of world social citizenship."[30] Addams's method of analysis is helpful today. Problems ranging from the global spread of infectious diseases to global warming and environmental degradation require multilevel responses, not simply new layers of international organizations and legal structures. Addams also rejected the idea that self-government could be exported or spread through military occupation, in contrast to the policies of Theodore Roosevelt and Woodrow Wilson.

Many have commented that the title of Addams's 1907 book, *Newer Ideals of Peace*, is odd, if not misleading, because so much of the book focuses on domestic social reform and not on issues of international peace. For Addams, peace was integrally linked to social justice. In "The Conceptual Scaffolding of *Newer Ideals of Peace*" philosopher Marilyn Fischer explicates how the chapters on domestic social reform function as an essential part of the conceptual scaffolding of the book's argument. Addams's thesis in *Newer Ideals* is that militarism is fundamentally opposed to democracy and yet is pervasive in American local and national institutions. Rooting out such institutional militarism at home is an essential part of working toward international peace. In *Newer Ideals of Peace* Addams used the experiences of subordinate groups, especially women and immigrants, to diagnose just how militarism functions domestically in government, industry, unions, and education. With a keen eye for evolving social trends, Addams found evidence of a new humanitarianism emerging among these subordinated groups that could address pressing physical and social needs democratically, cooperatively, and peacefully and replace the militarism then operating in social institutions. Once the conceptual scaffolding of the book is clear, we see how *Newer Ideals of Peace* as a whole presents Addams's conceptions of democracy, social justice, and peace as mutually defining concepts.

The need for democratic transnationalism as an alternative to imperialism and militarized nationalism has become ever more relevant in a post–9–11 world. In "A Global 'Common Table': Jane Addams's Theory of Democratic Cosmopolitanism and World Social Citizenship," Wendy Sarvasy presents Addams's argument that transnational and global ethics, institutions, and citizenship can be democratic only if they evolve out of, and are sustained by, inclusive nonhierarchical relations of daily nurturing, broadly understood. For Addams, U.S. urban immigrant neighborhoods prefigured these new global relations of mutual aid, generated a new cosmopolitan social ethics, and initiated new forms of democratic social politics. Addams advocated feminist bread or food politics as an arena in which women could create a new global social ethics, and new spaces for their own democratic participation in global affairs. Addams envisioned world social citizenship as a realistic, accessible democratic practice, and global social citizens as active synthesizers of local, national, and global relations. According to Sarvasy, Addams believed that where there is a mismatch between ideological concepts and experience, further experiences could lead to new concepts. Sarvasy is hopeful that there are now real opportunities to capitalize on the period of hopefulness that opened at the end of the Cold War.

Harriet Hyman Alonso's essay "Can Jane Addams Serve as a Role Model for Us Today?" is a meditation on how Addams's peace writings and activities on behalf of peace can help us think about peace today. Alonso presents parallels between the world conditions Addams faced a century ago and the international conflicts we face today, both at home and abroad. Through these parallels, Alonso identifies many ways in which Addams gives us patterns for living with hostility, while searching for peace.

Alonso begins with Addams's claim that she learned about seeking international peace while living in the cosmopolitan neighborhood of Hull-House. With *Newer Ideals of Peace* serving as a guide, Alonso surveys the rich ethnic mix of her own neighborhood and reflects on the ways it has and has not attained the sort of internationalism Addams identifies as the path toward peace. Alonso finds parallels to today's struggles addressed in *Women at The Hague: the International Congress of Women and its Results,* coauthored by Addams, Emily G. Balch, and Alice Hamilton, with its discussions of press censorship, the younger generation's revolt against war, and concern for the effects of war on women. Finally, *The Second Twenty Years at Hull-House,* in which Addams's focus moves from the European conflict to a true internationalism, gives Alonso a context for reflecting on the promise of new international institutions and brings her meditation back home to the internationalism present in her own community.

The work of the scholars represented in *Jane Addams and the Practice of Democracy* makes an important contribution to scholarship, elevating the stature and visibility of Jane Addams in intellectual history and social thought, and across many disciplines. Contemporary scholars and activists can take inspiration from Addams's commitment to work toward a more meaningful, ethically enhanced conception of democratic citizenship and find a guide for addressing a wide range of challenges.

Notes

1. Public Act 094-0796, Illinois General Assembly, May 22, 2006.

2. Shannon Jackson, "Toward a Queer Social Welfare Studies: Unsettling Jane Addams," chapter 7 in this volume.

3. James Weber Linn, *Jane Addams: A Biography* (New York and London: D. Appleton-Century Company, 1935). Linn's biography was reissued by the University of Illinois Press in 2000.

4. Violet Oakley, *Cathedral of Compassion: Dramatic Outline of the Life of Jane Addams 1860–1935* (Philadelphia: Press of Lyon and Armor, Inc., 1955).

5. Christopher Lasch, *The Social Thought of Jane Addams* (Indianapolis: Bobbs-Merrill Company, 1965), xv.

6. John C. Farrell, *Beloved Lady: A History of Jane Addams's Ideas on Reform and Peace* (Baltimore: Johns Hopkins Press, 1967).

7. Allen F. Davis, *American Heroine: The Life and Legend of Jane Addams* (New

York: Oxford University Press, 1973). A second edition of Davis's biography was published in 2000: *American Heroine: The Life and Legend of Jane Addams, With a New Introduction by the Author* (Chicago: Ivan Dee, 2000).

8. Davis, *American Heroine,* ix.

9. Davis, *American Heroine,* see pp. ix, 64, and 273, for example.

10. Daniel Levine, *Jane Addams and the Liberal Tradition* (Madison: State Historical Society of Wisconsin, 1971). Louis Hartz's *The Liberal Tradition in America* (New York: Harcourt, Brace, 1955) was the key work in depicting this liberal consensus.

11. Blanche Wiesen Cook, "Female Support Networks and Political Activism: Lillian Wald, Crystal Eastman, Emma Goldman," *Chrysalis* 3 (August 1977): 43–61.

12. Jean Bethke Elshtain, *Public Man, Private Woman: Women in Social and Political Thought* (Princeton, N.J.: Princeton University Press, 1981); Jean Bethke Elshtain, *Jane Addams and the Dream of American Democracy* (New York: Basic Books, 2002).

13. For this point, see Daniel T. Rodgers, "True Heroine, False Worshipper," *The American Prospect* 13, no. 22 (December 16, 2002): 33.

14. Shannon Jackson, in this volume, engages in a careful examination and critique of Elshtain's treatment of Addams along this dimension. Jackson stresses the pragmatic use of maternalism, just as Wendy Sarvasy stresses that Addams was a pragmatist and not an ideologue in her contribution to this volume, "A Global 'Common Table': Jane Addams's Theory of Democratic Cosmopolitanism and World Social Citizenship." See also Carol Nackenoff, "Gendered Citizenship: Alternative Narratives of Political Incorporation in the United States, 1875–1925," pp. 137–69 in *The Liberal Tradition in American Politics: Consensus, Polarity or Multiple Traditions,* ed. David F. Ericson and Louisa Bertch Green (New York: Routledge, 1999) for a nonessentialist reading of Addams's claims about unique contributions.

15. See, for instance, the reviews of *Jane Addams and the Dream of American Democracy: A Life* by Daniel Levine, *Journal of American History* 90, no. 1 (June 2003): 258–59; by Bart Schultz in *Ethics* 113, no. 2 (January 2003): 407–10; Daniel T. Rodgers, "True Heroine, False Worshipper," *The American Prospect* 13, no. 22 (December 16, 2002): 32–35; and Christine Stansell, "What a Woman Could Do," *New York Times Book Review* (January 27, 2002).

16. Rodgers, "True Heroine, False Worshipper," 34–35 for both quotes.

17. Victoria Bissell Brown, *The Education of Jane Addams* (Philadelphia: University of Pennsylvania Press, 2004); Louise W. Knight, *Citizen: Jane Addams and the Struggle for Democracy* (Chicago: University of Chicago Press, 2005).

18. Katherine Joslin, *Jane Addams: A Writer's Life* (Urbana: University of Illinois Press, 2004).

19. A wide selection of biographies for younger readers has also been published over the last decade. For early readers the following are significant additions to the field: *Jane Addams: People Who Made a Difference,* by David and Patricia Armentrout (Vero Beach, Fla.: Rourke Publishing, 2004); *Jane Addams,* by Lucia Raatma (Minneapolis: Compass Point Books, 2004); and *Jane Addams, a Photo Biography,* by John

Riley (Greensboro, N.C.: First Biographies, an Imprint of Morgan Reynolds, 2000). For older readers, recent titles include: *Jane Addams: A Biography,* by Robin K. Berson (Greenwood Press, 2006); *Jane Addams: Social Reformer and Nobel Prize Winner,* by Pam Rosenberg, (Chanhassen, Minn.: Spirit of America, 2003); and *Waging Peace: The Story of Jane Addams,* by Peggy Caravantes (Greensboro, N.C.: Morgan Reynolds Publishing, 2004). For young adult readers, *Jane Addams: Freedom's Innovator,* by Deborah A. Parks (Alexandria, Va.: TimeLife Books, 2000) is an especially rich addition to the field of Addams biography.

20. Marilyn Fischer and Judy Whipps, *Jane Addams's Writings on Peace* (Bristol, U.K.: Thoemmes Press, 2003).

21. Jean Bethke Elshtain, *The Jane Addams Reader* (New York: Basic Books, 2002).

22. For example, see: http://digital.library.upenn.edu/women/addams/hullhouse/hullhouse.html.

23. *The Jane Addams Papers* (Ann Arbor, Mich.: University Microfilms International (now ProQuest), 1984); *The Jane Addams Papers: A Comprehensive Guide,* ed. Mary Lynn McCree Bryan and Nancy Slote (Bloomington: Indiana University Press, 1996).

24. *The Selected Papers of Jane Addams, 1860–81* (Urbana: University of Illinois Press, 2003).

25. For the Swarthmore College Peace Collection, go to http://www.swarthmore.edu/Library/peace; for resources at the University of Illinois at Chicago, go to http://www.uic.edu/depts/lib/specialcoll. The University of Illinois at Chicago has also provided the Web site "The Urban Experience in Chicago: Hull-House and Its Neighborhood, 1889–1963," which contains transcriptions of primary documents about Hull-House (http://www.uic.edu/jaddams/hull/urbanexp/contents.htm).

26. Jane Addams, "The College Woman and Christianity," *Independent* 53(August 8, 1901): 1855, quoted in Louise W. Knight, "Jane Addams's Theory of Cooperation," chapter 3 in this volume.

27. Knight, "Jane Addams's Theory of Cooperation."

28. Elshtain, *Jane Addams and the Dream of American Democracy.*

29. Jane Addams, *The Second Twenty Years at Hull-House: With a Record of a Growing World Consciousness* (New York: Macmillan, 1930), 174.

30. Sarvasy, "A Global 'Common Table.'"

SECTION I

Addams's Experimental Method

1

The Sermon of the Deed

Jane Addams's Spiritual Evolution

VICTORIA BISSELL BROWN

In her autobiography, Jane Addams told her readers that she had been among the "few 'unconverted' girls" at Rockford Female Seminary in the late 1870s, but indicated that she bore that status with some pride. She had held herself "aloof" from evangelical appeals, she claimed, was "singularly unresponsive" to emotional tales of salvation and damnation, and drew comfort from her father's nondenominational ethics and Emerson's "rationalism."[1] Although this public version of her spiritual history had the virtue of assuring readers in 1910 that they could do good works without the certitude of orthodoxy, it did not capture Addams's complex, sometimes painful evolution from religious doubt to spiritual maturity in the years before opening Hull-House.

The private story that emerges from Addams's youthful essays and correspondence reveals a young woman who struggled to reconcile competing impulses and aspirations in the course of defining her religious and spiritual self. Never particularly drawn to organized, orthodox "religion," the young Jane Addams knew that her inability to take a leap of Christian faith conflicted with her personal ambition for a public life and her practical need, as a northern American female, for the mantle of religion to legitimize her ambition. At the same time, she knew that her unsanctified status conflicted with her genuine longing for spiritual transcendence and its ineffable sense of communion beyond the self.

These two aspirations—the desire for a public life and the longing for spiritual transcendence—coexisted in Jane Addams's youthful experience. But the record of her development as a young woman makes very clear that

Addams possessed a vaulting desire to *do* something in the world long before she stood firmly on the spiritual foundation that would ultimately guide her actions. That is to say, the young Jane Addams was enraptured with the notion of the "deed" before she had constructed, for herself, the meaning of "the sermon." In her life, the impetus to individual action preceded a grasp of the spiritual meaning in that action. Hers is not the story of a faithful young Christian who realized one day that she ought to enact her existing faith by doing some good on this earth; that is the often-interesting, often-noble story of many who joined the Social Gospel movement. It is not Jane Addams's story.

Jane Addams's story proceeded in the reverse direction: from desire to do the deed to the embrace of a faith. Inspired by ambition for a public life, Addams's youthful quest for spiritual guidance among variants of Christian philosophy was more intense and purposeful than we have always acknowledged. And her emergence—in her late twenties—as a devout, unflinching, resolute Christian humanist was the result of earnest struggle and a spiritual awakening to what, for Addams, was a lifelong and very earthly salvation.[2]

* * *

When Jane Addams was fourteen years old, living at home in Cedarville and attending the village school, she kept a fairly regular diary. It was not the sort of discursive, introspective record that other girls of her generation were keeping in the 1870s, not at all the secret, stormy site for self-examination and self-revelation that Jane Hunter has unearthed in her study of Gilded Age girls' diaries.[3] No, Jennie Addams used her diary to write newsy, unsentimental reports about social gatherings in the family parlor or hopscotch, horseback riding, chess games, croquet, and piano duets with her stepbrother George. But amid the bits and pieces about the "rather pretty" new dress her stepmother bought for her, the snowball fight George said he won "but didn't," and her dimwitted teacher, Mr. Moore, "ever lastingly picking his nose," Jennie made the occasional remark about church.[4] The Addams family, which was the wealthy, mill-owning family in the seven hundred–person town of Cedarville, did not actually belong to one church; Jennie's father, Illinois state senator John Addams, taught in the town's Union Sunday School and, along with his wife and children, alternated weekly attendance at the town's Methodist and Presbyterian churches.

Along with her friends, the fourteen-year-old Jennie Addams had "a big time with whispering" in church, but she did attend to the sermon admonishing her to remember the goodness of God, and she was impressed by a "very good sermon about Christians and their duties." While she thought the sermon on "what shall it profit a man if he gain the whole world and lose his soul" was "rather an old subject," she still felt she had "obtained a little good from it." And the warning issued by a visiting minister that theatergoing and card playing put one near the "precipice" to hell definitely caught her attention. The connection between card playing and sin was, for Jennie Addams, a "*new* view," which reveals something about her card-playing family's more liberal attitudes. Equally revealing is her report that her Sunday School class discussed Samson and "came to the conclusion that he was decidedly *not* a good man." But, Jennie noted, "Pa's class came to a somewhat different conclusion." Two weeks later, the Presbyterians' Rev. Mitchell preached what Jennie regarded as a "powerful" sermon in which *he* argued that Samson "was a good man," and though she felt the minister "had arguments . . . still," she wrote, "I do not know whether I am convinced or not."[5]

This adolescent reflection on Samson, the single longest comment on church in the one surviving diary from Jane Addams's youth, had, quite notably, nothing to do with Jesus or eternal salvation. The issue was moral conduct, and the medium was a group discussion in which good and reasonable people, even a loving father and daughter, might differ. It is a tiny moment in Jane Addams's youth, but one that serves to remind us she did not grow up in a doctrinaire environment, certainly not in a strict, orthodox household. Within her own family, Jennie was exposed to an array of views on faith and religious practice. At one end of the continuum stood her sardonic older stepbrother, Harry, who regarded churchgoers as "frigid souls" conned by a wicked clergy into trying to "wheedle Jove."[6] Quite a distance from Harry stood Jane's devout eldest sister, Mary, who believed that "our Father in heaven doth all things well." In that faith, Mary was joined by her husband, the Presbyterian minister John Linn, who reminded Jane that "Christ . . . gave up everything for . . . our woes."[7] The mere existence of this Protestant continuum within the extended Addams family telegraphed to an observant adolescent that religion was an individual choice, not a universal dictate. Underscoring that message, and standing at the center of the family, were Jane's father, Senator Addams, and his second wife, Anna Addams, the two most lasting family influences on Jane Addams's spiritual development.

Her father, Jane Addams told her nephew, was "not a professing Christian," and he was certainly not a Quaker.[8] Though she once confessed to a pacifist friend that she "wished with all my heart" that she could place her name on a roster of famous Quakers, she knew that her one Quaker grandmother on her deceased mother's side was "too slight a claim."[9] For ninety years, readers have clung to Jane Addams's autobiographical tale that when she was a seminary student she asked her father, "What are you? What do you say when people ask you?" and that he replied, with a twinkle in his eye, "I am a Quaker."[10] But in our desire to make much of that answer, we have not noted the oddity of the question. In constructing that scene, Jane Addams was asking us to believe that having grown up in this man's house, gone to church and Sunday School with him, been tutored by him in all sorts of subjects, she still had to ask him, "What are you?" The truth in this particular autobiographical fiction lies not in the Quaker reference but in what it telegraphs about John Addams's habitual reticence on doctrinal matters.

Interesting though it is to speculate on the cultural and political reasons that Jane Addams left us believing her father was a Quaker, the point for now is that Jane Addams grew up in a family that devoted relatively little attention to orthodox questions of heaven and hell. Her parents, if not her siblings, placed great value on Christianity as a guide to ethical conduct in this life, to figuring out if Samson was a good man or a bad man, and to discussing with neighbors the matter of one's Christian duty to others.

When John Addams was a young man, he confessed in his own diary that he hoped his brother-in-law, newly "enlisted under the banner of Christ," would "not become too much excited but keep within bounds that he may not . . . in his enthusiasm" be prevented "from doing good amongst his fellow beings."[11] Forty years later, Jane Addams's stepmother, Anna, would express her own belief that "to do good for our fellow beings . . . is all the religion worth one Christian thought."[12] In Anna's case, this view did not translate into any act of community service. But though Anna offered Jane no model for female stewardship, she did offer a consistent second to John Addams's focus on Christian conduct over Christian doctrine. For his part, Senator Addams loyally translated into daily action his convictions about "doing good amongst his fellow beings," and it was to his example that Jane Addams looked when she fashioned her own ambition for a steward's life of service, a leader's life of duty.

No evidence survives to suggest that earthly service was closely linked, in the Addams household, to eternal salvation. Apart from Mary and her husband, Rev. Linn, there is no record of any family member drawing theological connections between earthly duty and heavenly reward. John Addams bequeathed to his youngest child a recoil from unprovable presumptions about the afterlife; this life, he knew, was fleeting, God's ways unknowable, and obedience to the dictate of earthly service was the only honest path.[13] At the time of her father's death, twenty-one-year-old Jane Addams wrote nothing about him going to heaven; she wrote only about his legacy of good work in this life.[14] Four years later, when she was twenty-five and in the midst of a spiritual crisis, Jane Addams told her friend Ellen Starr that "for many years it was my ambition to reach my father's moral requirement," but now, she said, "I am needing something more."[15]

What Addams experienced at home in Cedarville, then, was a moral, not a religious, requirement. This spared her the burden of ever having to shed an uncomfortable orthodoxy, but it ill-equipped her for the intense "pressure to make a confession of faith" that she faced at Rockford Female Seminary, where she spent four years between age seventeen and twenty-one.[16] Emerging from the stack of essays, editorials, and letters she wrote during her Rockford years is Addams's eager longing for the deed and her equally eager search for a sermon to justify and elevate the deed.

Jane Addams's essays at Rockford were thick with the language of dramatic endeavor and heroic individualism that she was absorbing from her private reading of the Victorian idealists, especially Thomas Carlyle. Over and over again, she mimicked Carlyle by extolling the world's heroes for their "terrible earnestness," for their willingness to come "face to face with stern unflinching reality," for their possession of that "primary condition of greatness: oneness of purpose," for their "daring to express an honest opinion," for "never deviating" from principle, for their "absorption" in real work, and for following Carlyle's maxim: "the end of life is an action, not a thought."[17]

Carlyle, she wrote, "has a way of saying things that strikes me as it were my keynote." Senator Addams's diligent daughter thrilled to Carlyle's thundering cry: "Whatsoever of morality and of intelligence; what of patience, perseverance, faithfulness, of method, insight, ingenuity, energy; in a word, whatsoever of Strength that man has in him will lie written in the Work he does . . . Produce! Produce! Were it but the pitifullest infinitesimal fraction of a Product, produce it, in God's name!"[18]

Carlyle's high-flying idealism spoke to Jane Addams's youthful longing for a philosophy that could justify her ambition. Never relying on Christian dogma, Carlyle extolled heroes, heroism, and heroic action in terms that valorized individual integrity and individual destiny; he was exuberant in his belief that each soul craved and deserved meaningful work and just as exuberant in his corollary belief that such work was the vehicle by which human beings could discover their own divine essence and transcend the material world.

We can hear the echoes of both Senator Addams and Thomas Carlyle in Jane's Junior Exhibition speech, which was silent on the subject of one's duty to God, silent on the subject of one's submission to the church or embrace of Jesus, but quite eloquent in its announcement that "in labor alone is happiness . . . the only true and honorable life is one filled with good works and honest toil."[19]

The hunger for the deed was palpable in everything Jane Addams wrote at Rockford, and it was fed regularly by the words of ambitious, idealistic men. But along with that hunger there came, for Jane Addams, a very gendered dilemma—two dilemmas, in fact. First, she did not seek fulfilling work in the private realm; she never once imagined herself toiling as a wife, as a mother, in a kitchen, in a parlor. Work, for her, always wore a public face. But there were scant models, in Gilded Age America, of *non-Christian* women serving as respected public stewards. How could she possibly fulfill her desire to be a hardworking public servant like her father, and live a nondomestic, unmarried life, if she could not claim the mantle of Christian faith and divine inspiration? How else could an American woman justify nontraditional exertions in the public sphere?[20]

The second dilemma Jane Addams faced during her Rockford years was far more compelling: she had fully absorbed the belief, popular among agnostic Victorian idealists, that faith in something beyond oneself was requisite to the pursuit of meaningful work. Untethered to any transcendent ideal, work could too easily be sullied by egotism or greed. In the case of a female contemplating a life of work apart from domestic duties, the need for a spiritual calling, both for legitimacy and as a check on personal ambition, seemed obvious. With equal measures of arrogance and doubt, Jane confided to her friend Ellen Starr that she feared she could not "use my best powers" without settling the religious question; "could I but determine *that*," she predicted, "and have it for a sure basis . . . I could train my powers to anything, it would only remain to choose what."[21]

Blocking Addams's path to determining the religious question was her inability to accept the terms of the Christian offer of salvation; she regarded the Christian story as too literal to inspire a leap of faith. Her correspondence with Ellen Starr on this matter tells us that the two women shared a core conviction that faith resided in the realm of the abstract, but from that common ground, they went in different directions and would, years hence, find their differences irreconcilable. As young women, however, they built a relationship on the foundation of a dialogue about religion and spirituality. During Jane Addams's Rockford years, Ellen Starr was working in Chicago and exploring the ways in which Christian ritual could transport her beyond the tangible to the abstract. For Ellen, the capacity to accept mystery was advanced by her struggle to accept Jesus as divine. For Jane, however, the Christian focus on Jesus was an annoying distraction; "don't you see," she beseeched Ellen, "it doesn't make any difference whether you realize Christ or not, that is not the point." She was convinced that belief in the divinity of Jesus fettered spirituality rather than releasing it; Christians, she feared, missed the transcendent beauty of faith and stifled their chance to experience God by "lowering their ideal" to the most literal level.[22]

Assured as they sounded, these sorts of pronouncements did not take Jane Addams, at age nineteen, any closer to her own spiritual peace. Even as she disdained Ellen's path to transcendent faith, she envied her friend's journey, confessing, "I wish I was where you are. . . . There is a mystery and a beauty incomprehensible to me. . . . You long for a beautiful faith," Jane flattered Ellen, "I only feel that I need religion in a practical sense, that if I could fix myself with my relations to God and the universe . . . I could use my faculties and energy so much better. . . . *Mine* is preeminently selfish and yours is a reaching for higher things."[23]

A year later, Jane was feeling sufficiently concerned, and sufficiently pressured, about her spiritual status at the very orthodox Rockford Seminary to unburden herself to a liberal minister, T. H. Haseltine. In an intriguing reference to her reputation at Rockford, Haseltine tried to assure Jane that those who regarded her as "an atheist" simply did not understand that her lack of interest in Christianity meant she had moved on to a more abstract appreciation of the "greater Christ." His further advice, delivered at the end of Jane's junior year, that she "cease to blame" herself for "the rate" of her spiritual development suggests that she was not at all sanguine about her progress.[24]

The urgency in Jane's spiritual quest had nothing to do with gaining eternal salvation and everything to do with finding salvation in this life. She genuinely feared that her lack of faith meant that her life goals were bound to be prosaic and egocentric. She was caught between her intellectual view that religion was a human construct and her intimate belief that only an "expansiveness of soul" inspired people to do great work. Without a leap of faith, she feared she would never possess expansiveness or inspiration. "The great object of this age seems to be missionary works," Jane told a Rockford friend, Eva Campbell. As missionaries, Jane imagined that she and Campbell could "throw ourselves into the tide of affairs, feel ourselves swamped by the great flood of human action." Jane relished the idea of such vigorous endeavor, even going so far as to serve as vice president of the Home Missions Society at Rockford. But she saw herself as ineligible for the adventure because missionaries had to be believers. Left outside the circle of belief, she was "doomed" to a lifetime of "self-culture," and "self-culture," she sighed, "but impales a man on his personal pronoun," leaving "your soul spinning around on a great I."[25]

Jane experimented with a variety of alternatives to this unsavory, egocentric destiny, including a very public graduation tribute to feminine intuition, which, she claimed, could fulfill its potential as "one of the holy means given to mankind in the search for truth" if it could be tested and employed "in the active, busy world."[26] More privately, and poignantly, Jane Addams revealed to Ellen Starr that because "Christ don't help me in the least,"[27] she was exploring a rather different cosmology: "Lately it seems that I am getting back of all of it, superior to it I almost feel—Back to a great Primal Cause, not Nature exactly, but a fostering mother, necessity, brooding and watching over all things, above every human passion and yet not passive."[28]

Secret even from Ellen's eyes, Jane expanded on this goddess image in a private essay that began with Romola, the heroic "nature-goddess" in Jane's favorite George Eliot novel, who possessed "a power deeper and more primordial than knowledge." The essay went on to pay homage to the "life-giving power of moisture" offered by female goddesses dwelling in "silence and darkness," spoke reverentially of the "calm invisible circle of peace" that surrounded such goddesses, and extolled the ancient statues of ideal women whose "coldness and quiet" announced "they could be alone in the world and need no other support."[29]

Amid her search for a spiritual source that could sustain her ambitions for female stewardship, Addams lighted upon this goddess figure, "the kindly bosom of Mother Earth." But missing entirely from this image was any hint of intimacy or interdependence. Jane Addams's ideal female provided "life-giving" nurturance but then stood alone, above, and apart. She was not embedded in an interdependent web of giving and receiving. She fed others' bodies but was herself disembodied. Her origins were moist, but she was "cold." She invited others' dependence but was sufficient unto herself. Unable to embrace the submissive role of a bride of Christ, Addams turned to spiritual alternatives that emphasized individual heroism and superiority, even dominance and control.

Jane Addams's letters, essays, and editorials from her seminary years, 1877–81, constitute our most voluminous source of evidence on her struggles with religion and spirituality, but their richness must be qualified by their developmental limitations. These are, after all, the writings of a very young woman, and Addams did not cease her search for a spiritual home at age twenty-one. This makes the Rockford writings most useful for marking a base point from which to measure the ways in which Addams's thinking on these matters held firm and fast and the ways in which it changed. We can get a sense of her spiritual trajectory by looking ahead, to the end of 1891 and the summer of 1892, more than a decade after Addams's graduation from Rockford, more than two years after the opening of Hull-House. In that six-month period following her thirty-first birthday, Addams delivered two speeches that serve as representative sermons justifying the public deeds she had boldly embarked upon. They allow us to glimpse her mature relationship with Christianity and the spirituality that evolved out of that relationship.

In "The Subjective Necessity for Social Settlements," delivered in July 1892, Addams pointed to a "certain renaissance going forward" in what she called "Christian humanitarianism," whose expression of the "spirit of Christ" she carefully distinguished from "propaganda." Addams asserted that "Jesus had no set of truths labeled Religious" and she questioned whether the early Roman Christians considered his teachings a religion at all. "He himself," she said, "called it a revelation . . . a command to love all men," but Jesus taught that this revelation "must be put in terms of action," and action, she affirmed, "is found in. . . . social relationships, in the way [man] connects with his fellows . . . and [the] *affection* with which he regards his fellows." Jesus' achievement, argued Addams, was in creating "a deep enthusiasm for humanity," in making man "at once the organ and object of revelation; and by this process," she said, "came about that great wonderful fellowship, that true democracy of the early Church."[30]

This public address, delivered at the School of Applied Ethics in Plymouth, Massachusetts, gave Addams the opportunity to extol the "early Christians" for their uncompromising belief in "love as a cosmic force" and to insist that the social settlement "must be grounded in a philosophy whose foundation is on the solidarity of the human race, a philosophy which will not waver when the race happens to be represented by a drunken woman or an idiot boy."[31]

In the "Subjective Necessity" sermon, and in the one she delivered six months earlier called "Outgrowths of Toynbee Hall," Addams tied her Christian humanism to the positivists' belief that "the religious fervor of man can be turned into love for his race, and his desire for a future life [can be transformed] into contentment to live in the echo of his deeds. It seems simpler to many of us," explained a grown-up Jane Addams "to search for the Christ that is in each man and to found our likeness in Him—to believe in the brotherhood of all because we believe in His" brotherhood.[32]

Addams's adult, earthly reconciliation with Christianity is on full display in these sermons, providing a transcendent justification for the deed in its call to the most challenging faith of all: faith in other human beings. So, too, was there a reaffirmation of her family-bred belief that "deeds"—not an afterlife—offer the only certain immortality. At the same time, "Outgrowths of Toynbee Hall" offers up a significant reconciliation with the cold, aloof goddess figure of Rockford days. In this sermon, the figure called upon to aid in what Addams termed "the starvation struggle" was not standing apart and above, and was not without her own need. Now, the agent of help was *also* being helped; now, the act of service fueled the servant's own "powers of enjoyment." In trying to move her listeners away from the hierarchical, controlling image of stewardship she herself once held, and toward the communal, collective, democratic notion of interdependent transcendence she had come to embrace, Addams offered this corrective advice: "You pray in the common parlance . . . that you may never lose *your* hold on it all. You mean to pray that the great mother breasts of humanity, with its labor and suffering and homely comforts, may never be withheld from you."[33]

Between 1880 and 1891, between Rockford and Chicago, Addams's idealized fostering mother had ceased watching over or standing above and had become a part of "our common humanity"; the central image in the stewardship story was no longer control but inclusion. Addams made that point (and it was a spiritual point before it was a political point) crystal clear during the depression of 1894 when she told Chicago's business leaders, "we should consider not what shall we do with the unemployed, but what shall we and the unemployed do together, that we may all as brothers grow out into a wider and better citizenship than we have ever yet had."[34]

Among all of the changes Jane Addams had to undergo in her evolution from Rockford Seminary to Hull-House, none was more fundamental than her embrace of Christian humanism as a spiritual path to transcendence through daily, communal action with her fellow beings. This, for Addams, was the via media between her father's dutiful moral requirement and orthodoxy's supernatural salvation. The route she took, in the decade following her graduation from seminary, to reach this peaceful reconciliation is not so well documented as are the stresses at Rockford, but it is traceable. And though these strands of spiritual development intersected with numerous other familial, intellectual, and political strands, it is still possible to tease out the key threads of the story's spiritual aspect.

The death of Jane Addams's father, just weeks after her graduation from Rockford when she was only twenty-one, heightened her dilemma over doing the public deed into a genuine crisis. Her Presbyterian brother-in-law, John

Linn, tried to comfort her with the reminder that "your life aims were high enough and your plans broad enough so that [your Pa] could take an interest in them, and it was his great delight to prepare you for your mission."[35] Still, the fact remained that her beloved Pa's death had left her with two imperatives: a high moral requirement to do one's duty, and a very clear, if private, duty to take care of his needy widow, Anna Addams. Lacking a transcendent spiritual sermon that would justify a daughter's pursuit of a different duty, a public duty, Jane could see no alternative to serving what she later called "the family claim."[36] Anything else would be rank selfishness and, indeed, she fretted about a "selfishness eating out my very life" and had to command herself to "think of other people."[37]

So we must understand the eight years between Rockford Female Seminary and Hull-House as a time in which Jane Addams was caught between a masculine notion of public service that was hierarchical and controlling (and, in the hands of an unsanctified female could appear self-aggrandizing) and a feminine notion of private service that was self-denying and long-suffering. Neither one suited her maturing temperament, neither one offered a satisfying way out of her dilemma. Addams did not know at the time whether her efforts in these years were directed at making peace with a life of private duty or finding an escape into public service; her exact goal was by no means clear. But the surviving evidence testifies to her urgent curiosity about how it was that human beings rose above self-absorption. What, she wondered during these years of spiritual quest, pulled individuals out and beyond themselves; what inspired transcendence?

If we had footage of Jane Addams's first tour of Europe, when she was twenty-three and twenty-four, we would see her traipsing from art museum to art museum, clutching her John Ruskin, intent on discerning the moral character of each artist, squinting to see each painting's ennobling qualities, straining to understand how mere mortals translated their aspirations into tangible products that seemed to exceed human limitations. The religious painter who most engaged Jane's attention on that European tour was Fra Angelico, the fifteenth-century Florentine who painted on the walls of his cloistered monastery at San Marco, not caring if his work was "seen," not caring if it brought him fame. The very privacy of his labor made his paintings "sweeter," Jane thought, "unto themselves and peaceful that way." After a day viewing Fra Angelico's frescoes, Jane wrote to Ellen that artistic work performed for the sheer joy of the work itself—not for fame or self-aggrandizement—gave her a "tremor and a corresponding desire for the power arising from mere goodness."[38] Carlyle, Ruskin, and Jane's own father had equipped her with enthusiasm for solid labor, but the question Jane carried into every European gallery, church, and workshop was: how to engage in such labor "from mere goodness"? What secret motivated that sort of joyful selflessness?

Communication with Ellen Starr was vital to Jane Addams's religious process in these years. Except for the five months they spent together in Europe the year before Jane's move to Chicago, the two friends were seldom in one another's company, but we know from letters that Jane was increasingly open to and with Ellen, and that Ellen exposed Jane to the writings of an array of Christian thinkers from the American Protestant Episcopal bishop, Phillips Brooks, through liberal Anglicans like Arthur Stanley and William Frederic Farrar, to the Anglican-turned-Catholic, Cardinal John Henry Newman.[39] For all of their differences, these theologians shared a common insistence that a religious focus on the essential character of Jesus was more important than doctrinal conformity, church ritual, or denominational boundaries. Ironically, Ellen read these writers to say that embrace of Christ's *divinity* was at the center of the enterprise, while Jane read them as legitimating her sense that faith in a supernatural Christ was less important than faith in Jesus's moral example on earth. "I believe more and more," she told Ellen, "in keeping the . . . *facts* of Christ's life before us and letting the philosophy go."[40]

Independent of Ellen, Jane also began reading Leo Tolstoy's religious and social criticism in these years. His statement of faith, *My Religion,* was published in English in 1885 and Jane likely read it in the fall of 1886, a period for which her correspondence with Ellen is missing. Like the writers Ellen recommended, Tolstoy called for a focus on Jesus, not on the institutional trappings that had grown up around him. Tolstoy was more radical than Ellen's churchmen, however, because he insisted that true Christianity demanded faith in Jesus's message about human salvation on earth, not faith in a supernatural Jesus or promises of salvation after death. In *My Religion,* Jane encountered Tolstoy's argument that beyond the "mysteries of dogmatics, homiletics, patristics, liturgics, hermeneutics, apologetics," there was one, single "center of gravity" to Christ's teaching. That central message was "resist not evil," by which Christ meant "never do anything that is contrary to the law of love."[41]

The theologians Ellen was reading sought to clear wider spiritual pathways to experiencing faith in Jesus and, thereby, to increase individuals' access to eternal salvation. By contrast, Tolstoy derided faith in a divine Jesus and in eternal salvation as myths that distorted the teachings of Jesus. Human beings needed faith in the law of love, not in the divinity of Jesus, said Tolstoy.

Salvation was to be experienced only in this life, and the path to that salvation came through collective, not individual, action. So while Ellen looked to those who said faith in the supernatural was required for authentically selfless action in this world, Jane was attending to the sermon that said faith in human love would suffice to ensure that the deed arose from "mere goodness."

Jane Addams's reading in Christian philosophy in the 1880s prepared her in ways she could never have predicted for her 1888 encounter with Samuel Barnett, the Anglican canon who led London's settlement house, Toynbee Hall. Addams devoted just three sentences of her autobiography to her pivotal encounter with Barnett before recalling her relief that, at long last, her period of "passive receptivity," "ever-lasting preparation," and "curious inactivity" had come to a close and she was finally going to begin work too-long delayed.[42] For her own narrative reasons, Addams chose not to pause and reflect on the fact that without her period of preparation, she simply would not have understood what Barnett was up to at Toynbee Hall. She told her sister Alice, at the time, that she resonated to the settlement because "it was so free from 'professional doing good,'" and "so unaffectedly sincere."[43] Had she visited six years earlier, however, it is unlikely Addams would have discerned what was unique about Toynbee Hall. Thanks to her struggles, dilemmas, and delays, and thanks to her reading, Addams was able to perceive, beneath all the British propriety, that Toynbee Hall was fueled by Samuel Barnett's enduring faith in every individual's capacity to live by Christian ethics and to parlay those ethics, collectively, into the active creation of a civil society that dignified labor, culture, and religious diversity. Samuel Barnett's motto was "one by one," by which he meant that social reform and moral regeneration had to be rooted in direct and daily human encounters in which lives became entwined and from which grew a shared commitment to the common good.[44] When he spoke of "the best," Barnett meant not only Matthew Arnold's cultural best but the spiritual best envisioned by Balliol College's T. H. Green, a devout Christian ethicist who disavowed Christian dogma—and who Addams started quoting when she moved to Chicago. Green's philosophy infused Toynbee Hall with the idea, so similar to Leo Tolstoy's, that individuals found their "best selves" and their greatest joy when they identified their own happiness with that of the commonweal.[45] This meant that service to others was not a sacrifice, it was a choice to pursue happiness along a deeper, surer path; it was, as Addams would later explain, "a subjective necessity." It was, at the same time, a sufficiently transcendent ideal to justify the apparent selfishness of abandoning Anna and the family claim.

Addams finally committed herself to membership in a Christian church—

Cedarville's Presbyterian—in the months between her encounter with London's Toynbee Hall and her move to Chicago to start her own settlement with Ellen Starr. This act was not, she later explained, the result of any "emotional 'conversion.'"[46] Indeed, six months before joining the church, Jane told her sister Alice that when she read the testament of the Scottish believer Henry Drummond, she "felt more than ever before the vast difference between one who has once felt the inspiration and one who has not." Church membership was, for her, an earthly commitment to "start in the *footsteps* of Christ," it was not a leap heavenward.[47] When, on the eve of her move to Chicago, she pledged to Ellen to "love each other through thick and thin and work out a salvation," Jane did not mean, in either romantic or religious terms, what Ellen thought she meant.[48]

In the beginning, however, the two founders of Hull-House completely agreed that they were better off not affiliating with established Christian missionary organizations. It was not only that the power in those organizations centered around men or that those men, however kindly, were inevitably patronizing toward young women like Jane and Ellen.[49] Nor was it simply that affiliation with an existing mission put the new settlement at risk of being "swallowed up in a great organization."[50] It was a fundamental difference in assumptions that made a partnership impossible. Missionaries presumed themselves to be a saved people taking the gift of eternal salvation through Christ to the masses. Jane and Ellen assumed that they would not be saved, in any sense of the word, until they lived and worked among the masses, offering fellowship and whatever earthly gifts their education had given them. As Ellen explained to her sister, "Jane feels that it is not the Christian spirit to go among these people as if you were bringing them a great boon." It was, instead, Jane's belief "that one gets as much as one gives."[51]

Both Jane Addams and Ellen Starr refused to allow Hull-House to become a site for Protestant evangelizing and thereby nourished the trust of their Catholic and Jewish neighbors. Still, the Christian press of the day was full of articles that reveal how important it was to liberal adherents of the emerging Social Gospel movement to believe that Jane Addams was really "an earnest Christian."[52] Conservative Christians insisted that secular settlements like Hull-House were "necessarily antagonistic to Christianity and religion" because they aimed at "worldly results only" and did not bring their neighbors to Christ. But Protestants and Catholics who wished to move their congregations toward greater engagement with social problems pointed to Jane Addams as an exemplar of Christ's teaching on the "cosmic force of Love," argued that she stood for "the same idea which the carpenter of Nazareth first uttered," and insisted that she was a true Christian precisely because she did not proselytize.[53]

Such was Jane Addams's reputation by the early 1890s that Christian proponents of the Social Gospel thought it benefited their cause to claim her as one of their own. But wishing could not make it so. Addams did not simply refuse to impose Christian beliefs on her neighbors, she declined to identify with organized Christianity herself. Yes, she was a member of the Congregational Ewing Street Church in her neighborhood, but she expressed disappointment with the church's weak participation in Hull-House endeavors, and she aligned herself, on a daily basis, much more closely with Rev. Jenkin Lloyd Jones, whose liberalism ultimately felt confined by even the Unitarian pulpit. Yes, she continued to lead voluntary prayer services with Hull-House residents on Sunday evenings into the mid-1890s, but Chicago Christianity's inadequate response to the depression of 1894 so aggravated her that when a group of Congregational ministers in Oak Park grilled her on whether Hull-House took the place of a church, she rather snidely confessed, "there is in my mind a little ecclesiastical confusion with regard to the meaning of the word church."[54] Rescued from further self-incrimination by a liberal minister from Quincy, Jane departed the tree-lined streets of Oak Park and returned home to the bustling decay of Halsted Street. There, she faced no neighbors' demands to align herself with any religious organization, but she did face letters from Toynbee Hall's Samuel Barnett warning her that too much attention to the deed could obscure the sermon and admonishing her that "we need more of this faith in our Lord."[55] So, too, she faced Ellen's mounting concern that settlement life had not only failed to draw them closer together spiritually, but had also failed to draw Jane into Christian socialism.

The breach between Ellen Starr and Jane Addams was widened by multiple problems, but the religious differences evident from youth lay at the heart of their woes and encapsulate the very different sermons they preached to justify their deeds. By the mid-1890s, Starr was aligning with the Episcopal Order of the Holy Cross, where she could share her faith in Christian socialism with East Coast settlement leaders like Vida Scudder. The language of these women was rich with obedient references to "Him," "His will," and "the Master," terminology that Addams never employed. Starr, like Scudder, set the spiritual world apart from, and above, the physical world, while Addams presumed that one inhered in the other. In fact, Scudder conceded to the social Darwinist view that the laws of nature were "inexorable" in their cruelty and offered up the mystical mercy of Christ to *reverse* those nature's laws.[56] By contrast, Addams believed that kindness and cooperation were "primordial" and that Jesus set about to remind people of the goodness of their own nature, not to rescue them from the clutches of an enemy nature. What fundamentally separated Ellen Starr and Jane Addams, by 1894, was that Starr sought to transcend human nature through prayer and ritual while Addams sought to become fully human through unconditional love of her fellows, believing that that achievement would be transcendence enough.

Study of the second half of Jane Addams's life will surely bring many surprises, but it seems unlikely that we will find that she ever moved far from her core faith in the power of unconditional love for human beings. She became more sentimental on this point, and more candidly mystical, but never more literal, never more orthodox. The faith Addams fashioned in her twenties was not an easy one, but it suited her for all the reasons recounted here, and more. In giving her a transcendent sermon for participation in public life, her faith also gave her a more humane, democratic approach to that life than her youthful ambition for the deed had ever imagined—and gave her far more joy than she had ever dared to hope was possible.

Notes

SCPC = Swarthmore College Peace Collection
HJFP = Haldeman-Julius Family Papers, UIC
JAMC = Jane Addams Memorial Collection, UIC
EGSP = Ellen Gates Starr Papers, Smith College
SCHS = Stephenson County Historical Society
HHScrapbooks = Hull-House Scrapbooks, UIC

All letters to or from Jane Addams can be found in the Jane Addams Papers on microfilm, as can her speeches and the scrapbooks.

1. Jane Addams, *Twenty Years at Hull-House with Autobiographical Notes* (New York: Macmillan Company, 1910), 49–50.
2. For a more complete discussion of Addams's evolution, see Victoria Bissell Brown, *The Education of Jane Addams* (Philadelphia: University of Pennsylvania Press, 2004).
3. Jane H. Hunter, "Inscribing the Self in the Heart of the Family: Diaries and Girlhood in Late-Victorian America," *American Quarterly* 44 (March 1992): 51–81.
4. Jane Addams Diary, March 20, 1875; March 8, 1875; and May 31, 1875, SCPC.
5. Jane Addams Diary, January 24, March 14, January 17, March 21, May 9, April 25, May 2, and May 16, 1875, SCPC.
6. Harry Haldeman to Anna Haldeman Addams, February 16, 1873, SAH.
7. Mary Addams to Elizabeth Reiff, August 1, 1863, SAH; Rev. John Linn to Jane Addams, August 26, 1881, SCPC.

8. Jane Addams to James Weber Linn, February 2, 1935, SCPC. See the eulogy delivered by the local Presbyterian minister at the time of John Addams's death: "Hon. John H. Addams," *Freeport Budget,* August 27, 1881.

9. Jane Addams to William I. Hull, January 16, 1916, Swarthmore College Friends Historical Library.

10. Addams, *Twenty Years,* 16.

11. John Addams Diary, October 4, 1844, SCPC.

12. Anna Haldeman Addams to Harry Haldeman, November 30, 1882, HJFP.

13. John Addams to Anna Haldeman Addams, August 1, 1869, SCPC.

14. Jane Addams Diary, Summer 1881, JAMC.

15. Jane Addams to Ellen Gates Starr, December 6, 1885, EGSP.

16. Lucy F. Townsend, "Anna Peck Sill and the Rise of Women's Collegiate Curriculum" (PhD diss., Loyola University of Chicago, 1985), 235.

17. Jane Addams, "George Eliot's View of Savonarola," n.d.; "Follow Thy Star," February 26, 1879; "Hannibal," n.d.; "High Trees Take the Wind," n.d.; "The Notion of Conscience," n.d.; all Rockford Seminary essays, Detzer Collection, UIC.

18. Jane Addams to Eva Campbell, July 25, 1879, Eugene Goodrich Papers, York, Neb.; Thomas Carlyle, *Past and Present* (1843; New York: Charles Scribner's Sons, 1918), 183.

19. Jane Addams, "Opening Address of Junior Exhibition," *Rockford Seminary Magazine* 8 (April 1880): 110–11.

20. For a discussion of how Addams addressed this gendered dilemma, see Shannon Jackson, "Toward a Queer Social Welfare Studies: Unsettling Jane Addams," in this volume.

21. Jane Addams to Ellen Gates Starr, November 22, 1879, EGSP

22. Jane Addams to Ellen Gates Starr, August 1, 1879, EGSP.

23. Jane Addams to Ellen Gates Starr, November 22, 1879, EGSP; Jane Addams to Ellen Gates Starr, January 29, 1880, EGSP.

24. T. H. Haseltine to Jane Addams, June 13, 1880, SCHS. Jane Addams's letter to Haseltine did not survive.

25. Jane Addams to Eva Campbell, July 25, 1879, Eugene Goodrich Papers, York, Neb.

26. Jane Addams, "Cassandra," in Essays of Graduating Class, Thirtieth Commencement, Rockford Seminary, Wednesday, June 22, 1881, pp. 37–38, RCA.

27. Jane Addams to Ellen Gates Starr, November 22, 1879, EGSP.

28. Jane Addams to Ellen Gates Starr, August 11, 1879, EGSP.

29. Jane Addams, "The Nebular Hypothesis," January 28, 1880, and "Darkness vs. Nebulae," June 14, 1880, Rockford Seminary Essays, Detzer Collection, UIC.

30. Jane Addams, "The Subjective Necessity for Social Settlements," in *Philanthropy and Social Progress: Seven Essays Delivered Before the School for Applied Ethics* (New York: Thomas Y. Crowell & Company, 1893), 17–18. For a discussion of Addams's 1892 lectures for the School of Applied Ethics in terms of her engagement with the

cooperators' movement, see Louise W. Knight, "Jane Addams's Theory of Cooperation," in this volume.

31. Addams, "The Subjective Necessity for Social Settlements," 18, 23.

32. Jane Addams, "Outgrowths of Toynbee Hall," December 3, 1890, unpublished manuscript, p. 8, SCPC.

33. Addams, "Outgrowths of Toynbee Hall," 4.

34. Jane Addams, "What Shall We Do For Our Unemployed," Sunset Club *Yearbook*, 1893–94, pp. 81–82.

35. Rev. John Linn to Jane Addams, August 26, 1881, SCPC.

36. Jane Addams, "The College Woman and the Family Claim," *The Commons* 3 (September 1898), 3–7.

37. Jane Addams Notebook, entries undated, but internal comments indicate spring and summer of 1882. SCPC and Jane Addams Microfilm, Reel 27, Frames 0366, 0368.

38. Jane Addams to Ellen Gates Starr, March 9, 1884, EGSP.

39. Ellen Gates Starr to Jane Addams, December 3, 1885; December 8, 1885; and January 31, 1886, EGSP. Ellen Gates Starr to Jane Addams, March 10 and 13, 1886, SCPC.

40. Jane Addams to Ellen Gates Starr, March 30, 1885, EGSP.

41. Leo Tolstoy, *My Religion,* volume 17 in *The Novels and Other Works of Lyof N. Tolstoi* (New York: Charles Scribner's Sons, 1899), 77, 85, 87.

42. Addams, *Twenty Years,* 87–88.

43. Jane Addams to Alice Addams Haldeman, June 14, 1888, HJFP.

44. There is a rich literature on Samuel Barnett's philosophical approach to his work at Toynbee Hall. See, for example, Samuel A. Barnett, *Practicable Socialism: Essays on Social Reform* (London and New York: Longmans, Green and Company, 1888, 1894); Henrietta Barnett, *Canon Barnett: His Life, Work, and Friends by His Wife* (New York: G. P. Putnam's Sons, 1921); Henry Bradford Washburn, *The Religious Motive in Philanthropy* (Philadelphia: University of Pennsylvania Press, 1931), 31–41; Lois Ellen Shankman Nettleship, "The Settlement Rationale: A Comparative Study of Samuel Barnett and Jane Addams, 1870 to 1914" (PhD diss., University of Sussex, England, 1976); Standish Meacham, *Toynbee Hall and Social Reform, 1880–1914: The Search for Community* (New Haven, Conn.: Yale University Press, 1987).

45. Regarding T. H. Green, see James T. Kloppenberg, *Uncertain Victory: Social Democracy and Progressivism in European and American Thought, 1870–1920* (New York: Oxford University Press). Addams did not articulate her familiarity with Green until she delivered the speech, "Outgrowths of Toynbee Hall," 1890, SCPC. Her familiarity with Tolstoy's fierce, lyric tribute to these ideals prepared her for an appreciation of Green's less-accessible philosophical defense of them.

46. Addams, *Twenty Years,* 78.

47. Jane Addams to Alice Addams Haldeman, March 22, 1888, SAH.

48. Jane Addams to Ellen Gates Starr, January 24, 1889, EGSP.

49. After one memorable encounter, Jane wrote to Mary: "I met the entire board

of the Armour Mission last Sunday at four, about twenty gentlemen including some of the head teachers with Mrs. Beveridge to chaperone for me. Dr. Hollister himself introduced me, sat beside me and petted my shoulder encouragingly when I said anything that pleased him." Jane Addams to Mary Addams Linn, February 12, 1889, SCPC. Jane often seemed amused by her encounters with missionaries, as if she saw a secret joke in these earnest believers' interest in her and her project. Jane Addams to Mary Addams Linn, April 1, 1889, SCPC

50. Ellen Gates Starr to Mary Starr Blaisdell, February 23, 1889, EGSP.

51. Ibid.

52. "And Not Leave the Other Undone," *The Advance,* October 20, 1892; Hull-House Scrapbooks.

53. "Poor Are Ever Welcome: Growth and Work of Hull House, a Most Noble Charity," *Chicago Times,* September 26, 1892; "And Not Leave the Other Undone," *The Advance,* October 20, 1892; Rev. Theodore Crowl, "Hull House," *The Presbyterian Messenger,* 1894, p. 3; The "Editorial" in the *Unitarian* for March 1894 said that Addams and her coworkers were "applying literal Christianity." *Unity* magazine, untitled editorial, November 1892; "Social Settlements," *The Churchman,* November 24, 1892; "Men and Things," *Unity,* July 27, 1893, reviewed a criticism of settlements that was first published in the Episcopal publication *The Living Church* and then reprinted in the liberal magazine *The Independent. The Independent* editors wrote that if settlements are worldly, "give us more worldliness." Crowl, "Hull House," p. 3; "What Two Little Women Have Done," *Christian Register,* July 1894; Mary Josephine Onahan, in "A Social Settlement," described Hull-House as a "non-Catholic convent" and expressed regret that "the Church whose Madonna occupies the place of honor . . . that that church with all her tremendous leverage for good should remain a thing apart, not known, not understood" by the needy masses. *The Citizen,* end of 1894. Onahan argued that "though they have no religious exercises of any sort—at least none are evident to the casual guest—they are certainly animated by the true religious spirit." HHScrapbooks.

54. "Tells Ministers of Hull House: Miss Jane Addams Appears Before Congregationalists in Oak Park," no citation, May 22, 1894, HHScrapbooks.

55. Samuel Barnett to Jane Addams, December 26, 1892, and June 9, 1893, SCPC.

56. Vida Scudder, "The Socialism of Christ," *The Dawn* 3 (December 1890): 3–4; Addams, "The Subjective Necessity for Social Settlements," 10–12, 17–19; Ellen Gates Starr to Mary Allen, 1891 and August 13, 1892, EGSP; Ellen Gates Starr, "A Bypath to the Great Roadway," *The Catholic World* 119 (May 1924): 178.

2

The Courage of One's Convictions or the Conviction of One's Courage?

Jane Addams's Principled Compromises

CHARLENE HADDOCK SEIGFRIED

> Self-righteousness has perhaps been responsible for more cruelty from the strong to the weak, from the good to the erring than any other human trait.[1]

Jane Addams would be just as controversial today as she was in her own lifetime, idolized by some and reviled by others. Ideologically, she is something of a Rorschach test. For upholders of the status quo, she was branded a revolutionary, a socialist, and a tool of labor, while for ideological radicals she was too reformist and willing to compromise on principles and work within instead of against the system.[2] For the general public, Addams's positions were most often praised when they seemed to conform to a conventional feminine model of good works and attacked when she publicly supported unpopular causes. After raising her to the status of urban saint for her reform efforts to help the immigrant poor and clean up corrupt politics in Chicago, for example, they then reviled her as a traitor for remaining a pacifist after the United States entered the First World War.

Although it is not unusual for social activists to elicit such contradictory assessments depending on the perspective of the viewer, in Addams's case, her pragmatist aversion to ideology, to favoring a particular social, political, or religious orthodoxy to the exclusion of all others, was guaranteed to alienate her from those who solicited her allegiance.[3] It continues to provoke those who evaluate her theories and actions by how well they conform to some preconceived notion of what a radical theorist or reform activist ought to be or to have done. From the perspective of absolute truth and moral certainty that ignores the development of beliefs over time, anything less than complete assent to what is indubitably true and good is either an intellectual or moral failure. But as evidence mounts that human beings must struggle time and again to overcome the limitations of nature and culture to attain better, if not the absolute best, beliefs about the world, and that the moral judgments of one time and place are often questioned and deplored in other times and places, it could well be that conciliation and compromise in view of a more inclusive outcome is both the wiser and the better approach. In this essay, I will examine Addams's antipathy to dogmatism and her willingness to compromise as key components of her philosophic outlook and as evidence of a principled stance, rather than as an expression of indecisiveness or moral relativism that it might otherwise seem to be.[4]

Affirming Multiple Perspectives

In *Twenty Years at Hull-House,* Addams presented her resistance while at Rockford seminary to making a religious profession of faith as foreshadowing her resistance during the first decade of the Hull-House settlement to proclaiming herself a socialist. In both cases, she was being pressed to accept a particular version of what constituted the true (religious or political) faith, instead of being left free to "to select what seemed reasonable from this wilderness of dogma."[5] No one denomination or socialist party, which are essentially partial perspectives, could lay claim to the whole truth without distorting or denying other perspectives or aspects of truth. Rather than beginning with the assumption that one already has the truth or knows the good, pragmatists believe that particular truths and particular goods emerge from intelligent transactions between organisms and their natural and social environments. Addams's concern that this experiential learning not be distorted by assumptions of one-sided expertise or moral authority finds expression in her central antielitist principle of reciprocity.

She developed this principle of reciprocity in two papers given at the School of Applied Ethics in 1892 on the subjective and objective necessity for social settlements.[6] The miserable conditions in which the working-class immigrant poor lived and worked, and the obstacles they faced in trying to better their condition, made the activities of the Hull-House residents objectively necessary. This objective need was acknowledged by all who were concerned with social justice and who cared to examine the conditions surrounding rapid industrialization in the cities, but it needed to be more widely recognized. Addams's second claim, however, was less obvious but for her no less important. It was that privileged members of society were also in need of enlightenment of the sort that those supposedly less well-off were uniquely in a position to offer them. She argued that hierarchical exchanges, no matter how well-meant, and even when they seem to objectively remedy social problems, nonetheless demean the recipients and corrupt the upper classes. Because they either support or undermine the intrinsic dignity of the persons involved, the nature of the exchanges themselves, as much as the goals sought, constitute the moral worth of the engagements.

Addams argued that unless such interactions are subjectively recognized as beneficial to the caregivers as well as the caretakers, and efforts are consciously made to learn from and include those receiving aid at every possible stage of inquiry and services, the injustices that led to the oppressive conditions in the first place would persist. Her more radical friends, however, witheringly referred to *Philanthropy and Social Progress,* the book of collected papers from the School of Applied Ethics sessions, as "a fine Victorian example of rose water for the plague."[7] The problem was that Addams was not an ideological purist but joined other causes on her own terms, and so her approach was ridiculed. She recognized that identifying herself or Hull-House with any particular political party, religious denomination, or ideology would alienate those who represented other positions, and she steadfastly refused to do so. This was not just a politically savvy position, as her writings make clear, but followed from her belief that no one person or group and no one perspective or ideology has a monopoly on the truth. Demands for unwavering loyalty to set of beliefs—no matter how enlightened and well-meant—are counterproductive because they are responsive neither to the point of view of persons differently situated nor to changing circumstances. We ourselves are not immune to such changes. As Dewey succinctly put it: "Good things change and vanish not only with changes in the environing medium but with changes in ourselves."[8] Knowledge does not exist like apples on a tree that can be picked by anyone with a ladder, but emerges in situations in which sympathetic understanding opens the way for cooperative undertakings. Not surprisingly, each radical group in turn could question Addams's loyalty and doubt her long-term effectiveness.

Addams' conciliatory style did not serve her well when she was appointed, along with other reform-minded civic leaders, to the Board of Education of Chicago in an effort to reform the troubled Chicago school system.[9] Political controversies characterized her 1905–8 term of office. On the one hand, she and the other reformers were relentlessly attacked as too radical by the newspapers, one of which was benefiting from under-assessment of taxes due the public school system. On the other hand, Addams was later criticized by other reform school board members as giving in to the establishment. The Teachers' Federation plan to remove teacher promotion and salary from political manipulation provoked a massive controversy and was stigmatized as representing an opening wedge to socialism. Addams infuriated the head of the Teachers' Federation, Margaret Haley, by voting for a compromise proposal. Haley thought Addams should have had the courage to stand by her convictions and refuse to compromise on a fundamental democratic principle. Addams saw it as a matter of policy and not of principle. Allen F. Davis, responding to the incident as reported by Margaret Robins, insinuates that Addams was less than passionately involved in reform efforts when he says that "she did on occasion stand for a principle, but she preferred compromise, disliked conflict, and those who believed with all their hearts in an idea, as Robins and Haley did, were always disappointed in her."[10]

When the reform mayor was defeated for reelection and the new mayor demanded the resignation of almost every reform member on the board, the ousted members protested loudly that she did not come to their defense or resign in protest, but "again took the middle ground." Haley reported Addams's betrayal to the feminist activist, Anna Garlin Spencer, and said she was not the great moral leader the reformers expected because of her penchant for reflecting the feelings of those around her and her power of putting herself in the place of the other to an unusual degree. Davis's rather weak defense of Addams was that "[s]he was by nature a compromiser who preferred the middle ground." But Florence Kelley, a firebrand Marxist socialist resident of Hull-House, who alone among the residents did not scruple to criticize Addams and pushed her firmly away from philanthropy toward social reform, interpreted Addams's actions in a different light.[11] She asked her friend Lillian Wald, who was the founder of the Henry Street Settlement in New York, where Kelley lived for decades after leaving Hull-House: "Did you ever hear of anything so loony as Raymond Robins' systematic attack upon Miss Addams because she did not resign from the Chicago school board when he was dropped from it? Did you ever hear of a man resigning because a woman was dropped?"[12] The point is not that Kelley defended Addams's decision on feminist terms and Haley criticized it on socialist or moral terms, but that both Haley and Davis interpreted Addams as compromising when she should have stood on principle. That Kelley did not join in the criticism is a good indication that she understood the issue, not as one of principle versus compromise, but as forging principle through continuous communication and compromise, once compromise is understood as a recognition of multiple perspectives that need to be respected and examined.

Principled or Compromiser—Radical or Reformer?

Pragmatists are frequently accused of compromising by those who have no doubt of the righteousness of their cause and who assume that those who are not unquestionably with them are against them. In a world of moral certitude professing ethical universalism, it is an accusation of moral cowardice that is hard to shake off. It is vitally important to do so, however, in a world like ours where cultural, religious, moral, ethnic, and political differences are threatening the fragile stability of daily civility as well as the larger world order. Standing up for one's principles despite opposition has always been honored as an expression of moral rectitude, and when the opposition is extreme—as when Martin Luther King spoke out against segregation despite great personal danger—as heroic. But King's approach was not always directly confrontational. Indeed, his willingness to be conciliatory alienated him from Black Power advocates of more radical and intransigent solutions.

Addams is recognizably pragmatist in her opposition to dogmatism and ideological loyalty. Pragmatists oppose these attitudes because they bolster smug self-assurance and self-righteousness and lessen interest in inquiry and self-criticism and make it difficult to really hear or understand those who disagree with them. Such loyalist attitudes undermine interest in undertaking rational and imaginative inquiry into the causes, context, and cultural matrix of social problems that is at the heart of pragmatist philosophy. Addams seems to have been temperamentally predisposed toward nonconfrontational interactions with others and she was a natural peacemaker, but her experiences at Hull-House led her to deepen and broaden these tendencies into an experientially based theory.[13] What others might perceive as compromise, she understood as a profound respect for the individuality and dignity of all human beings that obliged her to see their point of view and work with them toward a mutually satisfactory resolution of whatever issue set them apart. Addams did not assume that she had a privileged approach to social betterment, and was willing to align herself with any nondiscriminatory ideology or group to resolve common societal problems. What she would not do was to affirm or take any position that in principle demonized some other group and excluded their participation. Because of the recurring tendency to assume ill will in those who disagree or oppose us, either personally or as members of nation-states, her attitude will continue to be unpopular and yet no less needed.

Too often missing in the current debate over how to situate Addams and the women of Hull-House on a political continuum, from radical anarchism on the left to a cult of femininity on the right, is any recognition of the existence of a pragmatist feminism.[14] From its own philosophical perspective, pragmatism criticized both the extreme individualism of liberalism and the Marxist socialist reductive materialist analyses and belief in the inevitability of the violent overthrow of capitalism. But it also sought to revivify the liberal emphasis on the importance of individual growth and development and to emphasize with Marxists the social nature of persons and the centrality of social ends to human flourishing. Pragmatist feminists analyzed the subjugated situation of women and minorities, developed emancipatory theories, and worked for a nonsexist, nonracist, nonclassist society, using pragmatist theory. The strengths and weaknesses of this feminist theory and practice mirrored somewhat those of pragmatist theory, but are not simply reducible to them.[15] In any case, first-generation women pragmatists like Addams cannot be adequately understood or evaluated in ignorance of their core theoretical beliefs.[16] The interdependency of all persons in society, from the local to the global, and the necessity for cooperation and mutual responsibility if all human beings are to realize their potential, are among these core beliefs of Addams's ethical theory.[17]

As Addams is brought back into current debates, the old controversies are reemerging, particularly those between radical socialists who aligned themselves with various factions and the pragmatic socialism of Hull-House. But this controversy over who has the right to radical credentials should not just blindly replay these earlier ideological clashes.[18] Contemporary feminist theories have developed significantly since their earlier formulations, and assessments of Addams's feminism should reflect these changes. Most significant among them is the recognition that just as there is no essential female experience, but a variety of ways that women incorporate or negotiate being female with being black, Latina, Asian, or white, with class, with sexual orientation, in a colonial context, and so forth, so there is no one feminist theory that is free from biases and that is adequate for all the varieties of women's experiences.[19] The terms of the debate about what is significantly feminist and what is counterproductive have shifted dramatically, and it is time to take a fresh look at the earlier controversies, rather than just repeating the earlier accusations and labels.

Dogmatism and Tolerance

Rivka Shpak Lissak criticizes Addams and other Hull-House residents for being elitist and ethnocentric.[20] But neither her arguments nor her examples demonstrate her case, which might be made with more accuracy about other settlement houses specifically designed to "Americanize" new immigrants as quickly as possible to make them pliable and docile workers. She does not recognize the way that Addams skillfully shaped her narrative in *Twenty Years at Hull-House* to emphasize that the cultured, religious views that the first generation of women college graduates brought with them were continually subverted by their experiences, and how they gradually and painfully learned to shed their preconceptions and prejudices. This ability to learn from experience, which pragmatists call the experimental method, is the central methodological approach in the book. Its antithesis is dogmatism, most often disguised as the plain expression of universal moral principles and self-evident truths.[21]

It is true that Julia Lathrop's first educational group at Hull-House was the Plato Club, sometimes presided over by John Dewey, but it is forgotten that such access to high culture was enthusiastically sought by the workers themselves, who occasionally extended the two-hour Sunday sessions, which were to end at six o'clock, to ten o'clock.[22] It is also important to recognize a learning curve. Addams and Lathrop at first sought to share with their immigrant, working-class neighbors what they themselves had learned as recent liberal arts graduates. But these very same neighbors soon demanded new and different skills. Instead of clinging to what they already knew, the Hull-House residents were exceptionally flexible and eager to continually move into new and even frightening areas. A recurring theme of *Twenty Years at Hull-House,* after all, is how poorly prepared the first generation of college women were to meet the extreme challenges brought about by the triumph of predatory, laissez-faire capitalism, including great waves of immigration, with their attendant poverty, misery, and class warfare, political corruption, and violent clashes between industrialists and labor.

In the early days when the Plato Club was meeting, for example, Addams and Lathrop were implored to attend a woman in the tenements who was in painful labor but whom no one would help because she was not married, and none of her neighbors would send for a doctor because they feared being stuck with the bill. Addams and Lathrop delivered the baby themselves, and on the way home Addams mused that midwifery was really carrying too far their willingness to relieve the misery of others, even when they had no particular knowledge or skills to do so. Lathrop promptly responded that even if they were to begin refusing to do what they were ignorant of, they could not at any rate start by cutting out humanitarian help, because if the work of Hull-House was not rooted in basic human kindness, it could do no good at all. Their courage and willingness to take on tasks beyond their knowledge and training were sorely tested in their very first winter, when they were called out to a transportation company that was ablaze in order to certify that their horses were seriously enough injured to be killed. The insurance company was too busy to send their own men, and they would not pay without a proper report. Both Addams and Lathrop were overcome with the suffering of a stable full of groaning, screaming horses, but forced themselves to witness it so that the horses could be more quickly put out of their misery.[23]

Addams's willingness to take on the social, economic, and political challenges of an extremely contentious Chicago at the turn of the twentieth century made her excruciatingly aware of the inadequacies of the beliefs, values, and expectations of her white, middle-class upbringing. She was predisposed to learning what she needed to know from those with whom she worked, and so intelligently self-reflective that she welcomed evidence of her own unconscious biases and began theorizing on how to overcome or at least mitigate their negative effects.[24] A recurrent theme in *Twenty Years at Hull-House* is the failure of the establishment, of the elites, of the better educated, and upper classes to understand or adequately deal with the problems created by industrialization, immigration, urbanization, ethnic diversity, and poverty. Addams demonstrates by concrete examples that reform efforts are sure to go wrong when imposed by those who claim superior moral integrity, class privilege, or political power, and can only succeed by cooperative efforts with those considered inferior on one or all of these grounds. The conviction of the righteousness of one's cause too often hinders rather than helps in overcoming unjust and oppressive economic, political, and social conditions. Care and concern for others is insufficient unless balanced with a sense of one's own inadequacies and the strengths even the poorest bring with them. Addams was therefore intent on developing attitudes that would encourage treating others as equal partners whose insights, labor, and good will were necessary for overcoming common social ills.

According to her nephew and biographer, James Weber Linn, Addams "sometimes resented the fact that tolerance seems to the fanatic either stupid or a crime."[25] He quotes her conviction "that nearly all the conflicts arising between men and peoples could be adjusted happily through a little yielding on both sides; that there were hardly any differences of opinion that might not be settled satisfactorily" were each side prepared to understand the issues involved.[26] Dewey shared the same belief, and it underlies his optimism about the pragmatic method. Both apparently thought that social conflicts arise all the time because of the diversity of interests operating in society, but a basic willingness to resolve these conflicts harmoniously, if at all possible, should provide a sufficient motive to work together. If solutions were not immediately forthcoming, as is not uncommon in long-standing, complex social problems, then the process itself of cooperative struggle among diverse groups becomes that much more important.[27]

Diversifying Pragmatist Theory

In an effort to characterize Addams's major strength as her effectiveness in changing public opinion on important issues, Daniel Levine downplays her intellectual contributions. He says she was not even more important than the other settlement workers "for the ideas she originated, because most of her ideas were not her own."[28] But a close reading of Addams's work, along with a knowledge of her participation in the major intellectual currents of the time, shows that such a dismissive judgment cannot be sustained. Her close collaboration with the other important figures in the Chicago school of pragmatism and interest in obtaining a "philosophical warrant" for her insights and practices distinguished the quality of Addams's philosophical contributions from that of the other women at Hull-House.[29] She shared this interest in explicitly integrating a coherent theory with and through practice with Kelley, whose socialism was thoroughly grounded in Marxist theory and was ardently acted on.[30]

In 1907, the same year that Addams published *Newer Ideals of Peace,* William James issued a ringing call for philosophy to return to concrete contact with life. He pointed out that dazzling intellectual acrobatics cannot satisfy people's needs; what is wanted is "some positive connexion [sic.] with this actual world of finite human lives." Academic philosophy, he complained, had come to resemble a classic sanctuary on a hill in which rationalistic thinkers take refuge from the confusions and distractions of everyday life. James wanted to develop instead a philosophy that does not shrink back from "the world of concrete personal experiences to which the street belongs," a world that "is multitudinous beyond imagination, tangled, muddy, painful and perplexed."[31] Addams's settlement work literally took philosophic reflection into the streets, and her writings demonstrate the value of interrelating theory and practice.

In *Twenty Years at Hull-House* Addams remarks that a settlement does not have the comfort adherence to dogmatic certainties would give, but "shares the perplexities of its times."[32] In recalling how the tumultuous early days of establishing the settlement left no time for its members to lose themselves in speculation, she tells of an incident in which she was standing near the foundations of the new gymnasium Hull-House was building. A Scottish neighbor passing by remarked that the settlement was spreading out, to which Addams responded that perhaps they were spreading too fast. "'Oh, no,' he rejoined, 'you can afford to spread out wide, you are so well planted in the mud,'" as he playfully glanced at the deep mire of the unpaved street on which they both stood.[33] She was indeed well planted in the muddy, painful, and perplexing world James and the other pragmatists were eager to address. In James's words, "She simply inhabits reality, and everything she says necessarily expresses its nature. She *can't help writing truth.*"[34]

Because Addams lived and worked among the tenements in an immigrant neighborhood, she was intimately acquainted with the problems of the working class. Other pragmatists like James, Mead, and Dewey were no less involved in social reform, but they were differently positioned. As astute students of, and collaborators in, the cutting-edge research of their times, these academics could base their theories on the best empirical data available. But they also learned from Addams, various Hull-House residents, and other social settlements and civic clubs, not only what worked and what did not, but how to put collaborative efforts and the needs of others at the center of their theory and practice. The close-knit Hull-House community, which approached problems from multiple perspectives and with different skills, embodied the multidisciplinary approach advocated by the Chicago pragmatists, in and out of the academy. Thus, their theories changed in response to changing conditions, not only in scientific findings but also in response to historical, social, and cultural changes.

Along with other pragmatists, Addams's philosophical approach can be summed up as the belief in the educational and socially transformative value of the continuing reconstruction of experience. One of her major contributions to pragmatist theory is her recognition and demonstration of the concrete diversity of such experience, with all this implies.[35] In expounding the significance of such diversity, she problematizes pragmatist appeals to experience and pluralism in which the barriers to shared experience are too easily glossed over. James, for example, has a suggestively challenging account of the many levels of reality that can peacefully coexist in one person's consciousness. When they happen to clash, they do so on the epistemological level and are usually resolved by being reflectively brought into compliance with beliefs and perceptions of the bodily self. For James, one's own hierarchy of realities is fluid and can be playfully and creatively rearranged, until there is a need to bring it in line with one's own dominant view of reality. Just how much this dominant view is thought to be pretty much the same for all, despite James's heartfelt recognition and valuing of diversity, can be seen when it is contrasted with Addams's viewpoint.

The many levels of reality Addams considers are concretely embodied in persons whose history, ethnicity, class, and gender lead to such different experiences from one's own that misunderstandings are inevitable and not easily resolvable. The conflicting perceptual and moral judgments engendered by such diverse realities are emotionally troubling and cannot be overcome by reflection alone. Moreover, the bodily self, which James un–self-critically assumes is male, white, Protestant, middle or upper class, and traditionally educated,[36] is in continuous process of renegotiation for Addams, whose heightened awareness encompasses her own female, Anglo-Saxon, Protestant, middle-class, traditionally educated self in interaction with male and female, young and old, ethnically diverse, Catholic and Jewish, upper class and working class, streetwise and culture-shocked, embodied selves. Inequalities of power, which Addams addresses in her concern to work with others instead of unilaterally imposing her worldviews and values on them, are minimized and ignored by James.

Especially in the early years of their relationship, Addams and Dewey worked closely together and shared insights. Nonetheless, Addams's recognition that experiences do not just happen but are had by someone in particular, often unanticipated, situations, and her analysis of how this specificity impacts the experiences themselves, greatly expand on and deepen Dewey's similar intention not to underplay either the role of the organism or the environment in his philosophy of experience. Dewey's view on communication and art is a case in point. He says that "[i]n the end, works of art are the only method of unhindered communication between man and man that can occur in a world full of gulfs and walls that limit community of experience."[37] But Addams recounts Hull-House efforts to break down the barriers between ethnically diverse factory workers and their middle-class detractors by introducing a number of their Hull-House neighbors to the high culture of the Art Institute of Chicago. The communication that ensued about a sculptured frieze of large skulls of oxen that symbolized classical Greek sacrifices to the resident, but that were simply depictions of skulls to the neighbors who "had no armor of erudition with which to protect themselves against such hideousness," revealed the lack of a common community of experience and showed that the works of art did not speak to the workers as it did to the residents of Hull-House.[38] But if museum art did not automatically lead to the unhindered communication predicted by Dewey, there were other forms of art that did, as Addams soon learned in her efforts to promote recognition of the beauty found in traditional skills such as weaving, music, and folk dancing.

Dogmatism and ideological fervor are the antithesis of communication. With deadpan humor Dewey points out that "communication is not announcing things, even if they are said with the emphasis of great sonority." He reimagines communication as "the process of creating participation, of making common what had been isolated and singular; and part of the miracle it achieves is that, being communicated, the conveyance of meaning gives body and definiteness to the experience of the one who utters as well as to that of those who listen."[39] Addams explores in great depth and detail the ways that genuine communication, communication that opens itself to the differing attitudes, values, and worldviews of others, profoundly changes the self-understanding, values, and experiences of those whose sense of moral superiority has habituated them to talking down to others. By implicating herself in this indictment, she slyly intimates that all of us are prone to fall into this sense of intellectual superiority and moral smugness without realizing it. In *Democracy and Social Ethics* she highlights this subjective aspect of the pragmatist method of inquiry through her emphasis on the perplexities inherent in it.[40]

Addams explains the women's movement, for example, as resulting from the growth of a new consciousness that seeks "to change political institutions that they might effectively give expression to the growth of new experiences."[41] Unlike domestic or cultural feminists with whom she is often identified, Addams does not assume essential gender differences. She argues that it is because of women's new experiences resulting from rapid industrialization and its dislocations, and not to their feminine natures, that women are coming together in varying ways in many countries and even across class lines. As women's intimacy with unsatisfactory and degraded social conditions has grown, so too has their social consciousness, and they become the obvious members of society to represent the interests neglected by men elected for supporting other interests. Addams believed that it is because women experience the need for "for better housing, for public health and education, for the care of dependents," because they are "'vividly aware' of the effects of chronic fatigue upon young working girls" and of stunted growth of children abused by a factory system fixated on profits, that they have been demanding their political rights.[42]

Inclusive participation in social and political decisions is not a luxury but a necessity for democracy to thrive because diverse experiences engender diverse viewpoints, which need to be heard and taken into consideration. A central argument for women's enfranchisement is that "in a complex community like the modern city all points of view needed to be represented; the resultants of diverse experiences need to be pooled if the community would make for sane and balanced progress."[43] Such a notion of progress should not be reduced to what progress means to a social Darwinist, despite the popularity, in Addams's day, of appeals to progress in the survival of the fittest as an excuse for predatory capitalism.[44] James argued that progress was one of the things that gave the deepest significance to life. But by progress he meant "that strange union of reality with ideal novelty which it continues from one moment to another to present."[45] So important is this dynamic sense of change characteristic of life that he defines intelligence as the ability to discern just which novelties are ideal and which just seem to be.

Mary E. McDowell, another of the pioneer residents of Hull-House, explained that she was attracted to settlement work because of its antiorthodoxy and dedication to change and progress. A more pervasive sentiment, as James explained it, was to identify ideals with "the older more familiar good." Instead, McDowell says: "We are ready to look at any situation on its merits, to study it and then to change it if it seems good." Seeking novelty may be a weakness, she continues, "but anyway it is a settlement weakness not to be afraid of a new thing, or a settlement strength, I mean." Her words gain particular resonance because she constantly contrasts this willingness to experiment with the ethnic and class prejudices with which she grew up, and that prevented the better-off members of society from challenging the conventions hindering social progress.[46]

The more unsettling and frightening situations are, the more likely it still is that confrontation will be preferred over self-criticism and cooperation in resolving them. Like Addams, Eleanor Roosevelt, during the Great Depression, publicly called for recognition of diverse viewpoints as a precondition for progress in democracy: "[W]e must learn to work together, all of us, regardless of race or creed or color; we must wipe out, wherever we find it, any feeling . . . of intolerance, of belief that any one group can go ahead alone. We go ahead together or we go down together." But her proposal, too, was greeted with "howls of protest."[47] And many decades later, during another crisis, in a speech to the graduating class of 2002 at the U.S. Military Academy at West Point, President George W. Bush reiterated his frequently expressed view that "[w]e are in a conflict between good and evil, and America will call evil by its name. By confronting evil and lawless regimes, we do not create a problem, we reveal a problem. And we will lead the world in opposing it."[48] Political rhetoric about the absolute evil of foreign governments and the absolute innocence of the United States, without any regard for the underlying economic, social, and political causes of international conflicts, is a chilling reminder that our prejudices are still not being recognized and that Addams's call for the need to open ourselves to the beliefs, attitudes, and values of those who profoundly disagree with us is more needed than ever, if sane and balanced resolutions are ever to be reached.

Social Ethics

Anna Garlin Spencer's complaint that Addams lost her claim to moral leadership because of her empathy with the feelings of others and her unusual ability to put herself in their place reflects a particular understanding of morality. Spencer must believe that morals are universal and invariant if she concludes that seeing the world as others see it and emotionally identifying with feelings other than those that spontaneously arise from one's own grasp of the moral law can only degrade or dilute moral purity. According to the pragmatist understanding of morality as evolving over time, as being culturally and situationally specific, and as subject to experimental verification, the very dispositions of Addams that Spencer criticizes are precisely what enabled her to become one of the great moral leaders and reformers of her time. Pragmatists have well-considered and deeply held values, such as the innate dignity and worth of all human beings and the necessity of making the means used to resolve troubling situations consistent with the ends sought. But they understand these moral principles as enunciating a naturalistic ethics, rather than a rationalistic ethics like Kant's. The difference is that a naturalistic ethics requires continued inquiry into the concrete conditions of human growth and development rather than rational arguments based on *a priori* principles.

Virginia Held contends that "[m]any feminist philosophers have questioned whether the reliance on abstract rules, rather than the adoption of more context-respectful approaches, can possibly be adequate for dealing with moral problems, especially as women experience them."[49] A naturalistic ethics, such as pragmatist feminist ethics, works to remedy unjust social relations, alleviate remediable sufferings, and extend experienced goods as widely as possible. In so doing, it modifies the very understanding of what constitutes such evils and goods. If good is experientially based, if it consists in human flourishing, then its concrete basis is an ongoing process of satisfaction or dissatisfaction with some state of affairs. The work of extending a good discoverable in a particular situation to others to which it is applicable, or of ridding the bad features that first come to light in a specific situation to others more broadly, is the method by which pragmatists have reconstructed universals. Instead of applying already recognized universals to particular situations, universals are generated out of situations only insofar as they are found after the fact to be of value in other situations. In the process of finding out if and to what extent they continue to be valuable, such ideals themselves undergo modification.

In her social ethics, Addams distinguishes between two viewpoints. One is that of autonomous decision making, based on the dictates of one's own conscience and following one's own ideals.[50] This model has been idealized in many ethical approaches. But because this model is also attractive to powerful business leaders, who have both a strong sense of self-worth and the power to unilaterally carry their decisions into operation, she calls this model "the commercial standpoint." In doing so, she begins developing the unacknowledged fallacy in the position, namely the assumption that autonomy, both as ideal and as fact, means self-sufficiency, detachment, the lack of binding relationships, and interdependency. She also draws out its inevitable corollary: namely, its justification of one-sided, hierarchical decision making and oppressive action.

The other viewpoint is consensual decision making. When consent is sought, compromise is inevitable. With a "feasible right" in sight, absolute right cannot be the criterion. In seeking together with people to attain a common goal, one's own view of what that goal should be will inevitably be challenged and modified in the process. Indeed, no one will see clearly where such consensual decision making will lead until the process is gone through and acted upon. In compensation for the clarity and certainty lost in such a process, the goals eventually arrived at will more likely be sustained because they are upheld by the sentiments and aspirations of many others besides oneself. As Addams puts it, progress will be "slower perpendicularly, but incomparably greater because lateral."[51]

Is Addams's Pacifism a Dogmatic Exception to Cooperative Methodology?

The one position Addams herself admitted to holding dogmatically was pacifism.[52] It was dogmatic because she held it to be an absolute value, one that she could not imagine ever relinquishing, no matter what the social or political circumstances. Although always willing to question her own beliefs when they clashed with contrasting beliefs held with equal self-righteousness by others, she could follow neither the rationale nor the actions of so many of her acquaintances and deeply respected friends like Dewey, who gave up or limited their pacifism for the sake of preventing greater evil after the United States entered the First World War. This exception disturbed her greatly as possibly undermining her own pragmatist cooperative approach developed through her Hull-House years. Contrary to her own self-doubts, I think that Addams's pacifism was not dogmatic. It not only exemplifies the pragmatic method but contributes to our understanding of how it should operate in practice.

After America entered the war, Addams was increasingly isolated and her words distorted by a media anxious to promulgate war propaganda. In periods of doubt she wondered whether it was not wrong to abstain from joining the majority who were convinced of the rightness of their cause. She remained convinced, however, that just as evolutionary growth requires variation from the mass, so moral changes in human affairs may begin with "cranks" who go their own way against the moral consensus. Friends told her that by her stubborn persistence in pacifism she was losing any power of influencing people in the future, and they questioned her pride in opposing her viewpoint to that of highly regarded statesmen and moral leaders. Addams pinpointed the crux of the dilemma in her article, "Reactions of a Pacifist in Wartime" (1922). She says, "[th]en, too, we were always afraid of fanaticism, of preferring a consistency of theory to the conscientious recognition of the social situation, of a failure to meet life in the temper of a practical person. Every student of our time had become more or less a disciple of pragmatism and its great teachers in the United States had come out for the war and defended their positions with skill and philosophic acumen." That temperamentally, this theory and her own practice were congenial is obvious, as Addams goes on to remark: "There were moments when one longed desperately for reconciliation with one's friends and fellow citizens. . . . Solitude has always had its demons."[53]

Addams ruefully continues: "We certainly had none of the internal contentment of the doctrinaire, the ineffable solace of the self-righteous which was imputed to us. . . . [W]e suffered from the fact that we were no longer living in a period of dogma and were therefore in no position to announce our sense of security! We were well aware that the modern liberal having come to conceive truth of a kind which must vindicate itself in practice, finds it hard to hold even a sincere and mature opinion which from the very nature of things can have no justification in works. The pacifist in war time is literally starved of any gratification of that natural desire to have his own decisions justified by his fellows."[54]

Addams was well aware that without such confirmation by others over time, there is nothing left of the pragmatic method. She had even contributed to this methodology by emphasizing that the relevant others were not limited to, or even principally made up of, intellectuals and scientists, but of those most harshly affected by cultural, social, religious, economic, and political norms and practices. But in glaring contrast to their earlier stance of neutrality, the American public left Addams behind when they overwhelmingly supported the war after it was declared.

It was particularly galling for Addams to have her principled stance for pacifism derided as mere dogmatic stubbornness when all her life she had been particularly outspoken in her criticism of dogmatism with its attendant fanaticism. Indeed, she says: "That, perhaps, was the crux of the situation. We slowly became aware that our affirmation was regarded as pure dogma. We were thrust into the position of the doctrinaire, and although, had we been permitted, we might have cited both historic and scientific tests of our so-called doctrine of Peace, for the moment any sanction even by way of illustration was impossible." Unable to fall back on her usual arguments for the evidence of experience justifying her belief, and unable to assert that many others were coming to see pacifism as she did—namely, as a new value worth upholding for its consequences for the betterment of life—Addams reverted to the very assertion of absolute moral values that her theory and practice rejected. She said: "It therefore came about that ability to hold out against mass suggestion, to honestly differ from the convictions and enthusiasms of one's best friends did in moments of crisis come to depend upon the categorical belief that a man's primary allegiance is to his vision of the truth and that he is under obligation to affirm it."[55]

I think that Addams, physically ill and under great social pressure, and frustrated that no one any longer wanted to hear her arguments for her position, heroically simply continued to assert her advocacy of pacifism. If this was considered to be dogmatic, so be it. Her detractors claimed the high moral ground of absolute values; so would she. After all, her position was no less principled than theirs, and held at much greater cost. In any event, even a pragmatist is under obligation to act on the truth as she sees it. Unless she does so, what good would it be to bring together persons with different persuasions with any hope that sharing their beliefs might eventually lead to a more insightful and nuanced understanding of contentious situations?

Moreover, unless they are prepared to act on these beliefs as they come to hold them, how is anything going to change? In fact, careful examination of Addams's writings before and after this period of depression and frustration demonstrates that she did, in fact, use the pragmatic method to enunciate, refine, and defend her position. Of the war being waged among nations, for example, Addams asked her characteristic question: "Has the experience any value?" that is, what can we learn from it that would be of value in future experiences?[56]

She had earlier pointed out that because existing international law was inadequate to deal with the underlying social and economic causes of the war, the Women's Congress at the Hague proposed "a conference of neutral nations composed of men who have had international experience so long that they have come to think not merely in terms but in the realities of internationalism. . . . Such a conference would represent not one country or another, but human experience as it has developed during the last decades in Europe. It would stand not for 'peace at any price,' but would seriously and painstakingly endeavor to discover the price to be paid for peace, which would if possible be permanent as well as immediate."[57] Addams's appeal to experience was not naïve, but critical; it was to be interrogated and its value weighed. If its lessons were worthwhile, they could serve as precedent or as incentive to new experiences; if not, they could serve as rebuke or warning.

Later, alluding to the historical connection of centuries of revolutionary wars fought to gain the freedoms of democracy, Addams argued that once genuine democracies are established, they can only be sustained through a constant effort that required a state of peace in order to be carried out. Revolutions and democracy might be experientially connected, but that did not necessarily make them valuable allies. She believed she could demonstrate that "[w]ar itself destroys democracy wherever it thrives and tends to entrench militarism."[58] Experiences are dynamically and not straightforwardly connected with interpretations. Addams comments that "[d]uring the decade of suffrage women have learned that ideas change less rapidly than events, with the result that much political thought is always out of date and inappropriate to changed conditions."[59] She suggests that women could take what they learned through the long years of agitating for suffrage to help the public see freshly, to interpret their own experiences more constructively, and thus not become deadened by stale political propaganda.

Experience is not always efficacious or helpful. Unless we are self-critical, it can also prevent us from hearing what others have to say, particularly if those others are thought to be inferior to us in some way. Addams astutely notes: "It is said that we can all like the young or envy them or fear them, but to learn from them is more difficult. The conceit of experience, the pride in having overcome difficulties, gets in the way," and adds humorously, "if we learn from them we almost hope they haven't noticed it."[60] But theory uncorrected by constant experience is dangerous, and Addams gives many examples from her Hull-House years of how easy it is to fall unwittingly into this trap.

Although Addams could imagine no possible conditions in which experience would undermine her belief in the absolute value of pacifism, her arguments in its defense were invariably drawn from experience, not by appeal to absolute or transcendent moral principles. In this, it shares affinities with the other basic moral principles Hull-House was grounded in, namely, the inalienable dignity and worth of all human beings and the reciprocal obligations demanded by our biological and social interdependency. All these principles, pacifism included, were summed up as the necessary constituents of democracy understood as a way of life. Diversified human experience and resultant sympathy—two factors that Addams constantly stressed—were taken by her to be not only the foundation but also the guarantee of democracy.[61] And because no one doubts that democracy itself is a historically developed political and social system, and its emergence and continuance contingent on both human factors and circumstances, it cannot be mistaken for a transcendent principle to be dogmatically proclaimed.

Addams's legacy of antidogmatic but deeply committed cooperation was evident in a commencement speech she gave at Rockford College, fifty years after her own graduation from there. She had not worked with young people all her life without realizing, as she told the students, that they would no doubt consider her generation of 1881 positively prehistoric. Nonetheless, she claimed kinship with them and gently warned "against doing good to people, and trying to make others good by law. One does good," she continued, "if at all, *with* people, not *to* people."[62] No wonder it had deeply troubled her when her isolation during the war years prevented her from working with others to peacefully resolve the issues that so inflamed the passions of war. Her continued assertion of pacifism in the face of what must have seemed at times to be a nearly universal opposition appeared too much like a dogmatic imposition of her views on others, whether they agreed or not. It is not surprising that as soon as she was able to do so, she redoubled her cooperative efforts to prove that peaceful means worked. Her pacifism was both principled and pragmatic; it was not dogmatic.

Notes

1. Jane Addams, *The Second Twenty Years at Hull-House* (New York: Macmillan, 1930), 301.

2. Examples of these contrasting criticisms can be found in *Eighty Years at Hull-House,* ed. Allen F. Davis and Mary Lynn McCree (Chicago: Quadrangle Books, 1969), 110–13. In the same book, Francis Hackett recalls: "The ruling class spoke of 'Unsettlement workers' with animosity, the socialists of a mealy-mouthed compromise." "Hull-House—A Souvenir," 71.

3. On this alienation, and the courage it took to withstand pressures to take sides, see Victoria Bissell Brown, *The Education of Jane Addams* (Philadelphia: University of Pennsylvania Press, 2004), 271–72.

4. Knight discusses Addams's aversion to dogmatism and her willingness to compromise in terms of her theory of cooperation. See Louise W. Knight, "Jane Addams's Theory of Cooperation," in this volume.

5. Jane Addams, *Twenty Years at Hull-House* (New York: Penguin Books,1981), 54–55.

6. The papers, originally called "The Subjective Values of Social Settlements" and "The Objective Values of Social Settlements," were published along with others given at the School of Applied Ethics in a book called *Philanthropy and Social Progress,* ed. Henry C. Adams (New York: Thomas Y. Crowell, 1893). They were also revised and incorporated into *Twenty Years at Hull-House.*

7. Jane Addams, *My Friend, Julia Lathrop* (New York: Macmillan,1935), 57.

8. John Dewey, *Experience and Nature,* in Dewey, *The Later Works,* vol. 1: 1925, ed. Jo Ann Boydston (Carbondale: Southern Illinois University Press, 1988), 298. Dewey makes this assertion while explaining the function of philosophy as criticism. My apple metaphor in the next sentence obliquely refers to his well-known passage on the same page, beginning: "If values were as plentiful as huckleberries . . ."

9. The ultimately unsuccessful efforts to reform the Chicago school system are recounted in Daniel Levine, *Jane Addams and the Liberal Tradition* (Madison: State Historical Society of Wisconsin, 1971), 79–86.

10. Allen F. Davis, *American Heroine: The Life and Legend of Jane Addams* (New York: Oxford University Press, 1973), 131–34. Margaret Robins's husband, Raymond, was a reformist member of the board.

11. Ibid., 77–78, 134.

12. Ibid., 134.

13. Brown suggests that Addams's mediation skills and preference for peaceful solutions were forged in family conflicts that arose from her father's second marriage. *The Education of Jane Addams,* 39–54.

14. See Carlin Romano, "Addams Family Values" ("Mulling [Not Hulling] Jane Addams"), *The Chronicle Review* magazine of *The Chronicle of Higher Education* (March 29, 2002), B11.

15. See Charlene Haddock Seigfried, *Pragmatism and Feminism* (Chicago: University of Chicago Press, 1996).

16. The situation is similar to that of W. E. B. Du Bois, whose Marxist affiliations late in life are often exaggerated to the extent of ignoring his pragmatist origins and its impact on his theories. See, for example, David Levering Lewis, *W. E. B. Du Bois: Biography of a Race, 1868–1919* (New York: Henry Holt, 1993).

17. See "Jane Addams," *Blackwell Guide to American Philosophy,* ed. Armen T. Marsoobian and John Ryder (Malden, Mass.: Blackwell, 2003) and Charlene Haddock Seigfried, introduction, *Democracy and Social Ethics,* by Jane Addams (Urbana and Chicago: University of Illinois Press, 2002). Dewey expressed most starkly the social nature of pragmatist ethics: "The moral and the social quality of conduct are, in the last analysis, identical with each other." *Democracy and Education,* in Dewey, *The Middle Works,* vol. 9: 1916, ed. Jo Ann Boydston (Carbondale: Southern Illinois University Press, 1980), 368.

18. Dorothy Ross, for example, argues that Addams's domestic feminism differs from Dewey's more radical pragmatism in regard to their approaches to sociology. See Seigfried, "Socializing Democracy: Jane Addams and John Dewey," *Philosophy of the Social Sciences* 29, no. 2 (June 1999): 217–19.

19. Summaries of contemporary views can be found in the entries, "Gender," by Linda Nicholson, "Sexual Difference Theory," by Rosi Braidotti, and "Human Nature," by Nancy Holmstrom in *A Companion to Feminist Philosophy,* ed. Alison M. Jaggar and Iris Marion Young (Malden, Mass.: Blackwell, 1998).

20. Rivka Shpak Lissak, *Pluralism and Progressives: Hull House and the New Immigrants, 1890–1919* (Chicago: University of Chicago Press, 1989).

21. For more on Lissak's misunderstanding of pragmatism and the Hull-House settlement, see Seigfried, introduction, *Democracy and Social Ethics,* note 8.

22. Addams, *My Friend, Julia Lathrop,* 50.

23. Ibid., 53–54. Florence Kelley was responsible for redirecting "the settlement's activities away from neighborly aid and toward larger issues in public policy." Her response to similar calls to be all things to all people was quite different from Lathrop's, telling Ellen Starr, who was leaving to bathe the corpse of a neighborhood child, "Sister Starr, if we [are to] bring about a change in this country peaceably, we've got to hustle. I believe it's a solemn duty to wash the dead, but its mighty incidental!" Kathryn Kish Sklar, *Florence Kelley and the Nation's Work: The Rise of Women's Political Culture, 1830–1900* (New Haven, Conn.: Yale University Press, 1995), 194–95.

24. Besides Addams's own experiences of benevolence and her exposure to ideas that helped her rethink her experiences, Louise W. Knight credits Addams's recognition of class bias and her growing feminist consciousness in part to the Pullman crisis and the writing of "Lear." "Biography's Window on Social Change: Benevolence and Justice in Jane Addams's 'A Modern Lear,'" *Journal of Women's History* 9, no. 1 (Spring 1997): 111–38. See also Louise W. Knight, *Citizen: Jane Addams and the Struggle for Democracy* (Chicago: University of Chicago Press, 2005).

25. James Weber Linn, *Jane Addams: A Biography* (New York: D. Appleton-Century, 1935), 432.

26. Ibid., 431.

27. See Charlene Haddock Seigfried, "The Dilemma of Democracy: Diversity of Interests and Common Experiences," in *Renascent Pragmatism: Studies in Law and Social Science,* ed. Alfonso Morales (Brookfield, Vt.: Ashgate, 2003), 31–48.

28. Levine, *Jane Addams and the Liberal Tradition,* 86.

29. For Addams's influence on Dewey and her role as one of the founders of pragmatism, see *The Social Thought of Jane Addams,* ed. Christopher Lasch (New York: Irvington, 1982), 176; Mary Jo Deegan, *Jane Addams and the Men of the Chicago School, 1892–1918* (New Brunswick, N.J.: Transaction Books, 1988); Charlene Haddock Seigfried, "Classical American Philosophy's Invisible Women," *Canadian Review of American Studies* (1992), 83–116; and Seigfried, *Pragmatism and Feminism,* 58–59, 73–79.

30. See Sklar, *Florence Kelley.*

31. William James, *Pragmatism* (Cambridge, Mass.: Harvard University Press, 1975; orig. 1907), 17–18.

32. Addams, *Twenty Years,* 307.

33. Ibid., 116.

34. William James, review of Jane Addams, *The Spirit of Youth and the City Streets,* in *American Journal of Sociology* 15, no. 4 (January 1910), 553.

35. Compare Addams's analysis of diversity with Dewey's in Charlene Haddock Seigfried, "John Dewey's Pragmatist Feminism," in *Feminist Interpretations of John Dewey,* ed. Charlene Haddock Seigfried (University Park: Pennsylvania State University Press, 2002), 47–77.

36. Seigfried, *Pragmatism and Feminism,* 111–41.

37. John Dewey, *Art as Experience,* in Dewey, *The Later Works,* vol. 10: 1934, ed. Jo Ann Boydston (Carbondale: Southern Illinois University Press, 1989), 110.

38. Jane Addams, "A Function of the Social Settlement" (1899), in Lasch, *Social Thought,* 191–92. Addams uses the incident to illustrate the futility of imposing middle-class cultural norms on the laboring classes, arguing that artists should cease slavishly imitating the past and start developing instead new artistic forms appropriate for contemporary social movements.

39. Dewey, *Art as Experience,* 248–49.

40. See Seigfried, introduction, *Democracy and Social Ethics,* xxii–xxxi.

41. Jane Addams, "The Larger Aspects of the Woman's Movement" (1914), in Lasch, *Social Thought,* 151–62.

42. For additional discussion on Addams and suffrage, see Pastorello, "The Transfigured Few: Jane Addams, Bessie Abramowitz Hillman, and Immigrant Women Workers in Chicago, 1905–1915" in this volume.

43. Jane Addams, "Why Women Should Vote" (1910), in Lasch, *Social Thought,* 150.

44. Lissak, for example, makes this mistake. See Seigfried, introduction, *Democracy and Social Ethics,* xxxv, note 8. Brown traces Addams's rejection of Herbert Spencer and social Darwinism back to her Rockford Seminary years. *Education of Jane Addams,* 85.

45. William James, *Talks to Teachers on Psychology* (1899) (Boston: Harvard University Press, 1983), 164.

46. Mary E. McDowell, "The Settlement as a Way of Life," *Neighborhood* 2 (July 1929), 150.

47. Blanche Wiesen Cook, *Eleanor Roosevelt,* vol. 2: 1933–1938 (New York: Viking, 1999), 185 and 187.

48. "Bush: U.S. won't wait for enemy strike," *Chicago Tribune,* sec. 1 (June 2, 2002), 14.

49. Virginia Held, "Feminist Reconceptualizations in Ethics," in *Philosophy in a Feminist Voice: Critiques and Reconstructions,* ed. Janet A. Kourany (Princeton, N.J.: Princeton University Press, 1998), 99. This paragraph is taken from Charlene Haddock Seigfried, "Kantian Autonomy Fails to Fulfill the Conditions of Practical Rationality," in *Kant und die Berliner Aufklärung Akten des IX. Internationalen Kant-Kongresses,* Band III: Sektionen VI-X. V, ed. von Volker Gerhardt, R-P. Horstman, and R. Schumacher (Berlin: Walter de Gruyter, 2001), 96–103.

50. Addams, *Democracy and Social Ethics,* 150–51.

51. Ibid., 152.

52. See Harriet Hyman Alonso's discussion of the development of Addams's pacifism in "Can Jane Addams Serve as a Role Model for Us Today?" in this volume.

53. Addams, "Reactions of a Pacifist in Wartime" (1922), in *Jane Addams: A Centennial Reader* (New York: Macmillan, 1960), 302.

54. Ibid., 303.

55. Ibid.

56. Addams, *Democracy and Social Ethics,* 31.

57. Jane Addams, "The Women's Congress at the Hague" (1915), in *A Centennial Reader,* 263.

58. Ibid., 273.

59. Jane Addams, "Aspects of the Woman's Movement" (1930), in *A Centennial Reader,* 130.

60. Addams, *My Friend, Julia Lathrop,* 60–61.

61. Addams, *Democracy and Social Ethics,* 7.

62. Addams, in Linn, *Jane Addams,* 387.

SECTION II

Jane Addams and the Practice of Democratic Citizenship

3

Jane Addams's Theory of Cooperation

LOUISE W. KNIGHT

For most people, cooperation is one of those ideas that seems too vague to be much use as a guide to living or to seeking social reforms, let alone substantial enough to constitute a theory. But in the nineteenth century in Great Britain and the United States, as scholars have shown, the critics of the dominant ideology of individualism—that is, those on the left wing of the political spectrum—embraced cooperation as a theory and developed methods for acting upon it in the economic realms of production and consumption, in the social realm of utopian community living, and in the political realm of democracy. Jane Addams first encountered some of these ideas as a teenage reader. By the time she moved to Chicago in 1889 to start a settlement house with Ellen Gates Starr, she was ready to be an enthusiastic cooperator. In this paper, I will trace the reform origins of the theory of cooperation in Great Britain, because those theorist-reformers influenced Addams the most, tell the story of Addams's developing fascination with the theory, and discuss the ways it influenced her first ten years of work in social reform and her own theories about that work.[1]

The Nineteenth-Century Theory of Cooperation

Cooperation as an idea cannot be said to have been invented by anyone, but in the nineteenth century it became the focus of a sustained enthusiasm for societal reform in both Europe and the United States. It was an enthusiasm that gave birth to multiple forms of socialism, new forms of utopian communities, and economic "co-ops," among other things. Beginning in 1817, the philosophical ideas of Charles Fourier, Claude Henri Comte de Saint-Simon, and Auguste Comte caused France to become one such flourishing center of cooperative theory and practice, while the ideas of Robert Owen sparked similar developments in Great Britain.[2]

An industrialist as well as a reformer and philosopher, Robert Owen promoted the idea of improving human character and escaping the evils of competition and individualism through his lectures, books, magazines, and experiments by forming "cooperative" agricultural and manufacturing communities.[3] A "cooperative motto" expressed his commitment to mutual service: "Each for all and all for each."[4] The vocabulary available to express these ideas was expanded in 1827, when an Owenite supporter introduced the word "socialist" as a synonym for "cooperative" and an antonym for "individualist." The new word would prove particularly protean.[5]

The next development in Great Britain was for the idea of cooperation to be Christianized. The social Christian, or Christian socialist (the terms were used interchangeably) movement arose in 1848, the brainchild of a young lawyer, John Ludlow, and two Anglican ministers, Frederick Denison Maurice and Charles Kingsley. Influenced by the ideas of the Owenite movement, as well as by the rise of Chartism—a prolabor movement—their cooperative ideal was both economic and spiritual. On the economic side, troubled by the injustices suffered by working-class people and rejecting the popular belief that competition was the law of the universe, followers of these young men founded a tailor cooperative, where shared investment and labor produced shared profit, and Maurice became president of a society for promoting workingmen's associations. On the spiritual side, troubled by the contemporary Christian emphasis on saving individual souls, Ludlow, Maurice, and Kingsley claimed that prosperous Christians had a primary duty to help the poor and to improve society, that salvation was a social undertaking.[6]

The ideas of the early cooperative movement produced a creative ferment in British society, and in time generated many of the most innovative British reform projects of the century—most notably the producer and consumer cooperative movements; an energetic labor movement; the British wing of the scientific, or Marxist, socialist movement; the workers' education movement; and the settlement house movement (all of these would have their American counterparts).

The reaction of British economists to cooperative theory was mostly, and not surprisingly, negative. The great majority thought the concept nonsense, being thoroughly devoted to the economic doctrine of laissez-faire, which argued that government should not interfere with commerce. But a few felt the idea's appeal. John Stuart Mill, for example, writing in 1848, foresaw a future when associations of workers would collectively own the capital that funded their economic production. He predicted that after society had transitioned from capitalism to a "cooperative socialism," individuals would have greater freedom because they would have greater economic equality and, therefore, greater opportunity to deliberate among themselves.[7]

In the United States, the movement found its earliest expressions in utopian communities. In 1825, Robert Owen founded his model American "co-operative" community, New Harmony, in Indiana, where all members did equal labor and shared the profits. Adin Ballou founded his Christian cooperative utopia in Milford, Massachusetts (renaming the town Hopedale) in 1841, even before Christian socialism had formally emerged in England. In 1854, Ballou, who was also committed to nonresistance, published *Practical Christian Socialism.*[8] In 1842, another cooperative community in Massachusetts, the famous Brook Farm, began. As early as 1845 at least one American labor union envisioned "a network of cooperatively owned stores and buying clubs."[9] And in 1847, John H. Noyes, a Christian perfectionist and a former enthusiast of Fourier's ideas, founded the communistic Oneida community in New York.[10] After the hiatus of the Civil War, a new generation of Americans revived these ideas. Farmers embraced economic cooperation in production and consumption in the 1870s and 1880s; idealists founded new utopian communities; the Knights of Labor encouraged the spread of "cooperatives" in the form of local assemblies; and reformers interested in women's issues started cooperative kitchens, day care programs, apartments, and factories, among other things.[11] In 1889, W. D. P. Bliss and others founded the Society of Christian Socialists.[12]

Jane Addams and the Theory of Cooperation

In her childhood, youth, and young adult years, Jane Addams encountered various cooperative and/or socialist ideas. Her first documented interest in the theory of cooperation was her fascination, which she mentions in her memoir, *Twenty Years at Hull-House,* with Robert Owen's New Harmony experiment. She first learned about it in 1873, when, at twelve, she read the *Atlantic Monthly*'s three-part series on the long-defunct utopian community.[13] She also knew about the farmers' cooperative movement. In 1875 the Stephenson County Farmers' Cooperative was founded in Freeport, Illinois, a city nearby to Addams's home of Cedarville. She first encountered the ideas of Christian socialism in 1881, when she read Charles Kingsley's novel,

Hypatia.[14] And in her twenties, she learned about the ideas of the French philosopher Auguste Comte, probably through the writings of John Stuart Mill, who wrote a book about Comte and was an enthusiast.[15]

Addams's interest in cooperation became more formal and focused in 1888, when, on a visit to London, she met two prominent British Christian socialists, Rev. Samuel and Henrietta Barnett. Just a few years prior they had founded the world's first settlement house, Toynbee Hall, in the city's East End, a low-income working-class neighborhood. Addams visited the settlement and became friends with the Barnetts, who were happy to mentor her. The Barnetts' left-leaning Christian socialism was manifest in several ways. First, the settlement was a new sort of community founded on social Christian ideals, making it a cooperative utopia of a sort.[16] Second, the Barnetts were concerned with economic issues and supported labor union organizing. At the same time, the Barnetts embraced the mainstream version of Christian socialism that, by the 1880s, was dominating the views of the Anglican Church leadership. This version offered a completely spiritualized critique of individualism. Concern for the poor and the suffering was primarily to be expressed through sympathy.[17] It was a version that held particular appeal to Addams, who had no interest in economic issues at this juncture.

Two books, by authors well known to the Barnetts, captured this version well; Addams likely read them in 1888 or soon after. One was by W. H. Fremantle, whom Addams had accidentally met just before arriving in London. He was the Canon of Canterbury, a social Christian, and a friend of Samuel and Henrietta Barnett. In his influential *The World as the Subject of Redemption* (1885),[18] Fremantle claimed that the goal was to "save the world" by abandoning selfishness and "imbu[ing] all human relations with the spirit of Christ's self-renouncing love."[19] The second book, by Brooke Foss Westcott, the Canon of Westminster, was *Social Aspects of Christianity* (1883). Westcott noted the suffering caused by "tyrannical individualism" and called for his readers to find a social fellowship with those in the household, the factory, and the warehouse. Thus they would find the "deeper, more abiding delight which comes from successfully administering to the good of others."[20]

For the Barnetts, the challenge was how to put their social Christian ideals into action. Their approach was to use cooperation as a primary method for the economic and social undertakings of the settlement house. They liked to say that "'with' not 'for,'" was their motto. To them, this meant not designing or running a program for people, but making it possible for people to design and/or operate it themselves. In the economic realm, the Barnetts worked with shoeblacks to launch a cooperative hotel and with teachers to found a cooperative traveling society. In the social realm, they approached school reform by seeking cooperation among parents, teachers, administrators, and students. Within the settlement house, the Barnetts considered cooperation best expressed through the principle of self-governance. Thus at Toynbee Hall the many boys and girls and adult clubs and the residents group were self-governing. The residents were a group of male college graduates who lived at the settlement house and spent their free time being sociable with, and offering structured programs to, the men and children of the neighborhood. The residents met weekly at a session that Samuel Barnett chaired, "the Grand," to settle policy questions relating to residential life at the house.[21]

Cooperation at Hull-House

A little more than a year after visiting Toynbee Hall, Addams and her friend Ellen Gates Starr cofounded Hull-House, a cooperative community modeled in most ways after the British settlement.[22] But while the Barnetts stayed focused on the principle of cooperation, Addams integrated the idea of nonresistance into her cooperative theory and practice. Her introduction to those ideas came from the writings of Leo Tolstoy in the 1880s, particularly his book, *My Religion*.[23] Certainly, the two ideas were complementary. Because cooperators rejected the idea of one person making decisions on behalf of others, they presumably also rejected the idea of one person using force to mandate the compliance of others.

In the early years, Addams tended to merge the two principles of cooperation and nonresistance. She wrote in 1892 that "the first residents" of Hull-House began with the conviction "that it would be a foolish and unwarranted expenditure of force to oppose or to antagonize any individual or set of people in the neighborhood." They intended, she explained, to live "with opposition to no man, with recognition of the good in every man, even the most wretched." In order to do this, the residents "must be emptied of . . . all self-assertion and be ready to arouse and interpret the public opinion of their neighborhood. They must be content to . . . grow into a sense of relationship and mutual interests."[24] A few years later she wrote that the settlement was "designed" to promote "co-operation with all [the] good which it finds in its neighborhood."[25]

Wary of labels, Addams did not call herself a social Christian, but it is clear she considered herself one. In a letter to her stepbrother, George Haldeman, during her first months at Hull-House, she predicted approvingly that "Christian socialism" would spread once prosperous people realized the extent of "the misery" of the poor. In 1892, she wrote that the settlement movement "is only one manifestation of that wider humanitarian movement which throughout Christendom . . . is endeavoring to embody itself, not in a sect, but in society itself." In 1895, she spoke of settlements as "an attempt in the direction of social Christianity," and quoted Samuel Barnett's views on the subject at length.[26]

Many of Hull-House's early cooperative projects were, like Toynbee Hall's, cooperative economic experiments conducted upon a principle often found in cooperative enterprises, the principle of self-governance.[27] Neighbors and Hull-House residents together organized the "coal cooperative" (1893), the public or "cooperative" kitchen (called the Coffee House)(1893), and the Jane Club, a "cooperative" workingwomen's residence possibly inspired by Toynbee Hall's shoeblacks hotel, with the same hope of providing inexpensive lodgings. Addams encouraged Mary Kenney, a working woman and union organizer, to form the free-standing club in 1892 (it was not, in its early years, a project of Hull-House's, although it was located in the neighborhood). To prepare Kenney and her friends for the responsibilities of self-governance, Addams read with them Beatrice Potter's book on economic cooperation, *The Cooperative Movement in Great Britain* (1891). Addams and the settlement residents even attempted to produce a product cooperatively. This was the book, *Hull-House Maps and Papers* (1895), which grew in part out of the papers several of the Hull-House residents had presented to the settlement congress of the World's Columbian Exposition, held at Hull-House in 1893.[28]

Addams's exploration of the social aspects of cooperation was equally energetic. She made sure that the principle of cooperation was applied to the management of the residential life of Hull-House and the management of the settlement's social clubs.[29] In imitation of what she had seen at Toynbee Hall, Addams delegated the decisions regarding resident life to the residents as a whole. Beginning in 1893, but possibly before (records are missing), the residents met more or less weekly (except in summer) as a policy-making, deliberative body.[30] As head resident, Addams chaired the residents meeting but, in keeping with Robert's Rules of Order, she could not, as chair, offer motions or speak on behalf of a proposal. When she wanted to do either, she vacated the chair. Decisions were made by vote and majority ruled. The resident group set resident fees for room and board, voted on whom to admit as a resident, on which duties would be required of all residents, and on which projects the house would undertake collectively.[31] For example, when the depression hit in 1893, the residents voted to organize a relief bureau; they rejected, however, Addams's proposal (which she made after vacating the chair) that the settlement set up a shelter for women and children.[32]

The residents meeting, as with all the cooperative efforts Addams entered into, tested the degree to which she was willing to give up power in order to be a true cooperator. As an upper-middle-class woman who had been raised to believe in the ethic of benevolence, she *felt* entitled when she first moved to Halsted Street to instruct others to do what she thought was best for them. But her belief in cooperation and in American social democracy compelled her to restrain her class-based instinct to control. Judging from the results and from the comments of those she cooperated with, she appears to have succeeded fairly well at this. The implications of the theory of cooperation for the reform practices of an upper-middle-class woman like Jane Addams were indeed revolutionary. More difficult to change than her behavior, however, was her related, internal sense of moral superiority, the quality she called self-righteousness, that she also brought with her to Hull-House. As I explore in my biography of Addams, *Citizen: Jane Addams and the Struggle for Democracy*, it would take her most of the 1890s to puncture this class-based delusion in herself.

Hull-House's numerous social clubs for children and adults were, like Toynbee Hall's, also run on the principle of cooperation and were self-governing groups. All the clubs, including the Working People's Social Science Club, elected officers and appointed a committee to arrange the weekly programs. Disagreements were debated and voted on. A Polish woman who grew up in the neighborhood, Hilda Satt Polacheck, recalled how the social and literary club for young people, which she helped organize, decided to devote one week to dancing and the next to studying some issue by listening to a member's paper on a subject—such as garbage, grand opera, clean streets, single tax, or trade unions—and then discussing it. Later they decided to organize a series of debates. Topics included, "Should women get the vote?" and "Which is stronger, the desire for fame or riches?" Still later, they took up book reviewing. For the children's and young people's clubs, an adult volunteer served as "leader" and was often elected president, which meant he or she would chair meetings (and model those skills) but make no decisions. The club members were cooperatively in charge.[33]

By 1895 Hull-House had this procedure working so well, it convened an annual congress of Hull-House clubs to take up common policy issues. That first year, the congress adopted the policy that all parties in the gymnasium would end at midnight. The second year, it took up the questions: Could one person belong to two clubs? How much visiting should be allowed between clubs?[34] The questions were the sort that staff or volunteers might be expected to decide, but at Hull-House the club members, acting as a collective body in a deliberative, no doubt representatively elected assembly, decided them.

In legislative bodies, including this one, the overlap between democracy and cooperation was 100 percent.

Political Cooperation

By the mid-1890s, Addams was consciously attempting to apply her theory of cooperation to the political realm. Sometimes Addams used the term "cooperation" to refer to nothing more complicated than Hull-House and another organization working together on a project. She liked to use the word "cooperation" in this loose way, simply because she liked to see herself being as "cooperative" as possible in everything she did. Some of the projects Addams described in chapter 13 of *Twenty Years* and labeled "cooperative" in the index were investigations undertaken with other groups—including an investigation of newsboys, and an investigation of the social value of saloons. Others were simply joint efforts, including an industrial exhibition, and the founding of the School of Civics and Philanthropy.[35] At yet other times the residents at Hull-House worked cooperatively with city and state governments on such issues as civil service reform, state colonies for epileptics, public baths, a public library branch, the aldermanic elections, juvenile justice, public education, and public charity, all described in chapter 14 of *Twenty Years*.

Addams also engaged in more formal kinds of true political cooperation. In all of these cases, as with her practice of social cooperation, the central tenet she sought to advance and practice was self-governance. Some of her earliest political cooperation was labor unions. At first, she simply lent unions space to organize in, helped distribute flyers, and assisted workers who wished to bring their disputes before a judge for arbitration. But by 1893, she was working alongside trade union leaders to urge public and legislative support for state legislation on sweatshop reform, believing that citizens who best understood the issues ought to have a voice in shaping new policies. The Pullman Strike drew her in further. In 1894, as a member of the Civic Federation of Chicago's Conciliation Board, she sought to bring the American Railway Union and the Pullman Company to the arbitration table, so that both the employees and employer could share in the task of governing the industrial workplace. Her efforts on behalf of labor deepened two years later, in 1896, when she chaired a rally to raise money for a strike fund for the tailors, and spoke at another rally to rouse support for federal sweatshop reform legislation that the trade unions favored.[36]

Another aspect of the labor movement that appealed to her was that it was itself built on the principle of cooperation. Unions were simply workers coming together to act cooperatively. She saw in the trade union movement an example of the power of cooperation, or association, as she and others were beginning to call it by the end of the nineteenth century, to lead society. "Association is the method of the future," she observed in 1898, in a speech about the significance of the labor movement. "Labor," she added, "is the association fit to change the state."[37]

Political cooperation also involved the practice of coalition building to tackle reforms. Addams was a cofounder in 1904, for example, of the National Child Labor Committee, which sought to bring into one cooperative political alliance all the people and organizations committed to ending child labor at the state and federal levels.[38] She was also involved in the formation and work of the Women's Trade Union League, another coalition of diverse individuals and groups all seeking to advance the cause of trade union women.[39] Often, these efforts brought together individuals and organizations from different classes, states, and professions. Cooperation involved mutual agreement on a policy goal, and an ability to set aside other differences to work effectively together.

The Limits of Political Cooperation

Jane Addams did not believe that political cooperation should be pursued at any cost. Throughout the 1890s and beyond she wrestled with the question of when she should cooperate and when she should not. A commitment to political cooperation, she learned, required not just a willingness to be cooperative but also some well-thought-out criteria for limiting one's cooperation. Refusing to cooperate always remained a difficult and perplexing choice for her.

Typically, middle-class reformers refused to cooperate with politicians or others who were thought to be "corrupt." But Addams found this analysis too narrow. Sometimes, politically corrupt politicians are "the real leaders of the people," she observed, because "they minister directly to life and to social needs and because they have not "lost their faith in the people." Indeed, without ignoring their corruption, she believed these leaders were often engaged in "the great moral effort of getting the mass to express itself and of adding this mass energy and wisdom to the community as a whole."[40] Again, the principle of self-governance lay at the heart of her goals. Living in a ward that was represented in the city council by such a politician, John Powers, Addams knew the depth of support among her neighbors for him and respected his democratic function even though he was notorious among middle-class and trade union reformers in the city for taking bribes for city jobs and votes.

Addams's ability to understand and respect the nature of Powers's political support did not mean that she wanted him to remain in office. She joined Florence Kelley and others in opposing Powers's reelection twice in the 1890s. But she was also willing to cooperate with him when it benefited the neighbors. During the early months of the depression of 1893, Powers proposed to Addams that Hull-House cooperate with him on the distribution of Christmas turkeys to the neediest. Not wishing to be associated in the public mind with Powers in any way, a majority of the Hull-House residents at the residents meeting voted down the motion, which Addams offered after vacating the chair.[41] She apparently was unconcerned that others would interpret the arrangement symbolically. To her, the important thing was that cooperation with Powers would insure that more inhabitants of the ward would receive turkeys.

Some potential cooperators, while not corrupt, were simply less than pleasant to be around, or inept in their reform efforts. Addams cooperated with them too. "[M]oral results are often obtained through the most unexpected agencies," she wrote in 1922, "[I]t is very easy to misjudge the value of an undertaking by a critical or unfair estimate of the temperament and ability of those undertaking it."[42]

The more complicated question for Addams was whether she should cooperate on projects when the moral principle being applied was not one she agreed with or was one on which her own views were not yet sorted out. A tragic example occurred in 1893–94, during the first winter of the depression, when she enforced the Charity Organization Society rules in dispensing charity and inadvertently sent an unemployed clerk she had known for years, a married man with two children, to his death. The COS rules required that all able-bodied men should "earn" relief by doing construction work on the city's sanitary canal project.[43] The gaunt clerk was technically able-bodied but, as Addams well knew, physically unfit. He had worked indoors all his life and, having been unemployed for months, was weak from hunger. He told her he was not sure he was capable of working outdoors in winter. Still, she insisted he go. He caught pneumonia and died a week later. In *Twenty Years,* where Addams tells the story, she concludes that general rules need to be modified by knowledge of individual circumstance, but she avoids the larger question of why she suspended her own judgment so completely.[44] One suspects she had not fully analyzed the differences between her highly flexible, individualized settlement approach and the rigid requirements of

COS. In this case, practicing cooperation without reflection proved a horrible mistake.

Deciding not to cooperate politically was difficult for Addams, but when she did it was usually because she disagreed with a major policy being set by a collective body of which she was a member. During the first year of the 1893–97 depression, for example, she resigned from a wages subcommittee of the mayor's relief committee rather than support the policy it recommended of paying street cleaners a wage of $1.00 for a day's work rather than $.75 for a half-day's. Addams knew that the minimal wage a man with a family could survive on was $1.50 a day. She did not want to be part of a decision that restructured wages.[45]

Addams resigned from membership in a governing body again in 1914. In that case, the policy she objected to was the Shafroth American Amendment and the governing body was the national board of the National Woman Suffrage Association, on which she served as vice president. To pragmatists like Addams, the amendment seemed initially appealing because it would have authorized citizens in a state to give women the vote (or adopt any other policy) through a referendum, and thus dismiss the necessity of a state constitutional amendment. But to many others, the amendment symbolized either a rejection of the beloved "Susan B. Anthony" federal suffrage amendment strategy or a devious way to allow state associations of the NAWSA in the South to push for racist versions of women's suffrage. Addams voted for the amendment when it came before the national board, but when, after a subsequent heated debate at the convention that educated Addams on the opponents' views, the attendees voted to endorse the amendment, Addams resigned as vice president.[46]

But she did not always resign when she disagreed with a policy. One example when she stayed on a governing body was in 1905–8, when the Chicago Board of Education, of which she was a member, failed to provide better working conditions for teachers in the ways sought by the Teachers Federation; another was in 1912, when the Platform Committee of the Progressive Party, of which she was a member, failed, despite her determined efforts, to require the party to seat the mixed-race, instead of the all-white, delegations from four southern states.[47]

Why did Addams resign sometimes and other times not? One explanation is that Addams needed her good friend, the feisty and confrontational Florence Kelley, to stiffen her resolve when symbolic action was required. Kelley was available to coach in the first two cases—she was living at Hull-House in 1893–94 and attended the NAWSA convention in 1914. In the latter two cases, she was absent. She was no longer a resident at Hull-House in

1905–7 and was not involved with the Progressive Party in 1912 (she joined the Socialist Party to support the candidacy of Eugene Debs).

But it is also true that Addams was generally reluctant to resign on principle; she deeply believed in working incrementally, in taking half a loaf and then continuing to push for more, rather than withdrawing from the scene altogether. "Life [has] taught me," she wrote in 1910, "that existing arrangements and the hoped-for improvements must be mediated and reconciled to each other, that new must be dovetailed into the old, as it were, if it [is] to endure."[48] Most of all, the principle of cooperation authorized Addams's belief in a pragmatic, rather than symbolic, approach to political reform.

Jane Addams and Cooperation: Refining an Understanding of Her Theory

Jane Addams never set forth, in a coherent way, the theory of cooperation she put into practice in the economic, social, and political realms during her first decade at Hull-House. But in her first book, *Democracy and Social Ethics* (1902), while unfolding her larger argument, she repeatedly touches on the need to abandon the out-of-date, narrow ethic of individualism and to embrace the emerging ethic of cooperation/association. The message is presented poetically in her obscure "introduction" and in her metaphoric references in other chapters to "marching" with one's fellow human beings on the road of life, to taking "a more active share in community life," and to shaping industries to be more "in line with associated effort."[49] In one chapter, Addams camouflages her underlying thesis as a popular view. It "is many times stated . . . [that] we are passing from an age of individualism to one of association." In another, she attaches ethical value to the trend. "[U]nless all men and all classes contribute to [achieving] a good, we cannot even be sure that it is worth having."[50] In yet another chapter she is more direct about the challenge to individualism that cooperation, which she also sometimes referred to as corporate effort, poses. Speaking of reformers of every class, she wrote, "A large body of people feel keenly the present industrial system is in a state of profound disorder and that there is no guarantee that the pursuit of individual ethics will ever right it. They claim that relief can only come through deliberate corporate effort inspired by social ideas and the study of economic laws."[51]

Beyond this, Addams notes in the book some of the lessons to be learned from the practice of cooperation. In keeping with her growing pragmatism, the lessons were about its usefulness. In one place, she stresses the harm that can come to a person if he or she fails to cooperate. "The man who disassociates his ambition," she writes, "however disinterested [it is], from the cooperation of his fellows, always [runs] the risk of ultimate failure."[52] In another, she writes about the benefits from being cooperative. "An action [may] appear ineffective [but] if it is carried out . . . [as] an associated effort, [it] may . . . have a greater social value than the more effective individual action."[53] Her belief in cooperation in all of its forms also lies behind her suggestion that "those who desire [social morality should be] . . . brought in contact with the moral experiences of the many in order to procure an adequate social motive."[54] And we see the same belief in her observation that we "are under a moral obligation in choosing our experiences, since the result of those experiences must ultimately determine our understanding of life."[55] Cooperation, Addams was arguing, produced the best social reform because it engaged people's enthusiasm and challenged them to gain new skills. In *The Second Twenty Years at Hull-House* she writes, "What we want is not mere argument but the release of energy and the evocation of new powers in common action." When people see the "necessity for united action" and understand that discussion should be replaced by "mutual interests," she writes, then "cooperation [is] easier than ever before."[56]

The emotional benefits of cooperation are also a subtle theme in her writings. She endorsed those benefits in remarks on the occasion of her sister suffrage advocate Anna Howard Shaw's passing in 1919. "There is no affection and no friendship so complete," Addams observed, "as that which develop when two people merge their energies in a common cause. It is very much greater . . . than whe[n] two people merely try to come together through their own personalities[.]"[57] In less intimate ways, cooperation provided her with a much appreciated antidote to discouragement. In "A Modern Lear," for example, she writes about taking "strength and cheer from [feeling] a hundred connections" to one's fellow citizens.[58]

Conclusion

Addams's ideas about cooperation and the history of her cooperative activities are widely scattered in her writings. As we have seen, her most determined efforts to write about them were *Twenty Years at Hull-House* and *Democracy and Social Ethics*. But she does not attempt to set out a coherent theory in either. Sadly, she never gave a speech about cooperation.

Despite these difficulties, it seems possible to formulate Addams's theory of cooperation from her efforts and ideas. In the economic realm, she believed in shared ownership of profits (the coal cooperative) and shared responsibility for production (the cooperative kitchen; the *Maps and Papers* book). In the social realm, she believed in shared responsibility for decisions affecting the group. In the political realm, she believed in shared effort to advance the reform agenda of those with the clearest vision of society's better future. More philosophically, to cooperate meant to choose to work on mutual interests with others rather than work on one's own project, to enter into every conversation with an open mind, and to ask how she could help. Cooperation meant stepping back, creating space, but also connecting with others' hopes, trusting, and moving forward on a collectively determined agenda.

On a personal level, Addams's theory of cooperation meant the need to set aside any desire for personal accomplishment. Her famous modesty was the surface manifestation of her more private efforts to feel no pride in her accomplishments. That this was a conscious discipline is apparent from her strikingly radical observation, made in *Democracy and Social Ethics,* that in seeking "a higher morality in our social relations, we must demand that the individual be willing to lose the sense of personal achievement, and shall be content to realize his activity only in connection with the activity of the many."[59] She makes the point more subtly in a passage in "A Modern Lear." Although she does not mention cooperation, she both highlights the need to sacrifice personal goals in working with others and sums up all that she understood the theory of cooperation to mean. "The man who insists upon consent, who moves with the people," she writes, may "often compromise [his] best convictions. . . . He has to discover what the people really want." What he attains, she notes, will not be his personal accomplishment but something "upheld by the sentiments and aspirations of many others."[60] While we can be sure that Addams did take pride in her accomplishments at times, being only human, we can only honor her remarkable desire to tamp down that pride and find the greater pleasure in the larger accomplishments of those with whom she cooperated.

Given the centrality of the theory of cooperation to Jane Addams's reform work in all its dimensions, it is puzzling, at least at first glance, that she did not highlight the theory more. But at second glance, the reason becomes clear. Addams believed that action unshaped by theory was a bad thing, but she was also convinced that theory had no meaning if it was not applied. She summed all this up neatly in the pungent observation, "There is too much analysis in our thought and too much anarchy in our action."[61] She therefore distrusted theoretical statements as evidence of conviction. Words, she knew, were cheap. "Action," she wrote in 1902, "is the sole medium of expression for ethics" and "[S]peculation in regard to morality is but observation and must remain in the sphere of intellectual comment[.]"[62] A few years before, she observed, "We judge [a living institution] not by its creed . . . but by its blundering efforts to apply its principles to living affairs."[63] Perhaps Jane Addams gave us no succinct theoretical statement on cooperation because she wanted her commitment to the theory to be judged by her deeds.

Notes

1. This essay is not intended to provide either a complete history of the cooperative movement in the nineteenth century in Great Britain or the United States. Nor do I highlight the early role of women in those movements. Though it seems plausible that Addams would have been interested in the 1880s in that part of the movement's history, this is merely conjecture because I have no evidence to document it. She was very familiar, of course, with women's roles in the movements in both countries in the 1890s, a subject that deserves more exploration than I have space to devote to here. I do mention (see note 28 below) that she read Beatrice Potter [Webb's] book, *The Cooperative Movement in Great Britain* (London: Sonnenschein, 1891); she knew the author, who visited Hull-House in the 1890s.

2. Fourier published his first socialist work, *l'Industrie,* in 1817. Owen presented his plan for a socialistic community to the Parliament the same year. For more on Fourier and Saint-Simon, see Francois Dagognet, *Trois Philosophies Revisitees: Saint-Simon, Proudhon, Fourier* (New York: Hildesheim/G Olms, 1997). For more on later developments in France, see John C. Cort, *Christian Socialism: An Informal History* (Maryknoll, N.Y.: Orbis Books, 1988), chapter 7, "France"; and W. D. P. Bliss, ed. *The Encyclopedia of Social Reform* (New York: Funk and Wagnalls, 1897), under the word "Christian Socialism: France." W. D. P. Bliss was a leader of the social Christian movement in the United States in the second half of the nineteenth century, which makes his encyclopedia a particularly appropriate source for this essay.

3. Robert Owen's books included *Lectures at Washington* (1825), *A New View of Society: Essays on the Formation of Character* (1825), and *Report on the County of Lanark* (1832). For other publications on the early Owenite movement, see "List of Some Books and Publications," in *Industrial Co-operation: The Story of a Peaceful Revolution*, 4th rev. ed., ed. Catherine Webb (Manchester: The Cooperative Union, 1910), 278–80. Regarding Robert Owen and his ideas, see Edward K. Spann, *Brotherly Tomorrows: Movements for A Cooperative Society in America, 1820–1920* (New York: Columbia University Press, 1989), chapter 2, "The Prophet of New Lanark," and Webb, *Industrial Cooperation,* chapter 6, "Life and Work of Robert Owen." For reasons of space, I do not give a complete early history of the English cooperative movement, which also had a separate point of origin among the cooperative economic efforts of working men. See Webb, *Industrial Co-operation,* 13.

4. Cort, *Christian Socialism,* 139–46; Webb, *Industrial Co-operation,* 2.

5. Spann, *Brotherly Tomorrows,* 77; Cort, *Christian Socialism,* 141, 145. Regarding first use of term "Christian Socialism" in England, see also Bliss, *Encyclopedia,* under the word "Christian Socialism: England." The first use of the word "socialism" in France was apparently in 1831. Ibid., 101. The equating of socialism and cooperation continued in some circles throughout the nineteenth century. See James Russell Lowell, "Democracy" (1884) in James Russell Lowell, *The Works of James Russell Lowell, Vol. VI, Literary and Political Addresses* (Boston: Houghton, Mifflin and Co, 1886), 35.

6. Regarding the earliest activities of Maurice, Kingsley, and Ludlow, see Bliss, *Encyclopedia,* under the word "Christian socialism: England." Regarding Christian Socialism later in the century, see Peter d'A. Jones, *The Christian Socialist Revival, 1877–1914: Religion, Class and Social Conscience in Late-Victorian England* (Princeton, N.J.: Princeton University Press, 1968); Norman R. Edward, *The Victorian Christian Socialists* (New York: Cambridge University Press, 1987); Webb, *Industrial Cooperation,* 72–73; Cort, *Christian Socialism,* 139–50.

7. Cort, *Christian Socialism,* 254; Nadia Urbinati, *Mill on Democracy* (Chicago: University of Chicago Press, 2002), 198–99.

8. Regarding New Harmony, see Spann, *Brotherly Tomorrows,* 25–48. This is an incomplete sketch of the community, which also promoted equal, liberal, education for all. It adopted a common-property policy in its second year, and closed shortly thereafter. Regarding Ballou, see Bliss, *Encyclopedia,* under the word "Hopedale"; Adin Ballou, *Practical Christian Socialism* (New York: Fowlers and Wells, 1854).

9. Steve [sic] Leikin, *The Practical Utopians: American Workers and the Cooperative Movement in the Gilded Age* (Detroit: Wayne State University Press, 2005), 2.

10. Jane Addams's father, John Huy Addams, had an interesting, if indirect, connection to the Oneida community. He himself was a Christian perfectionist, as was one of his closest friends, Luther Guiteau, the manager of his bank in Freeport, Illinois. Guiteau took a great interest in the Oneida community, and his son, Charles Julius, lived there for a time. This son later assassinated President James A. Garfield. Knight, *Citizen,* 27, 111.

11. Regarding the farmers' cooperative movement, see Lawrence Goodwyn, *Populist Moment: A Short History of the Agrarian Revolt in America* (New York: Oxford University Press, 1978). Regarding the history of the consumer cooperative movement in Illinois in these years, see Colston Estey Warne, *The Consumer's Co-operative Movement in Illinois* (Chicago: University of Chicago Press, 1926). Regarding post–Civil War utopian communities, see Robert S. Fogarty, *All Things New: American Communes and Utopian Movements, 1860–1914* (Chicago: University of Chicago Press, 1990), chapter 3, "'Hard Times': Common Land and Common Labor," 98–175. Regarding the Knights of Labor, see Leikin, *Practical Utopians,* 71. Regarding women's issues and cooperation, see Mary Livermore, "Cooperative Womanhood in the State," *North American Review* 152 (September 1891): 283–95; Frances Willard, "The Dawn of Woman's Day," *Our Day* 2 (November 1881): 345–60; Eileen V. Wallis, "The Woman's Cooperative Movement in

Utah, 1869–1915," *Utah Historical Quarterly* 71 (Fall 2003): 315–31; Caroline A. Huling, "Activities of Chicago Women," *Woman's Journal* 21, no. 44 (November 1, 1890): 346. Regarding later developments in the American cooperative movement, see Florence Evelyn Parker, *The First 125 Years: A History of Distributive and Service Cooperation in the United States, 1829–1954* (New York: Cooperative League of America, 1956). Livermore was a founding member of the Society of Christian Socialists in 1889 (see below). Regarding British women and cooperation in the first half of the nineteenth century, see Barbara Taylor, *Eve and the New Jerusalem: Socialism and Feminism in the Nineteenth Century* (1983 repr., Cambridge, Mass.: Harvard University Press, 1993).

12. Regarding Bliss, see Joseph Dorfman, *The Economic Mind in American Civilization,* vol. 3, *1865–1918* (New York: Viking Press, 1959), 155. For more about the American movement, see James Dombrowski, *The Early Days of Christian Socialism in America* (New York: Columbia University Press, 1936); Phillips, *Kingdom on Earth*; Gary Scott Smith, *The Search for Social Salvation: Social Christianity and America, 1880–1925* (Lanham, Md.: Lexington Books, 2001); Fogarty, *All Things New,* chapter 3, "Hard Times"; A. J. Behrends, *Christianity and Socialism* (New York: 1886); Richard T. Ely, *Social Aspects of Christianity and Other Essays, New Edition* (New York: Thomas Y. Crowell, 1889); Philo Sprague, *Christian Socialism: What and Why* (New York: EP Dutton, 1891). It is beyond the scope of this essay to address the complicated question of how the American social Christian movement and the American Social Gospel movement relate and intersect. The best discussion I have seen, one that acknowledges the complexities, is by Paul T. Phillips, *A Kingdom on Earth: Anglo-American Social Christianity, 1880–1940* (University Park: Pennsylvania State University Press, 1996), xviii–xx, xxiii–xxiv, 12n31, 34, 74–76. For a different view, see Gary Dorrien, *The Making of American Liberal Theology: Imagining Progressive Religion, 1805–1900* (Louisville: Westminster John Knox Press, 2001); Ronald C. White Jr. and C. Howard Hopkins, *The Social Gospel: Religion and Reform in Changing America* (Philadelphia: Temple University Press, 1976). All that can be said at this juncture is that there was a group of people in the 1890s, Jane Addams among them, who considered themselves social Christians and did not themselves use the term, "Social Gospel." Addams is often described as a Social Gospeler. See, for example, Richard Wightman Fox and James T. Kloppenberg, eds., *A Companion to American Thought* (Malden, Mass.: Blackwell Publishers, 1998), under the word "Liberal Protestantism"; White and Hopkins, *Social Gospel,* 102.

13. Jane Addams, *Twenty Years at Hull-House with Autobiographical Notes* (New York: Macmillan, 1910), 143. The three articles were by Robert Dale Owen, the son of Robert Owen. "Robert Owen at New Lanark," *Atlantic Monthly* 31, no. 185 (March 1873): 310–21; "The Social Experiment at New Harmony," *Atlantic Monthly* 32, no. 190 (August 1873): 224–36; "My Experience of Community Life," *Atlantic Monthly* 32, no. 191 (September 1873): 336–48.

14. *Freeport Weekly Journal,* June 27, 1877, 6, col. 4. This advertisement for the cooperative gives the date of its founding. Regarding *Hypatia,* see Jane Addams to

George Haldeman, May 29, 1881, Jane Addams Papers Microfilm (hereafter cited as JAPM). Addams certainly read about the history of social Christianity at some point. See her reference to Maurice and Kingsley in *The Second Twenty Years at Hull-House* (New York: Macmillan, 1930), 12.

15. Comte influenced both the cooperation and the Christian Socialist movements. Regarding Comte and social Christianity, see Phillips, *A Kingdom on Earth,* 10, 16–17. Regarding Jane Addams and Comte, see *Twenty Years,* 83; Knight, *Citizen,* chapter 6, "Culture." In college, Addams's interest in Charles Darwin's ideas—he too favored cooperation, though that fact has been long ignored—was yet another influence, but there is no space to discuss it here.

16. I use the word "utopia" here advisedly. Toynbee Hall was indeed intended to be "a visionary system of . . . social perfection." *Random House Unabridged Dictionary,* second edition, 1987. Of course, it was not like most nineteenth-century utopian communities, which generally were located in the countryside in order to be completely isolated from corrupting influences on community members.

17. J. A. R. Pimlott, *Toynbee Hall: Fifty Years of Social Progress, 1884–1934* (London: J. M. Dent and Sons, 1935), 32. See S. A. Barnett and Mrs. S. A. Barnett, *Practical Socialism: Essays in Social Reform* (London: Longmans, Green, and Co., 1888). One of the Oxford philosophers who most influenced the settlement movement was the social Christian, T. H. Green, a friend of the Barnetts'. See Phillips, *Kingdom of God,* 10–11. For more on the Barnetts' social Christian views, see Knight, *Citizen,* chapter 7, "Crisis."

18. Regarding Jane Addams meeting Fremantle, see Addams, *Twenty Years,* 87; Jane Addams to Alice Addams Haldeman, June 14, 1888, JAPM; Henrietta Barnett [Mrs. S. A.], *Canon Barnett: His Life, Work and Friends* (Boston: Houghton Mifflin, 1919), 1:13, 22. The book is W. H. Fremantle, *The World as the Subject of Redemption* (London: Rivington's, 1885). The title page identifies him as Canon of Canterbury. Phillips, *Kingdom on Earth,* 17. Regarding the influence of Fremantle's book, see Dombrowski, *Early Days of Christian Socialism,* 18.

19. Fremantle, *World as Subject,* 1, 8. Fremantle mentions poverty and politics in passing (96) and even notes that in the most advanced stages, Christian society calls for giving up personal property (99), but the reader is not required to attend to these radical points. See also Phillips, *Kingdom on Earth,* 16–17. Regarding Fremantle and the settlement movement, see Barnett, *Canon Barnett,* 2:34.

20. Brooke Foss Westcott, *Social Aspects of Christianity* (London and New York: Macmillan, 1883), 138, 146–48, 90–91. The title page identifies him as Canon of Westminster. See also Phillips, *Kingdom on Earth,* 16–17. Regarding Samuel Barnett's knowing Westcott, see *Canon Barnett,* 2:34. My evidence for Addams's reading the book is indirect, that is, that Westcott was a friend of the Barnetts, that his book was influential in the social Christian movement, and that it was just published the year before Addams met the Barnetts.

21. Regarding "with," not "for," see Samuel Barnett, "Town Councils and Social Reform," in S. A. Barnett and Mrs. S. A. Barnett, *Practicable Socialism*, 181. Regarding the various cooperative Toynbee Hall projects, see Barnett, *Canon Barnett,* 1: 139–40, 221, 256, 287–88, 335; 2: 73. Regarding "Grand," see 1:315, 2:37, 38, 41. On these subjects, see also Pimlott, *Toynbee Hall,* 47–48, 49. The references in *Canon Barnett* to the clubs' decision-making powers are vague. It is possible that Hull-House's clubs were more formally self-governing (see below) than were those of Toynbee Hall.

22. For another conceptualization of Hull-House's many cooperative practices, see Shannon Jackson, "Toward a Queer Social Welfare Studies: Unsettling Jane Addams," in this volume.

23. Leo Tolstoy, *My Religion [What I Believe],* trans. from French by Huntington Smith (New York: Thomas Y. Crowell & Co, 1885). Addams recalls she read this book "immediately after I left college." *Twenty Years,* 261. She graduated in 1881. The book was first published in Russian in 1884 and in English in 1885. Tolstoy's version of nonresistance differed from hers in many ways. For one thing, he believed its tenets included not cooperating with governments that made war. For another, he was not opposed to moral force, only physical force, as Addams was shocked to discover when she visited him in 1886. See Knight, *Citizen,* 373–74. Tolstoy may have introduced her to the idea, but that did not mean she agreed with him in how she interpreted the idea or practiced it.

24. Jane Addams, "The Subjective Necessity of Social Settlements," in *Philanthropy and Social Progress,* ed. Henry C. Adams (New York: Thomas A. Crowell, 1893, repr., Freeport, N.Y.: Books for Libraries Press, 1969), 20, 23. She recycled the first passage in *Twenty Years,* 273, and in "A Book that Changed my Life," 1196.

25. "The Settlement as a Factor in the Labor Movement," in Jane Addams, *Hull-House Maps and Papers,* Residents of Hull-House (New York: T. Y. Crowell, 1895), 187. See also Addams, *Twenty Years,* 133. It is beyond the scope of this essay to consider how Addams's views on nonresistance developed. Certainly, she still thought of it as central to her work on Halsted Street as of 1896. Knight, *Citizen,* 374.

26. Jane Addams to George Haldeman, November 24, 1889, JAPM; Addams, "Subjective Necessity," 19; Addams, "Social Settlements," in an unidentified publication, March 28, 1895, JAPM, 55: 0059.

27. Self-governance has a checkered history in the cooperative movement's many branches. Many economic co-ops and utopian communities in the nineteenth century embraced the principle, and were governed by all members or by elected representative councils, but others were governed by an autocratic founder or nonelected governing committees.

28. For details on Hull-House's cooperative projects, see chapter 7 of *Twenty Years.* The full citation for the *Maps* book is: The Residents of Hull-House, *Hull-House Maps and Papers: A Presentation of Nationalities and Wages in a Congested District of Chicago Together with Comments and Essays on Problems Growing out of the Social*

Conditions (New York: Crowell & Co, 1895). The Hull-House kitchen was another consciously cooperative venture. It served both the coffee house and the settlement dining room. Dorothea Moore, "A Day at Hull-House," *American Journal of Sociology* 2, No. 5 (March 1897): 634. Regarding the Jane Club, see Addams, *Twenty Years,* 136. Addams writes that the club was founded in 1891, but it was actually founded in 1892 ("The Objective Value of a Social Settlement," in *Philanthropy and Social Progress,* ed. Adams, 48; Scrapbook 1, 18, 24, 26, 48, "Clippings," JAPM, Addendum Reel 10 [Reel 81]). For a copy of the Jane Club's 1894 constitution, see Scrapbook 2, 39, "Publications," JAPM, Addendum Reel 10 [Reel 81]. The book they read was Beatrice Potter [Webb], *The Cooperative Movement in Great Britain.* For more on Mary Kenney [O'Sullivan], see Kathleen Banks Nutter, *The Necessity of Organization: Mary Kenney O'Sullivan and Trade Unionism for Women, 1892–1912* (New York: Garland Publishing, 1999). The club was independent of Hull-House in its early years but later absorbed into the settlement's operations.

29. Residential life was not the same as the settlement's program operations. The latter were not administered cooperatively. Addams, as head resident, had overall responsibility for day-to-day program operations. For details, see Knight, *Citizen,* chapter 11, "Baptism."

30. How long the residents meetings continued is difficult to say. The minutes of the group survive only for the period 1893–96, but an entry in Jane Addams's personal calendar notes a meeting for April 25, 1898. Apparently the absence of minute books after 1896 in the historical record cannot be interpreted as signaling the end of the residents meeting. The Hull-House Meeting Minutes are on the JAPM, Reel 50. See Jane Addams Calendar, April 25, 1898, JAPM, 29: 0419. The lack of records for the later years apparently owes to the fact that many Hull-House documents were destroyed in 1963 when the University of Illinois bought the settlement's land for its new Chicago campus, with the result that all but two of the settlement's thirteen buildings and much of their contents were abandoned to the wrecking ball. Mary Lynn McCree Bryan, Nancy Slote, and Maree de Angury, eds. *The Jane Addams Papers: A Comprehensive Guide* (Bloomington: Indiana University Press, 1996), 72.

31. For examples, see Hull-House Minutes for 1893 and 1894, particularly December 10, 1893, JAPM. See also Louise Wilby Knight, "Jane Addams and Hull House: Historical Lessons on Nonprofit Leadership," *Nonprofit Management and Leadership* 2, no. 2 (Winter 1991): 127–28. Regarding residents' admission process, see *Hull-House Maps and Papers,* 229. Regarding Toynbee Hall's similar practices, see Barnett, *Canon Barnett,* 1:315, 325. Hull-House probably did not need to have a formal residents meeting in its first two years, when there were only three residents. By the fall of 1891, it had six. For details, see Knight, *Citizen,* 226.

32. Hull-House Residents Meeting Minutes, September 24, 1893, November 25, 1893; Addams, *Twenty Years,* 161. Regarding the women's shelter, see Hull-House Residents Meeting Minutes, December 10, 1893. Instead Addams cooperated with the Chicago Woman's Club. *Annals,* 117, 122–23; Scrapbook 3, 3–4, "Clippings," 1894–1987, JAPM,

Addendum Reel 10 [Reel 81]; Hull-House Residents Meeting Minutes, January 14, 1894.

33. Regarding clubs being self-governing, see Alzina Stevens, "Life in a Social Settlement—Hull-House, Chicago," *Self-Culture* 9 (March 1899): 49; Scrapbook 3, 3; "Hull-House Description January 1, 1894," JAPM, 46: 0608; W. D. Johnston, "The New Social Movement" *Brown Magazine* (November 1894): 56; Stuart Joel Hecht, "Hull-House Theatre: An Analytical and Evaluative History" (PhD diss., Northwestern University, 1983), 24. Regarding Polacheck's recollections and the club leader being president, see Hilda Satt Polacheck, *I Came a Stranger: The Story of a Hull-House Girl* (Urbana: University of Illinois Press, 1989), 94–95, 215n6.

34. Regarding the congress, see *Hull-House Bulletin* 1, no. 4 (April 1896): 4.

35. See chapter 13, "Public Activities and Investigations," *Twenty Years.* The chapter title lacks the word "cooperative" but it reappears in the book's index, in the place where these investigations are referenced. The pages listed in the index under "Hull-House Cooperative Activities," mostly refer to the pages of chapter 13 (see page 458).

36. For details, see Knight, *Citizen.* Regarding sweatshop legislation rally, see also *Chicago Times-Herald,* March 9, 1896, 1, col. 7. For a detailed discussion of Addams's engagement with labor unions, see Karen Pastorello, "The Transfigured Few: Jane Addams, Bessie Abramowitz Hillman, and Immigrant Women Workers in Chicago, 1905–1915" in this volume.

37. Addams, "Significance of Organized Labor," *Machinist's Monthly Journal* (September 1898): 552.

38. Knight, *Citizen,* 391.

39. For details, see Elizabeth Anne Payne, *Reform, Labor and Feminism: Margaret Dreier Robins and the Women's Trade Union League* (Urbana: University of Illinois Press, 1988).

40. Jane Addams, *Democracy and Social Ethics* (New York: Macmillan, 1902), 224, 225, 270.

41. Hull-House Residents Meeting Minutes, December 10, 1893, Hull-House Minutes, Residents Meeting, Hull-House Association Records, Special Collections, University Library, University of Illinois at Chicago.

42. Jane Addams, *Peace and Bread in Time of War* (New York: Macmillan, 1922), 37.

43. Michael B. Katz, *In the Shadows of the Poorhouse: A Social History of Welfare in America* (New York: Basic Books, 1986), 71; Richard D. Brown, *The Strength of the People* (Chapel Hill: University of North Carolina Press, 1996), 122–23.

44. Addams, *Twenty Years,* 162.

45. Addams, *My Friend,* 74–76; Addams, *Twenty Years,* 161. Regarding minimally survivable wage, see John Albert Mayer, "Private Charities in Chicago from 1871–1915" (PhD diss., University of Minnesota, 1978), 448.

46. Aileen S. Kraditor, *The Ideas of the Woman Suffrage Movement 1890–1920* (New York: Doubleday, 1971), 163–65; Ida Husted Harper, ed., *The History of Woman Suf-*

frage, vol. 5, 1900–1920 (New York: National American Woman Suffrage Association, 1922), 422–24.

47. Daniel Levine, *Jane Addams and the Liberal Tradition* (Madison: State Historical Society of Wisconsin, 1971), 193–94.

48. Addams, *Twenty Years,* 336.

49. Jane Addams, *Democracy and Social Ethics* (New York: Macmillan, 1902), 69, 73, 136.

50. Ibid., 137, 220.

51. Ibid., 165–66.

52. Ibid., 153.

53. Ibid., 138.

54. Ibid., 5.

55. Ibid., 9–10.

56. Jane Addams, *The Second Twenty Years at Hull-House: September 1909 to September 1929, with a Record of A Growing World Consciousness* (New York: Macmillan, 1930), 202–3. See also p. 379 for another comment about cooperation.

57. Jane Addams, "Address," National Council of Women Voters, St. Louis, November 13, 1919, typed manuscript, page 6, JAPM: 48: 0138.

58. Jane Addams, "A Modern Lear," *Survey* 29 (November 2, 1912): 123.

59. Addams, *Democracy,* 275.

60. Addams, "A Modern Lear," 122–23. Although published in 1912, Jane Addams wrote the final version of the essay in 1895 and delivered it often as a lecture in 1896 and 1897. The evidence suggests that she did not revise it before she published it in 1912. For details, see Knight, *Citizen,* chapter 14, "Justice." Regarding Addams's refusal to seek credit for her accomplishments, see Dunn, "Jane Addams as a Political Leader," 151–52.

61. Jane Addams, "A Function of the Social Settlement," *Annals of the American Academy of Political and Social Science* 13 (May 1899): 48 (second numbering system: 338).

62. Addams, *Democracy,* 273–74.

63. Addams, "Significance of Organized Labor," 551.

4

A Civic Machinery for Democratic Expression

Jane Addams on Public Administration

CAMILLA STIVERS

Among Jane Addams's many gifts to American civic philosophy and institution building, her philosophy of public administration is probably one of the least known. Yet her thinking on administration was both unique and profound: unique among Progressive reformers in seeing that what public agencies do and the way they are run have significant implications for democracy; profound in its lasting contribution to a theory of administration that is political in the deepest sense. In order to convey the importance of Addams's ideas on public administration, I begin by filling in some necessary historical and theoretical background, against which Addams's ideas will stand in bold relief.

At the turn of the twentieth century in America, administrative governance was rudimentary. Private corporations far outweighed government at all levels. For example, the amount of money raised to organize the billion-dollar steel trust in 1901 was nearly enough to fund two years' worth of federal government operations. One large railroad company employed eighteen thousand people, while the commonwealth of Massachusetts had only six thousand employees. Large changes were, however, rapidly making urgent the question of government's capacity to stabilize and steer society: cities swollen by massive influxes of immigrants, economic cycles of boom and bust, and new mechanisms of communication and transportation that linked once isolated communities. In this context, the issue of government capacity became pressing. This pressure was particularly acute in cities, controlled by political party organizations ("machines") that rewarded immigrants' and other workers' party loyalty with government jobs.

Throughout the nineteenth century, political parties had fostered public activity. They linked together the national government with local areas, and brought a measure of cohesion to the nation. Parties also provided a mechanism for poor and working-class white men to participate in politics. The vacuum created by the absence of all but an embryonic administrative capacity was filled by the courts.

In 1883, patrician reformers, their political influence impeded by the machines, succeeded in getting a merit-based civil service established at the federal level. At the start, the civil service only covered about one-tenth of federal employees, and for many years the service grew a little at a time by extending its reach to certain political appointees. But the idea of merit gained strength. Over time, state and local governments followed the federal government's lead. Today, except for politically appointed top executives, who now constitute only about one-tenth of the federal workforce, employees in public agencies have to meet standardized qualifications regarding education, training, and relevant experience. Because the roots of the idea of merit lie in an ideology of nonpartisanship and neutrality, it has become common to think of the civil service as a nonpolitical institution.

Municipal reform followed on the heels of the civil service. Toward the end of the nineteenth century, concern grew among the upper middle class over the power of the working class in city councils and party organizations. Groups of reformers, the majority of them businessmen, launched efforts to wrest control of city governments away from the machines. Their initial strategy, which was to get business-oriented candidates elected mayor, met with little lasting success. The reform mayors generally failed to master the art of quid pro quo politics and thus could not get reelected. Reformers began to wonder whether another strategy might be more effective.

Their new tack was to start from the bottom rather than the top: to offer city agencies technical expertise provided by municipal research bureaus established for the purpose. The businessmen aimed to reshape city government and its day-to-day activities, and to change administrators' understanding of their work. The bureaus provided advice to city agencies on such matters as the most efficient way to organize personnel, keep records, develop budgets, and track revenues and expenditures. A good many mayors and appointed agency heads liked the prospect of being able to cut costs and/or do more with less, and the reformers' idea of a stronger role for the executive in city governance had irresistible appeal. What became known as the "bureau movement" spread rapidly from its beginnings in New York City in 1905. More and more, running government agencies came to be seen as a matter of "management."[1]

After a few years, the New York bureau launched a training school for administrators, and the professionalization of the government workforce began in earnest. Merit took on a more specific connotation. Over time, it came to entail possession of knowledge and technical expertise requiring specialized education; civil servants began to claim status as "professionals." Today, the legacy of the bureau movement is visible not only in the dozens of undergraduate and graduate public administration programs in universities around the country, but even more fundamentally in the norms that guide government administrative work. More than ever, agencies are expected to conduct themselves in a businesslike way, to attain high levels of efficiency, to keep costs down, and to meet measurable performance standards. More and more, individual clients and the citizenry-at-large are seen as customers.

These reforms—a merit-based nonpartisan civil service, professionalism, and management expertise—have become the pillars supporting the edifice of public bureaucracy. Most experts on modern public administration take their cues from the Progressive Era reformers. They justify the presence of tenured, unelected bureaucrats wielding power in a representative democracy on the basis of the need for expert, public-spirited leadership in a fractionated governmental system that apportions authority among federal, state, and local levels; separates power among legislative, judicial, and executive branches; and includes checks and balances. Without the bureaucracy, apologists ask, would such a machine run at all? They argue that citizens can trust public administrators because the latter know what they are doing (they are experts), because they have passed the test of merit (an advanced degree rather than connection to the party boss), because someone needs to steer the ship of state (we need leaders), and because civil servants are dedicated to the public good.[2]

This philosophy of administration relegates ordinary citizens to various peripheral roles, depending on the circumstances: voter, onlooker, customer, client, once in a while giver of "input." In twenty-first-century America, if we citizens trust the bureaucracy it is because we must. Direct democracy has been deemed unworkable, perhaps even dangerous. In fact, from Alexander Hamilton on down, thinkers on American government have argued that what ordinary people want is not participation in government but results: a well-run machine that leaves them free to pursue private interests. The recent "reinventing government" movement, known at the federal level as the National Performance Review, built its successes around the idea of results, arguing that well-run government means freeing bureaucrats from red tape so that they can be entrepreneurial and serve their customers.[3]

Jane Addams had a different vision of public administration. She was leader and shaper of a distinctive stream of municipal reform thinking, one grounded in the experience of the settlement houses. From this practical foundation, she articulated a view of government, including administration, as animated by ideas of home and community. In addition, she specifically rejected the management reformers' idea that efficiency was the key to effective administration.

The idea that cities were first and foremost homes for their residents was one that grew naturally from the settlement mission, which was to develop an understanding of the conditions and causes of city poverty by living with and learning from residents of poor neighborhoods. By becoming neighbors, settlement residents would gradually become their friends; by sharing the experiences of the poor, they would be able to interpret neighborhood problems to policy makers and push governments to do more to ameliorate them.

Jane Addams, founder of Hull-House, one of the earliest American settlements, used "family" as a metaphor for the wider society in order to argue for a notion of governance rooted in the kind of caring and nurturing seen as typical of the home. In arguing for the importance of women's involvement in urban reform, Addams implicitly outlined the qualities of a good public administrator: "The very multifariousness and complexity of a city government demand the help of minds accustomed to detail and variety of work, to a sense of obligation for the health and welfare of young children, and to a responsibility for the cleanliness and comfort of other people."[4] Addams criticized approaches to administration that lost sight of the human impact of bureaucratic rules in the interests of efficiency. She indicted the county relief agency for being so fearful that public support for the poor would expand endlessly that when needy couples were placed in the poorhouse, they were separated into men's and women's units and allowed to talk to each other only once a week, and then with heavy screening between them. "Such a state of mind," Addams commented, "affords one more example of the dangers of administering any human situation upon theory uncorrected by constant experience."[5]

In 1895, when Addams served on a mayoral commission investigating conditions in the county poorhouse, she likened the experience of listening to testimony to "a tearing of living tissue that . . . can scarcely be endured." After each commission meeting, she came back to Hull-House to find waiting throngs of inmates' friends and relatives, who poured out stories of what people in the poorhouse had to endure and begged for her help in finding another place for them to stay. Addams's personal interaction with the friends and relatives brought home to her the "piteous dependence of the poor upon the good will of public officials."[6] Such experiences shaped Addams's philosophy of public administration; she came to believe it had to be grounded first and foremost in commitment to treat people with the kind of respect and care due real human beings, as opposed to abstractions and statistics. A man she knew, desperate for work, took a job digging outdoors during a severe winter and as a result died of pneumonia. Addams, who had advised him to take the job despite his having declared that he could not endure hard weather, reflected: "I cannot see [his two children] without a bitter consciousness that it was at their expense I learned that life cannot be administered by definite rules and regulations; that wisdom to deal with a man's difficulties comes only through some knowledge of his life and habits as a whole. . . ."[7]

Such experiences helped shape Addams's views on the role of administration in the overall system of governance, and the relative importance of political versus managerial values. In a little-remembered essay called "Problems of Municipal Administration,"[8] Addams attributed what reformers referred to as the "shame of American cities" not to the amateurishness and corruption of party loyalists but to the persistence among reformers of outmoded eighteenth-century ideas. She charged the founders of cities, like the founders of the United States, with lack of faith in the people. She saw those who wrote state constitutions and municipal charters as the kind of "humanitarian who loves the people without really knowing them."[9] Basing the organization of city government on ideals like the "rights of man," said Addams, municipal leaders have reflected the kind of idealism "that is afraid of experience. . . . They depended upon penalties, coercion, compulsion, and remnants of military codes to hold the community together" rather than perceiving the potential in "social capacity" and the "efficiency of the popular will."[10] Compounding this error, Progressive reformers had tried to give increasing "power to administrative officers" instead of having the imagination to invent new machinery that allows the people's voice to speak. The result: despite the lip service given to the people, government had become more and more remote from them. With fine irony, Addams noted:

"Having staked so much upon the people, whom they really knew so little, [city founders] became eager that they should appear well, and should not be given enough power to enable them to betray their weaknesses; as a kind lady may permit herself to give a tramp five cents, believing that, although he may spend it for drink, he cannot get very drunk on so small a sum."[11]

This governing strategy had broken down, however, according to Addams, under the pressures of industrialization, urbanization, and the arrival of large numbers of immigrants from a variety of cultures. City governments lacked the capacity to weave this complex social fabric together. Instead, all they could do was pass more and more ordinances, to try to control the "vicious," to provide only minimal help to the needy, and to defend themselves against taxpayers who resent "the fact that they should be made to support that which, from the nature of the case, is too barren to excite their real enthusiasm."[12] Addams noted that the existing mechanisms of government "inevitably [produce] the indifferent citizen and the so-called 'professional politician.'"[13] The first just wants to be left alone, the second claims that he knows what the people want and can represent them in the halls of government. In neither case is the voice of the people heard in public.

When it comes to administering the laws, corrupt politicians appoint their friends, who in turn are bought off by those, such as businessmen seeking city contracts, whom the laws are supposed to control. The resulting ineffective and corrupted administration can only continue as it does, Addams argued, in the absence of "civic machinery for simple democratic expression." Railing against corruption, reformers had failed to notice what was utterly apparent to Addams and other settlement workers: "simple people, who carry in their hearts the desire for mere goodness, who regularly deplete their scanty livelihood in response to a primitive pity, and who . . . have an unquenchable desire that charity and simple justice shall regulate men's relations."[14] The potential to improve government administration, in other words, lies in the goodness and civic-mindedness of ordinary people. This goodness was obvious to Addams and other settlement residents because they lived in urban neighborhoods, in contrast to civic leaders and officials who knew the residents of such neighborhoods only as abstractions.

Similarly, Addams argued, government concentrates on the needs of the poorest and most vulnerable, building hospitals and almshouses but doing nothing for the average citizen. Governments are afraid, she said, of taking on functions that benefit the population at large, so ordinary folk are left to their own devices, then "scolded for staying at home on election day."[15] "What broad basis has been laid," she asked, "for modification of their most genuine and pressing needs through their own initiative?"[16] In another critical thrust, Addams noted, "So conservative an economist as Marshall has pointed out that, in the fear of erasing 'individual initiative,' we every year allow to go to waste untold capacity, talent, and even genius, among the children of the poor, whose parents are unable to shelter them from premature labor; or among the adults, whose vital force is exhausted long before the allotted span of life. We distrust the instinct to shelter and care for them, although it is as old and as much at the foundation of human progress as is individual initiative itself."[17]

Whereas European countries had instituted social policy measures to ensure adequate standards of living for wage earners, Addams argued, in the United States these policies had been blocked by industrialists clinging to an outmoded idea of the role of government. She speculated that the zeal with which the founders of the country fought to limit government intervention in daily life may have locked us, their descendants, into antiquated patterns of thought. Ideas, she said, were part of the spoils of the revolution, but they had turned into theories that afflict us today with "a sort of disease of responsibility for [their] possession."[18]

Addams concludes with this vision: "If we could trust democratic government as over against and distinct from the older types—from those which repress, rather than release, the power of the people—then we should begin to know what democracy really is, and our municipal administration would at last be free to attain Aristotle's ideal of a city, 'where men live a common life for a noble end.'"[19]

There are several aspects of Addams's argument worth emphasizing. They offer vivid contrast to mainstream theories of American government generally, and public administrative theory in particular.

First, Addams rejected the idea that government should be the province of the specialist, whether this be an elected representative or a professional administrator. Though she would no doubt bow to the force of the argument put forth during the constitutional convention that in an extended republic the room in which political deliberation takes place will not hold everyone, her respect for the knowledge and goodness of ordinary people makes her unwilling to give up on the idea that the wisdom people gain from daily living is as valuable a resource for governing as are technical expertise and objective analysis. A striking difference between settlement residents, including Addams, and other Progressive reformers was that the settlers were actually living in the neighborhoods hardest hit by what we have learned to call "urban problems," and witnessed firsthand the ingenuity and mutual support with which their neighbors dealt with them. Because she knew poor immigrants as individuals and families, not merely as statistics, Addams could see their capacity to contribute to civic life. From her perspective, everyone is an expert on the conditions of his or her life, and the biggest challenge of running a government is to tap this expertise.

Second, Addams rejected what has become known in public administration as the politics-administration dichotomy, that is, the idea that administering government agencies is somehow outside politics or that good administration is carried forward objectively and neutrally. Woodrow Wilson had planted the seeds of this idea in an 1887 essay entitled "The Study of Administration," which argued that administrative standards were the same for public agencies as they were for private corporations.[20] Municipal reform efforts led by business groups built on this idea that the precepts of management were essentially the same regardless of the nature of the work. In both cases, good management meant being as businesslike and efficient as possible. This precept supported the notion that politics not only could, but should, be removed from administration, leaving only the issue of how to make administration maximally efficient and effective, a purely technical question. As Addams noted in *Democracy and Social Ethics,* "The well-to-do men of the community think of politics as something off by itself. . . . As a result of this detachment, 'reform movements' started by business men and the better element are almost wholly occupied in the correction of political machinery and with a concern for the better method of administration, rather than with the ultimate purpose of securing the welfare of the people. They fix their attention so exclusively on methods that they fail to consider the final aims of city government."[21]

In reuniting public ends and means within administration, Addams put forth a broad understanding of the work that goes on in government agencies, one that contrasts sharply with present-day notions that public administration consists of competently implementing laws passed by legislative bodies. The view of public administration as an implementation tool obscures the many complex judgments that administrators have to make in carrying out legislated mandates, judgments that are as much about conflicting public values as they are about technical correctness in the service of economic efficiency—in sum, judgments about matters that have no technical right answer. As roundly as it has been rejected by contemporary theorists of administration, the idea that politics and administration can be separated reappears in, for example, recommendations that much government work can be contracted out to private businesses because it is "purely technical." Ultimately, listening to Jane Addams would lead one toward the position that which government functions are technical and which political is a political rather than a technical question.

The paramount issue for governments, Addams held, was not how they should be run, but what they should do. The shame of the cities was not corruption, it was that city governments had lost sight of the need to turn the great body of their residents into real communities, each one a "civic machinery for democratic expression." This failure was grounded in a lack of trust in the ability of citizens to understand and judge the issues facing their governments. Problems of municipal administration were not only procedural or technical, they were substantive—or rather, the technical and the substantive were inextricably intertwined. Cities would never be well run unless they addressed matters that would improve the quality of life for all their residents, matters, in other words, that cannot be decided technically by experts but must be weighed and wrestled with by the people themselves. Addams's position suggests that in addition to technical expertise, professional administration requires expertise in forming and maintaining relationships with citizens so that *their* expertise, drawn from daily life, can contribute to finding solutions to the complex problems of governance.

Today is a time when the question of what governments should do to improve the lives of citizens has dramatically lost ground. National leaders send citizens the message that government is the problem, not the answer. Regulatory and service delivery functions are contracted out to the private sector to such an extent that the issue of public administrative capacity is once again an urgent concern (witness, to take just one example, government's failure during and after the catastrophic hurricanes in 2005). Public administrators are being assured that what ordinary people want, if they want anything at all from government, is customer-friendly, entrepreneurial management and contractors who produce results.

In these times, Jane Addams's legacy to public administration is worth remembering. Perhaps her advice to us today would be that the most important challenge facing public administrators is not to make government work more efficiently but to make it more human and caring. Perhaps, as she believed, the results people really want are not reached through management by objectives or greater entrepreneurialism but through fostering the conditions under which ordinary people, sometimes in collaboration with administrators, can pursue public-spirited activities that enable them to "live a common life for a noble end."[22]

Notes

1. Camilla Stivers, *Bureau Men, Settlement Women: Constructing Public Administration in the Progressive Era* (Lawrence: University Press of Kansas, 2000).

2. The literature is vast. For a broad argument in defense of the legitimacy of public administration in a representative democracy, see Gary L. Wamsley, Robert N. Bacher, Charles T. Goodsell, Philip S. Kronenbert, John A. Rohr, Camilla M. Stivers, Orion F. White, and James F. Wolf, *Refounding Public Administration* (Newbury Park,

Calif.: Sage, 1990). For examples of arguments based on the need for professionalism and technical expertise on the part of bureaucrats, the classic statement after Woodrow Wilson is Carl J. Friedrich, "Public Power and the Nature of Administrative Responsibility," in *Public Policy,* ed. C. Friedrich, 221–45 (Cambridge, Mass.: Harvard University Press, 1940). See also John Nalbandian, "Tenets of Contemporary Professionalism in Local Government," *Public Administration Review* 50, no. 6 (1990): 654–62; Ruth DeHoog and Gordon Whitaker, "Professional Leadership in Local Government," *International Journal of Public Administration* 16, no. 12 (1993): 2033–49; R. C. Kearny and C. Sinha, "Professionalism and Bureaucratic Responsiveness: Conflict or Compatibility," *Public Administration Review* 48, no. 1 (1988): 571–79. Arguments based on the need for leadership include Philip Selznick, *Leadership in Administration* (Evanston, Ill.: Row, Peterson, 1957); Robert D. Behn, "What Right Do Public Managers Have to Lead?" *Public Administration Review* 58, no. 3 (1998): 209–30; Jameson Doig and Erwin C. Hargrove, *Leadership and Innovation: A Biographical Perspective on Entrepreneurs in Government* (Baltimore: Johns Hopkins University Press, 1987). Arguments grounded in public spirit or commitment to the public interest include Terry L. Cooper and Dale Wright, *Exemplary Public Administrators: Character and Leadership in Government* (San Francisco: Jossey-Bass, 1992); Douglas F. Morgan and Henry D. Kass, "Constitutional Leadership, Phronesis, and the American Administrative Ethos," *Dialogue: The Public Administration Theory Network* 12, no. 1 (1991): 17–60; Larry D. Terry, "Leadership in the Administrative State: The Concept of Administrative Conservatorship," *Administration and Society* 21, no. 4 (1990): 395–412; George F. Frederickson and David Kirkwood Hart, "The Public Service and the Patriotism of Benevolence," *Public Administration Review* 45, no. 5 (1985): 547–54.

3. See, e.g., David Osborne and Ted Gaebler, *Reinventing Government* (New York: Penguin, 1992).

4. Quoted in Carol Nackenoff, "Gendered Citizenship: Alternative Narratives of Political Incorporation in the United States, 1875–1925" (paper presented at the Annual Meeting of the American Political Science Association, San Francisco, 1996), 10.

5. Jane Addams, *My Friend Julia Lathrop* (New York: MacMillan, 1935), 70–71.

6. Jane Addams, *Twenty Years at Hull-House* (1910) (New York: Penguin Books Signet Classic, 1981), 125–26.

7. Addams, *Twenty Years,* 123.

8. Jane Addams, "The Problems of Municipal Administration," *American Journal of Sociology* 10, no. 4 (January 1905): 425–44. Addams incorporated much of the material from this article into *Newer Ideals of Peace.* To see how Addams used this material in constructing the relation between social justice and peace, see Marilyn Fischer, "The Conceptual Scaffolding of *Newer Ideals of Peace,*" in this volume.

9. Addams, "The Problems of Municipal Administration," 425.

10. Ibid., 426–27.

11. Ibid., 427–28.

12. Ibid., 428.
13. Ibid., 429.
14. Ibid., 438.
15. Ibid., 440.
16. Ibid., 441.
17. Ibid., 441–42.
18. Ibid., 444.
19. Ibid.
20. Woodrow Wilson, "The Study of Administration," *Political Science Quarterly* 2, no. 2 (1887): 197–222.
21. Jane Addams, *Democracy and Social Ethics* (Urbana and Chicago: University of Illinois Press, 2002), 98–99.
22. Addams, "The Problems of Municipal Administration," 444.

5

"The Transfigured Few"

Jane Addams, Bessie Abramowitz Hillman, and Immigrant Women Workers in Chicago, 1905–15

KAREN PASTORELLO

Learning of the proposed demolition of Hull-House in the spring of 1961, Amalgamated Clothing Workers of America (ACWA) vice president Bessie Abramowitz Hillman pleaded with Chicago mayor Richard Daley to do everything in his power to save the institution she regarded as "not only hallowed and venerable," but as "sacred to every American with the slightest understanding of the social forces that have given America its internal strength and vitality. . . . In the fullest sense," Hillman elaborated, "it is woven into the fabric of America." Bessie Abramowitz Hillman joined "a concerted effort by labor unions, civic organizations, and leading citizens that raised over three hundred thousand dollars to preserve the historic building" and, in the process, paid a lasting tribute to the valuable lessons she learned at Hull-House.[1] As a young immigrant in the early 1900s, Hillman's interactions with settlement residents determined her life's work. The middle-class women centered at Hull-House not only taught her how to work with political officials such as Daley, but also provided a foundation for the skills that enabled her to engage in cross-class collaborations and effectively organize workers for more than half a century.[2]

Immersion in the community of women reformers at Chicago's premier settlement transformed a number of young immigrant women from passive victims into determined activists. Hull-House associates introduced Abramowitz and other women who were novice working-class activists to progressive endeavors in the fields of labor, education, and politics. Hillman's lifelong admiration for Hull-House and particularly for its founder, Jane Addams, began during the 1910 Chicago Men's Garment Workers' Strike.

The pair's acquaintance evolved into an enduring friendship when Addams served as a negotiator between the Hart, Schaffner, and Marx Company and a group of striking employees led by the young Russian garment worker, Bessie Abramowitz. Abramowitz, along with other strike leaders, who met at Hull-House frequently during the strike, affectionately began to refer to it as the "House of Labor."[3] The strike marked both the birth of the Amalgamated Clothing Workers of America—once heralded as the largest men's garment workers' union in the country—and the emergence of Bessie Abramowitz as a labor leader. Addams's twenty-year-old protégé proved instrumental in initiating the largest strike of its kind by clothing workers and, ultimately, in the founding of the union that she helped guide for the next sixty years.

Historians studying the early years of women's activism within the American labor movement have long recognized that middle-class women and their organizations often joined working-class women in the struggle to better the lives of workers. A number argue that the middle-class "allies" were merely patronizing the so-called "girls" as they pushed their own agendas forward.[4] Obvious class tensions in the female support networks suggest that this may have been true in some cases, especially in New York City, where the male-dominated labor movement complicated matters by never fully endorsing the efforts of working women to improve their working conditions.[5] In Chicago, however, the relationships between Hull-House residents and the working women who frequented the settlement appeared genuine. This study explores the nature of the bonds established among Hull-House reformers and the young immigrant women they befriended by analyzing the early years of the lifelong friendship between Jane Addams and Bessie Abramowitz Hillman.

By the time Bessie Abramowitz met Jane Addams in the opening decade of the twentieth century, Addams presided over Chicago like a "mythical Amazon of social reform."[6] To fully understand the evolution of the relationship between Addams and Abramowitz requires tracing Addams's perceptions of and actions toward foreign-born workers. This process will explain how immigrant workers, particularly immigrant women workers like Abramowitz, shaped Addams's own activism and, conversely, how she shaped theirs. Moreover, it will reveal the ways in which both Addams and Abramowitz were transformed by their relationship and what transpired because of it.

When twenty-nine-year-old Jane Addams launched Hull-House in 1889, she purposely situated it in the midst of the "large foreign colonies which so easily isolated themselves in American cities." Hull-House's proximity provided both a refuge for immigrants and the opportunity for direct interaction between residents and the immigrant poor whose lives they sought to improve.[7]

Settlement workers helped immigrants adjust to life in their new country by assisting those seeking to become Americans through a humanitarian approach that included English and naturalization classes. By 1912 Hull-House residents established a citizenship school where immigrants could first receive and then contribute to "what is best in American civilization."[8] The settlement workers accommodated the immigrants' work schedules and demanding family lives. Citizenship opportunities presented at the settlement meant that even the most recent immigrants could readily become active citizens.

Jane Addams quickly earned a reputation as a staunch supporter of immigrants. Hilda Satt Polacheck, a young Polish immigrant, one of the thousands who frequented Hull-House, credited Jane Addams with being the first person to "[wake] the conscience of America to the debt that it owed to the great masses of people pouring into America" by introducing the idea that immigrants were producers who made the clothing that Americans wore, cut the lumber to build their homes, and grew the crops and worked in the stockyards to put food on American tables.[9] Addams encouraged the value of self-determination, arguing that "all human beings were equal and therefore worthy of being "train[ed] into good citizenship."[10] Accordingly, the responsibility for training future citizens rested squarely upon the shoulders of middle-class women. Addams emphasized the reciprocal aspect of cross-class relationships, so that once working-class women became empowered citizens, they too would be expected to assume the rights and obligations that followed. Addams believed that "citizens' access to direct participation in the state was vital to national progress."[11] She hoped that eventually, as many immigrants as possible would join the ranks of what she called "the transfigured few," who broke out of the dreary slum sweatshops, usually by getting an education.[12]

In the meantime Addams set out to learn all she could about her Nineteenth Ward neighbors. Attempting to see things from their perspective, she singled out those most in need, intending through "sympathetic understanding" to "secure the consent of all concerned" so that she could involve those affected from the first formulation of the problem in offering suggestions for resolution, carrying the solution forward, and assessing its impact. She stood back and observed, bent and swayed, in a conscious attempt to reject "top-down patrician political reform."[13] Others around her watched as Addams and her colleagues worked to equip the immigrant poor with the skills necessary to survive in Chicago's tough urban neighborhoods. Mary McDowell, a worker at Hull-House and later at the University of Chicago settlement, recounted one such incident when she invited a trade union woman to dinner at Hull-House. The young woman was reluctant to accept what she felt was probably another effort "to patronize a working girl." When she arrived late, Jane Addams stood to welcome her, explaining that she had asked her to come to see "what we could do with each other for the girls in your trade." Addams's use of the word "with" rather than "for" made all the difference to the young girl, who had "been with her ever since."[14] The settlement leader's willingness to learn from experience and consequently, to modify her approach accordingly, were counted among her most admirable qualities.

Unlike New York, where "sustained conflict between upper-class and working-class women," whose diverse lives and political agendas all but defeated efforts to build a reform coalition, class tensions seemed to dissipate in the cooperative environs of Progressive Era Chicago.[15] The high degree of social cohesion proved to result from the organizations and personalities enmeshed in the nascent reform community. Hull-House leaders like Jane Addams, Ellen Gates Starr, Julia Lathrop, and Florence Kelley went to great lengths to ensure that their actions took the form of cross-class discussions predicated on ameliorating the problems of the poor through empowering them rather than doling out charity. Advancing self-determination and mutuality, they managed to create a space where women's political culture flourished. By living and working together in a neighborhood of the poor and disenfranchised and communicating with them across class lines, they "campaigned as a united force" to set the stage for "radical social change."[16]

Addams recognized that those around her helped her overcome her own class and ethnic prejudices. Julia Lathrop's extensive investigative work into the poorest homes within a ten-block radius of Hull-House first helped Addams realize she should "not set the agenda for Hull-House but instead she should meet the needs of the neighborhood." Florence Kelley, best known for her quest for protective legislation for women and children, also worked behind the scenes to help Addams appreciate her neighbors' high regard for drama, art, literature and music, and learning.[17] While these women and many others shaped and implemented social policy based on their activities, Jane Addams was, without question, the preeminent woman among her allies. Her conciliatory approach to moral and ethical problems allowed her to broaden the progressive reform circle by allying with business, civic, and labor leaders.

Addams's connections outside the settlement entailed many of the city's reform-minded men and women affiliated with the University of Chicago, which by 1890 boasted the nation's first school of sociology. Rather than remaining distant elitists mired in theory, faculty and administrators at the University of Chicago such as Marion Talbot, John Dewey, and George H.

Mead directed their convictions toward a constructive social effort. They were examples of the many who helped alleviate tensions between community-based activists and academic theorists by challenging the existing system and advocating female participation in combinations of research, community service, and teaching.[18] Talbot, dean of undergraduate women and assistant professor of sanitary science at the University of Chicago, fought for the integration of female students and faculty into the academic community while proposing that homemakers could also be involved in social reform. Philosophers John Dewey and George Herbert Mead supported women's advancement as well and regarded Hull-House as a laboratory already practicing what they sought to theorize. The team approach to problem solving and social research employed by Hull-House residents echoed the principles embodied in Mead's "working hypothesis." Jane Addams adopted pragmatism, including Dewey's vocabulary and ideas, because it provided a means for understanding and transforming experience. Though it is difficult to gauge the degree of influence the academics and reformers had on one another, it is clear that the three themes of experiment, experience, and democracy informed their writings and activities.[19]

With the climate conducive to reform, Addams began to put her principles into practice and, in doing so, made a definitive transition from an ardent observer to an impassioned activist. The exchange of pragmatic ideas with the men and women of the Chicago school, the compilation of investigative reports by social workers, and the economic hardship following the depression of 1893 surely helped to pull Addams toward meaningful reform. However, the most compelling reason for Addams's transformation from a sociologist to a full-fledged political activist was the exploitation and industrial debasement of the immigrant that she and her fellow Hull-House residents witnessed on a daily basis. Addams related that, "Even when the immigrant escapes industrial disaster he still faces a higher death rate" than his American neighbors, "and increasing insanity, due to the complexity of his new occupations and the nervous strain of maladjustment, added to the fact that his cheap food is too often filled with dubious preservatives and the imitation of his native drinks is drugged by poisonous stimulants." The common expression in the neighborhood was "something always happens to the greenhorn."[20]

By choice, Addams and her colleagues observed, experienced, and, ultimately, confronted the overwhelming challenges that characterized progressive Chicago. Likewise, Addams's interest in industrial reform piqued as a consequence of her first encounter with working women. She recalled that shortly after moving to Chicago, "fresh from the country," and having "little idea of the social and industrial conditions . . . a dozen girls came from a neighboring factory with a grievance in regard to their wages."[21] Addams watched, intrigued, as a progressive judge successfully arbitrated a settlement.

Addams's talents as a negotiator were evident from an early age. As a young adult, Addams often played the self-appointed mediator, resolving minor family conflicts. She learned that successful arbitration involved more than a mere compromise, it meant understanding all sides before undertaking negotiations.[22] Her first professional attempts at arbitration dated to the days of the 1894 Pullman Strike. As a member of the Civic Federation's special Board of Conciliation, Addams met with the workers and American Railway officials to investigate possibilities for ending the strike. Later, when she tried to confer with Pullman Palace Car Company managers so that she could have a more complete account of the conflict, her attempts proved futile. Afterward, in a paper entitled "A Modern Lear," Addams chronicled the strike, focusing on company owner George Pullman's refusal to arbitrate. According to James Linn, her nephew and early biographer, once the controversial paper was finally published in 1912, it "began to make Jane Addams a figure of national importance in the philosophy of social progress."[23]

However, while Addams pinned her hopes on arbitration as the most peaceful and effective strategy for settling conflicts between employers and workers, she realized that the unions "saw more to be had from a fight." On the surface, her early perspective on labor unions seemed tinged with ambivalence. She admired the labor movement's struggle to better the lives of workers, but she objected to the use of the strike as a tactical weapon because of the violence often associated with it, and more importantly, because of the "distinct cleavage of society" it caused.[24] After all, labor leaders had initiated a number of strikes, the majority of which were unsuccessful, violent, and rarely represented women's interests.

Yet by 1899, in "Trade Unions and Public Duty," Addams came to the defense of unions. She explained that she was impressed with their "noble purposes" and faulted the state, the public, and employers for the violence and disorder that accompanied union efforts.[25] Addams realized that involvement in trade unions enabled many immigrants to begin "to secure a more orderly existence." Hoping to further labor's cause, she began to promote the labor movement as an indispensable "part of the general reorganization of society," and urged "first, the organization of working people" so that they might "carry out the aims of higher living."[26] She agreed with labor leaders that appealing to the immigrants' most immediate needs would be the most effective way to organize immigrant workers. Once these "primal necessities" were met, Addams theorized that immigrants would begin to display "the first indication of idealism," and she hoped that "it may be sturdy enough and sufficiently founded upon evidence to make some impression upon the tremendous immigrant situation." Like those at the English settlement Toynbee Hall, Addams championed the idea of self-governance among the working class. Once imbibed with the "tonic of self-help," Addams believed that the immigrant workers themselves would begin to direct the process of social evolution toward securing greater government responsibility for workers' welfare.[27] In Addams's mind, social and industrial democracy were inextricably linked.

From the beginning, "it was generally understood that Hull-House [was] on the side of the unions."[28] Disregarding the objections of a few settlement associates who equated the labor movement with anarchy, almost from its inception, Hull-House residents made overtures to the fledgling labor movement. Seeking to avoid class conflict at all costs, Addams viewed the interests of the working class and women as synonymous.[29] Under her direction, settlement workers provided much-needed meeting space for early women's unions, which had been forced to meet over saloons, and soon offered financial assistance as union leaders mounted organizational campaigns. "Sorely in need of help," it seemed "perhaps natural [to Addams] that the unions organized at Hull-House should have been those in the sewing trades." Among the first to organize were the shirt makers in the spring of 1891, followed by the cloak makers in 1892, and the citywide Dorcas Federal Labor Union (later the Woman's Union Label League).[30]

While a number of settlement residents concentrated their efforts on facilitating the organization of women into unions, others, including Jane Addams and WTUL president Margaret Dreier Robins, continued to advance the cause of working women by reaching beyond the immediate neighborhood. In 1900, with the financial support of Hull-House, Addams opened the Jane Club, offering cooperative living arrangements to young working women so that they would have a residence from which they could not be evicted, in the event of a strike. In the first decade of the twentieth century, female reformers forged a long-lasting alliance with the Chicago Federation of Labor and its president, John Fitzpatrick. Addams believed that during "industrial disturbances" workers tended to be suspicious of all but their "own kind," and that by offering multiple levels of assistance to workers, she could bring the settlement "into fellowship with . . . trades-unions."[31] Hull-House's longstanding tradition of involvement with workers also encouraged amicable relations between the working girls and their middle-class allies. Mary Kenney, an Irish bookbinder who grew up in Missouri, and Alzina Stevens, a former typesetter and Hull-House resident, both helped to educate Jane Addams about organized labor. They too contributed to her experiences, which eventually encouraged her move from seeking to understand the working poor to mitigating their problems. Florence Kelley's advocacy of trade unions also encouraged Addams's activism and facilitated her understanding of working-class politics.[32] They worked together for labor legislation and to organize women into unions.

Addams's escalating activism on behalf of workers reflected her awareness of their mounting difficulties. She drew on her direct experience in the Pullman Strike to educate various classes about labor, constantly stressing the mutual interdependence of classes, remarking: "No part of society can afford to get along without the others." She explained that unions moved in the direction of industrial democracy, all the while carving "tiny paths of progress" that would ultimately lead to a "type of government founded upon peace and fellowship."[33] Her work as an arbitrator during the Teamsters' and garment workers' strikes in 1905 led to her pronouncement that the existing industrial system "thwarts our industrial demands, not only for social righteousness but for social order." Addams pledged to "go as far as possible" to abolish "the evils of the sweating system."[34]

Their drive gained cross-class support throughout the Progressive Era. Addams in particular used the time between strikes to agitate for protective labor legislation. Her introduction to the concept of protective legislation can be traced to her mentor at Toynbee Hall, Rev. Samuel Barnett, who believed "that higher moral standards in industrial life must be somehow attained, that as rapidly as any advance in standards can be perceived it must be embodied in legislation so that it may be as fair for one as for another." As a member of Chicago's Civic Federation in the wake of the depression of 1893, Addams helped secure the passage of the Illinois Factories and Workshops Inspection Act, which established eight hours as the legal limit of the working day for women, restricted child labor, and created a factory inspection office.[35] Years later, addressing the topic of "The Relation of Women to Industry and Social Legislation" at a 1908 Boston meeting, she suggested that: "We should look more carefully to the protection of our most valuable asset—the human being that works, and especially the woman who works." Calling for the government to afford the necessary protection, Addams emphatically stated, "Legislation must shape itself to these ends." The cohesive nature of their network enabled Chicago reformers to univocally add the quest for legislation to their cross-class drive for worker organization.[36]

The U.S. Senate's *Report on Conditions of Women and Child Wage Earners in the United States, 1911–1915,* validated Addams's pragmatic principles and her quest for protective legislation. She touted its findings, insisting that the comprehensive nineteen-volume report "ought to be familiar to every woman in the Nation." Addams viewed the report as the culmination of the maternalist's protective argument: "This illuminating study makes it seem impossible that any employer should unwittingly place the profits of industry above the health and virtue of the future mothers of the Nation, or fail to see the moral implication of exhausting hours and starvation wages." More adamantly than ever, Addams invoked the social responsibility of women to the common good: "Certainly it is the business of women to prevent 'an impaired second generation,' above all if we are living in a republic whose very continuance depends upon the intelligence and vigor of its future citizens."[37]

Addams's concern for working women was all-encompassing. Women's vulnerability outside the workplace also troubled Addams. She observed that, "Many a working girl at the end of the day is so hysterical and overwrought that her mental balance is plainly disturbed. Hundreds of working girls go directly to bed as soon as they have eaten their suppers. They are too tired to go from home for recreation, too tired to read, and often too tired to sleep."[38] For working women, Hull-House afforded a respite from the chaos of urban life. Hilda Satt Polacheck remembered the settlement as "an oasis in a desert of boredom and monotony" where one could rejuvenate after a hard day of factory work.[39] Structured recreational activities offered reformers ample opportunities to protect, and ultimately empower, working women who, as an added benefit, would be less conscious of class distinctions in a relaxed atmosphere. Having experienced the pangs of relocation herself, Addams believed that young immigrant women were often "bewildered by the change from an old world village to an American city."[40]

For newly arrived immigrant women like Bessie Abramowitz, Hull-House provided a fundamental source of support as well as an introduction to American life. Born in 1889, Abramowitz was the fourth daughter in a large Jewish family that eventually included eight children. The Abramowitzes resided in Linoveh, a tiny shtetl deep within the Russian Pale of Settlement. Abramowitz's father, Emanuel, was a commission agent who sold wholesale goods in the countryside while her mother, Sarah, supplemented the family income by occasionally taking in boarders who were passing through the hamlet on the rail lines. Abramowitz and her siblings were educated by a private tutor in their two-story wooden house.[41] At the age of fifteen Abramowitz abruptly left her comfortable family to escape an arranged marriage to a local butcher's son. Accompanied by two young cousins, Bessie Abramowitz sailed into New

York harbor on December 14, 1905. Assuring Ellis Island officials that she was well past the legal age for immigration, she listed her age as twenty-one.[42] Following the path of countless others before her, Abramowitz immediately traveled to Chicago, where recently arrived Russian Jews, Italians, and Greeks displaced more prosperous American, German, and Irish residents in densely settled ethnic enclaves. She stepped off the train into a city in the process of undergoing a transformation from a prairie transportation capital to the second largest metropolis in the country. Yet Chicago still suffered from many of the ills that Addams first described in 1892: "the streets [were] inexpressibly dirty, the number of schools inadequate, sanitary legislation unenforced, the streetlighting bad, the paving miserable . . . and the stables [defied] all laws of sanitation."[43]

Despite this perplexing environment, Abramowitz found a job hand-sewing buttons on men's suits in a local garment factory. Immersion in the Jewish American community on Chicago's northwest side facilitated her acculturation into American society. Residing in a distant cousin's boardinghouse, she enrolled in English classes at Hull-House where, as in the garment shop, she met immigrant women in situations similar to her own. For Abramowitz and for thousands of other young immigrants, "Hull-House came to represent everything good that America stood for."[44]

The prevailing spirit of reform offered hope to disheartened immigrant women. An optimistic Abramowitz not only sponsored the emigration of her two younger sisters in 1908 but attempted to protect them from the rigors of factory work by planning to open a dress shop with them when they joined her in Chicago. Probably owing to lack of money, the shop never opened, but Abramowitz saw to it that her sisters did homework—making men's bow ties in their boardinghouse rather than working in a factory, as she was forced to do. In the meantime Abramowitz confronted her own workplace dilemma by trying to organize her coworkers in 1908. Fired and blacklisted for her efforts, she worked outside Chicago for about a year. Upon her return, she obtained a job under an alias at Hart, Schaffner, and Marx, the largest men's clothing company in the city, where she began her activism in earnest.

On September 22, 1910, Bessie Abramowitz and her coworker, Hannah Shapiro, led a small group of young women out of Hart, Schaffner, and Marx Shop Number 5 to protest an arbitrary cut in the piece rate.[45] Abandoned by the only union in the industry, the United Garment Workers, whose president Thomas Rickert refused to organize unskilled immigrants, Abramowitz turned to Hull-House in sheer desperation. Addams embraced the cause of the striking women, providing financial assistance and meeting space. Hull-House became "a citadel of hope and strength from then on."[46] With the resources of the women's network based at Hull-House enabling them to maintain the strike, thirty-eight thousand clothing workers followed Abramowitz's lead in the monumental strike that paralyzed the Chicago garment industry.

Intervening in the conflict at Abramowitz's request, both Jane Addams and Ellen Gates Starr maintained unusually high profiles during "the struggle which brought [the Amalgamated Clothing Workers of America] into being."[47] For many, the mere association of the middle-class reformers with the strike lent credibility to the striking workers. Addams tried to influence the business owners and successfully persuaded Hart, Schaffner, and Marx owner Joseph Schaffner to go into the factory to experience the conditions firsthand. Appalled by what he saw, Schaffner admitted that he was surprised the strike had not happened much sooner.[48] In addition, Addams oversaw the creation of the Citizen's Strike Committee, the negotiating body eventually responsible for ending the five-month-long strike. Unwilling to risk negative public opinion against Hull-House, Addams refrained from public activities such as picketing. The strike yielded mixed results, yet due largely to Addams's efforts, approximately eight thousand Hart, Schaffner, and Marx workers returned to work with a guarantee for an arbitration board that would attempt to settle future disputes in the workplace.[49]

Meanwhile Addams took a personal interest in the young strike leader. At the time of the strike, Addams had moved from speaking to writing, having just published *The Spirit of Youth in the City Streets* and the autobiographical *Twenty Years at Hull-House*. In addition to its optimistic answer to the problem of juvenile delinquency, *The Spirit of Youth* offered a fundamental cause for the discontent of urban youth—the industrial system that employed them in monotonous jobs for long hours. In her book, she offered suggestions for young people so that they could adjust to the system and perhaps be happier in the process.[50] Perhaps most important, she encouraged young workers to become union members so they could benefit by the advances made by the labor movement. The publication of these works not only lent insight into Addams's ever-evolving philosophy but, on a practical note, it also meant that she had more time to devote to activism. Mentoring Abramowitz during the strike enabled Addams to reveal the principles of mutuality by integrating cross-class cooperation with working-class advocacy.

Addams taught Abramowitz to "use connections for the cause," introducing her to influential men and women, including WTUL president Margaret Dreier Robins.[51] Addams offered unconditional support as Abramowitz organized unskilled immigrants in the men's garment trade. Later Bessie recalled the maternal nature of her relationship: "During the long weeks of the strike Hull-House was a home to me, and Jane Addams was like a mother. Many of our meetings were held there, and when they did not end until late at night, she would not let me go home alone so I slept at Hull-House. When she suspected that I had not eaten properly she would ask me if I had and see to it that I did."[52]

Impressed by Abramowitz's initiative and intense dedication to the strike, Addams agreed with arbitration board chairman John E. Williams's assessment of Abramowitz as "Earnest and sincere in word and act, she is a power among the women workers. . . ."[53] Above all, Addams identified with many of the qualities Abramowitz possessed. Seemingly worlds apart, the two women shared similar traits. Abramowitz was not only from a middle-class family, she was educated, cultivated, and single. She proved a model immigrant, undergoing the process of Americanization by preserving what she deemed most valuable about the Old World while quickly absorbing the New. For Addams, Abramowitz personified the potential of youth. Abramowitz's serious demeanor served as a valuable asset in crossing the class divide to act as a liaison between the working-class women and the middle-class allies. She enlightened Addams further on the harsh realities of immigrant life while making her aware of her political acumen. Perhaps what Addams found most impressive was Abramowitz's relentless drive to improve her circumstances. Abramowitz learned to work for wages from her biological mother, Sarah Abramowitz, but it was from her surrogate mother, Jane Addams, that she learned to effect social justice.

Moreover, Addams's goal of social justice through Christian responsibility—or, as Addams practiced it, neighbor helping neighbor—closely paralleled Abramowitz's Old World tradition of *tsodeka:* acts of charity performed by Jewish women.[54] During the harsh winter that followed the 1893 Chicago Exposition, Addams "became permanently impressed with the kindness of the poor to each other." She was fond of recounting the story of a "hard up" family with seven children whose upstairs neighbor shared her breakfast with them and whose boarder paid their rent in the hardest month. Even the struggling baker sent three loaves of stale bread across the street "because he had seen the faces of the children looking longingly into his window."[55] Eastern European Jewish women's activism translated to the United States as an interest in promoting the welfare of working women and vigorous support of women's suffrage. Its deep roots could be traced to a prophetic Judaism that highlighted the individual's obligations to the social good, to communal responsibility and justice.[56]

In the midst of the nurturing Chicago reform community and influenced by her orthodox heritage, Abramowitz redefined her vision from one that considered primarily her own well-being to a proactive ethic of social justice concerned with the general welfare of all working people. She believed that in America, if nowhere else in the world, workers—including women—had rights. Empowered by her alliance with women reformers in this highly charged climate, Abramowitz emerged an activist.

In the name of women's suffrage, Abramowitz and Addams entered the formal political arena. They viewed the vote for women as a fundamental aspect of social justice, particularly for working women who had "been carried along with the stream of industrial development from its source in home work up to the present specialization involved in factory methods."[57] For Addams, who served as vice president of the National American Woman Suffrage Association from 1911 to 1914, political activism was a logical step on the progressive continuum toward direct action. She suggested that the working woman "has parted with her old normal power of controlling the conditions of her life industrially to a much greater extent than has the working man, who has become equipped with the ballot."[58] Taking this rationale one step further, Addams argued that women's suffrage was imperative for them to perform their civic duty. She believed that "the ballot would afford the best possible protection to working women and expedite that protective legislation which they so sadly need and in which America is so deficient." She maintained that if political rights were "given to women, if the situation were theirs to deal with as a matter of civic responsibility, one cannot imagine that the existence of the social evils like child labor and sweatshop conditions would remain unchallenged."[59] Both Addams and Abramowitz drew a direct connection between the vote and their work for social amelioration, including the passage of protective legislation.

Although Abramowitz became a naturalized citizen in 1913, her true education in citizenship was not defined by a naturalization paper but by the accumulated experiences of life in the new country. Abramowitz and other working-class women saw the vote as a way to exert control over their own lives, for "woman's suffrage was not a detraction from class struggle but a part of it." Suffrage would empower women workers by allowing them to influence labor laws that directly affected their working lives. Immigrant women spoke of "industrial citizenship," which entailed decent wages, safe conditions, and reasonable hours as only the first step in working women's battle to win their larger "right to citizenship." Working-class women like

Rose Schneiderman, former cap maker turned labor activist, envisioned an expanded notion of citizenship, defined "as a complex entitlement that included 'the right to be born well, the right to a carefree and happy childhood, the right to education, the right to mental, physical and spiritual growth and development.'"[60] In Chicago, working women and middle-class reformers at Hull-House saw suffrage as a gender rather than a class issue. Their unified reform agenda, along with the cooperation from women of all persuasions, enabled Chicago women to pursue their ends free from the divisive class tensions that inhibited reformers' progress in New York and elsewhere.[61]

Bessie's political activity was directly linked to her responsibilities as a newly naturalized American. Citizen Abramowitz fulfilled her obligation by speaking at suffrage rallies and fund raisers to promote suffrage. To mark the 1913 suffrage victory of women in Illinois, she spoke at Lincoln Center on the "Rights of the Newly Acquired Franchise for Women of Other Races." Abramowitz modeled her skills after Addams, whose clear and confident public speaking demeanor often drew praise. Although the exact text of the speech no longer exists, one can rest assured that Abramowitz, Yiddish accent and all, knew how to arouse a crowd by appealing to women workers' most immediate needs.[62] Amplifying the voice of the working class from the suffrage podium, she polished the oratorical talents that she relied heavily on her entire life.

These skills would be tested again in the fall of 1915 when the ACWA leadership called a strike in Chicago in an attempt to organize twenty thousand more workers, mostly women and girls, who remained outside the union fold. Without the right to bargain collectively, they were still subjected to low wages and long hours. To avoid a confrontation with the American Federation of Labor and the Women's Trade Union League, both of which officially still supported the United Garment Workers, Abramowitz and the other Amalgamated leaders turned to Hull-House once more for assistance. Again Addams, Starr, and Hull-House residents rallied to labor's cause by walking the picket lines, collecting strike funds, distributing clothing, and exposing the workers' plight to the local press. After the shooting death of one of the strikers on the picket line, Addams organized a mass meeting to arouse the public conscience, and successfully headed a delegation that appeared before Mayor William Hale Thompson to ask him to become chairman of an arbitration board and to end the strike.[63]

Abramowitz learned from Addams, at the time "regarded as one of the Progressive Era's most effective organizers and most articulate philosophers," how to organize effectively and speak persuasively. Addams "demonstrated her capacity for cross-class cooperation" in her daily interactions with the thousands of immigrant neighbors who visited Hull-House.[64] Like Hilda Polacheck, Abramowitz admired Addams's magnetism and charisma, but never considered her a "lady bountiful" bestowing charity but rather a progressive steward committed to the common good. Renowned political journalist Walter Lippmann expressed the thoughts of many: "She had compassion without condescension and pity without retreat into vulgarity."[65] Although people from all walks of life regarded Jane Addams as an American icon, she never distanced herself from the masses. Among immigrants, her fame was attributed to the fact that despite national acclaim, she modeled useful citizenship while remaining accessible to all throughout her life.[66]

While still in her early twenties, Abramowitz learned that worker empowerment, in part, resulted from cultivating contacts with influential persons and building support networks, as Addams did during the 1910 and 1915 strikes. The young organizer's vision of industrial democracy closely resembled Addams's grand scheme for a new social order founded on the premise that it was no longer sufficient to feel responsible only for the well-being of one's own family when the welfare of the entire industrial society was a stake. First Addams, and later Abramowitz, pushed for the expansion of the nation's political democracy—an ethical society where an enlightened government would assume the responsibility for arbitration and provide benefits to all workers.[67]

Worker education was a vital part of Hull-House's mission. It would be a priority for Abramowitz in her own union, the Amalgamated Clothing Workers of America, where as education director in the 1930s and eventually as vice president from 1946 to 1970 she designed union education programs to help educate workers, especially women workers, to become useful citizens. Addams's faith in immigrants was well founded. On numerous occasions, Addams praised the efforts of Abramowitz and the other Amalgamated officials who generated impetus from within their organization: "No other union in the country has done as much as this group to educate its members, to place within their reach the most varied possibilities and opportunities for intellectual advancement."[68]

Although Abramowitz relocated to New York upon marriage to Amalgamated Clothing Workers' president Sidney Hillman in 1916, her years in Chicago predicated her commitment to labor feminism. Abramowitz expressed her gratitude to Addams on numerous occasions. In turn, Addams continually held up the immigrant-led Amalgamated Clothing Workers of America as "one of the most successful experiments in giving a measure of self-rule to workers." Until her death in 1935, Addams considered the Amalgamated to be a shining example of industrial democracy or, as she rendered, "what could be accomplished with the right intentions."[69]

Under Jane Addams's tutelage, Bessie Abramowitz rose from the ranks of exploited workers to help found one of the leading unions in the country. Following in Jane Addams's footsteps, Amalgamated Clothing Workers education director Bessie Abramowitz Hillman mentored a young black laundry worker, Dollie Lowther Robinson. With Hillman's help, Robinson went on to law school, and after graduation served as the New York State secretary of labor and special assistant to the director of the Women's Bureau in the United States Department of Labor.[70] Educated in the locus of the progressive women's network in Chicago, Hillman became a committed labor feminist, dedicating her life to advancing the cause of working women.

Addams, too, was transfigured by her interactions with young women immigrants. In the years that elapsed between the founding of Hull-House and the 1910 Chicago strike, she gradually narrowed the gap between thought and deed. She moved from observing and articulating specific social problems at the local level to direct political participation in the national reform movement. Intimate interaction with neighborhood immigrants allowed Hull-House reformers to readily "identify with the common lot." Addams accurately predicted that from that vantage point residents were "bound to see the needs of their neighborhoods as a whole, to furnish data for legislation, and to use their influence to secure it."[71]

Working-class women and middle-class reformers centered at Hull-House collaboratively campaigned for, and eventually achieved, improved working and living conditions for immigrant workers and their children, and in doing so, contributed to a larger sense of community. For one of the first times in American history, workers, particularly women workers, were definitively linked to the wider political arena. Although she did not live to see it through, Addams made a significant contribution to the creation of the New Deal welfare state, helping to infuse its policies with a "sense of social obligation," while Abramowitz, concerned with working women's welfare, assisted in determining the meaning of industrial democracy for women, replete with its broad notion of citizenship for immigrant workers.[72] Undoubtedly, the exceptional friendship between Addams and Abramowitz exemplified the possibilities of cross-class cooperation.

Notes

1. "ACWA Helped Save Hull House From Axe," *Advance,* July 7, 1961, p. 7. Only the original Hull-House mansion escaped demolition. It currently serves as a museum. The surrounding annexes were torn down and the University of Illinois built a new campus on the site.

2. For a full account of Bessie Abramowitz Hillman, see Karen Pastorello, *A Power among Them: Bessie Abramowitz Hillman and the Making of the Amalgamated Clothing Workers of America* (Urbana: University of Illinois Press, 2008).

3. "A House of Labor," *Advance,* September 15, 1963, p. 12.

4. Ann Schofield, *"To do and to be": Portraits of Four Women Activists, 1893–1986* (Boston: Northeastern University Press, 1997), 14 and 151, note 21. Schofield offers a synopsis of the literature concerning class tensions between workers and allies.

5. Male unionists viewed working women as threats to their own jobs. A number of male labor leaders, such as the American Federation of Labor's president Samuel Gompers, not only had difficulty relating to working women but were especially suspicious of middle-class women reformers. See Nancy Schrom Dye, *As Equals and as Sisters: Feminism, Unionism, and the Women's Trade Union League of New York* (Columbia: University of Missouri Press, 1980), 6–7.

6. Victoria Bissell Brown, "Jane Addams," in *Women Building Chicago, 1790–1990: A Biographical Dictionary,* ed. Adele Hast and Rima Lunin Schultz (Bloomington: University of Indiana Press, 2001), 14.

7. Addams, "The Subjective Necessity of Social Settlements," in *Philanthropy and Social Progress,* ed. Henry C. Adams (New York: Thomas Crowell and Company, 1893), 1. See also Addams, *Twenty Years,* 89 and 173.

8. Jane Addams, "The Waste of Talent Among the Poor or Our Waste of Nationalities," May 18, 1907, Jane Addams Papers (Microfilm), hereafter JAPM.

9. Hilda Satt Polacheck, *I Came a Stranger: The Story of a Hull House Girl,* ed. Dena J. Polacheck Epstein (Urbana: University of Illinois Press, 1991), 96–97 and Jane Addams, "Miss Addams on the Protection of Immigrants," *Ladies Home Journal* 30 (May 1913), 27. Polacheck's account is one of the only commentaries on Hull-House by an immigrant woman. For more on progressive policies toward immigration, see Rivka Shpak Lissak, "Liberal Progressives and Immigration Restriction, 1896–1917," Annual Lecture at the American Jewish Archives, Jerusalem, 1991, 25.

10. Addams, "The Waste of Talent Among the Poor," n.p.

11. Victoria Bissell Brown, "Jane Addams," in *Women Building Chicago,* 18.

12. Addams, *Twenty Years,* 76; and Philip Davis, *And Crown Thy Good* (New York: Philosophical Library, 1952), 86.

13. Charlene Haddock Seigfried, *Pragmatism and Feminism: Reweaving the Social Fabric* (Chicago: University of Chicago Press, 1996), 78 and 200–201.

14. Mary McDowell, "The Settlement as a Way of Life," *Neighborhood* 2 (July 1929), 156–57. Quoted in Seigfried, *Pragmatism and Feminism,* 264. Victoria Brown relates a

similar episode involving Mary Kenny, an Irish bookbinder in Victoria Bissell Brown, *The Education of Jane Addams* (Philadelphia: University of Pennsylvania Press, 2004), 245–46.

15. Nancy Schrom Dye, *As Equals, As Sisters: Feminism, the Labor Movement, and the Women's Trade Union League of New York* (Columbia: University of Missouri Press, 1980), 56–60; and Annelise Orleck, *Common Sense and a Little Fire: Women and Working-Class Politics in the United States, 1900–1965* (Chapel Hill: University of North Carolina Press, 1995), 44. Former shirt worker and New York WTUL member Leonora O'Reilly saw Alva Belmont and Anne Morgan as prime examples of socialities whose participation in and financial donations to the league marked them as philanthropists acting out of patronizing benevolence rather than sincerity toward building a reform coalition.

16. Seigfried, *Pragmatism and Feminism,* 59 and 308, note 55. Kathryn Kish Sklar defines "women's political culture" as the political culture specific to a particular group of women in a particular time and place when they come together outside the home. For a more detailed definition, see Sklar, "The Historical Foundations of Women's Power in the Creation of the American Welfare State, 1830–1930," in *Mothers of a New World: Maternalist Politics and the Origins of Welfare States,* ed. Seth Koven and Sonya Michel (New York: Routledge, 1993), 79–80. See also Louis Menand, *The Metaphysical Club* (New York: Farrar, Straus and Giroux, 2001), 311–14; and Ann Schofield, *"To do and to be",* 24–25. See also Kathryn Kish Sklar, "Hull House in the 1890s: A Community of Women Reformers," *Signs* 10 (Summer 1985): 658–77.

17. Seigfried, *Pragmatism and Feminism,* 78; Addams, *Twenty Years,* 220; and Mary Jo Deegan, *Jane Addams and the Men of the Chicago School, 1892–1918* (New Brunswick, N.J.: Transaction Books, 1988), 293–94.

18. Seigfried, *Pragmatism and Feminism,* 264–65.

19. Ibid., 59–78.

20. Jane Addams, "On the Protection of Immigrants," *Ladies Home Journal* 30 (May 1913): 27.

21. Addams, *Newer Ideals of Peace* (New York: Macmillan, 1907), 119–20 and 134–45.

22. Brown, *The Education of Jane Addams,* 46–47, 152–53, 158–59.

23. Ibid., 281–84 and 290–93; Seigfried, *Pragmatism and Feminism,* 229; and James Weber Linn, *Jane Addams: A Biography* (New York: D. Appleton-Century Company, 1935), 164–67.

24. Linn, *Jane Addams,* 163–64.

25. Ibid., 162 and 198–99; and Jane Addams, "Trade Unions and Public Duty," *American Journal of Sociology* 4 (January 1899): 448–62.

26. Jane Addams, "The Settlement as a Factor in the Labor Movement," in *Hull-House Maps and Papers,* ed. Jane Addams, Agnes Holbrook, Florence Kelley, et al. (New York: Thomas Y. Crowell and Company, 1895), 187, 191, and 203.

27. Jane Addams, "Recent Immigration: A Field Neglected by the Scholar," *Educational Review* 29 (March 1905): 245–63; and Jane Addams, *A New Conscience and an Ancient Evil* (New York: Macmillan, 1912), 80–81 and 93.

28. Addams, "The Settlement as a Factor in the Labor Movement," *Hull-House Maps and Papers*, 214.

29. Seigfried, *Pragmatism and Feminism,* 44; and Brown, *The Education of Jane Addams,* chapter 14, especially 253.

30. Addams, *Twenty Years,* 157. See also Ann D. Gordon, "Alzina Ann Parsons Stevens," in *Women Building Chicago,* 842–44.

31. Addams, *Twenty Years,* 106–7 and 166–67.

32. Davis, *American Heroine,* 78–79; and Florence Kelley, "Industrial Democracy: Women in the Trade Unions," *Outlook* 84 (December 15, 1906): 926–31.

33. Addams, *Newer Ideals,* 30; and Addams, "The Settlement as a Factor," 203.

34. Addams, *Twenty Years,* 166.

35. Linn, *Jane Addams,* 159–60 and 162–63; Kathryn Kish Sklar and Jamie Taylor, "How Did Florence Kelley's Campaign against Sweatshops in Chicago in the 1890s Expand Government Responsibility for Industrial Working Conditions?" Document 13, "Factories and Workshops," Laws of the State of Illinois, Passed by the Thirty-Eighth General Assembly (Springfield, Ill.: H.W. Roker, 1893), 99–102. Women and Social Movements in the United States, 1600–2000. www.alexanderstreet6.com.

36. Addams quoted in Kathryn Kish Sklar, Anja Schuler, and Susan Strasser, *Social Justice Feminists in the United States and Germany: A Dialogue in Documents, 1885–1933* (Ithaca, N.Y.: Cornell University Press, 1998), 123. Coverage of speech contained in the *Boston Globe,* March 23, 1908, and "The Relation of Women to Industry and Social Legislation," *Woman's Journal* 38 (March 28, 1908): 52. For more on reform goals, see Alice Kessler-Harris, *Out to Work: A History of Wage-Earning Women in the United States* (New York: Oxford University Press, 1982), 205. In New York much more so than in Chicago, the WTUL moved away from organizing as it began to concentrate its efforts on securing protective legislation. Kessler-Harris dates this transition as occurring between 1912 and 1915.

37. Jane Addams, "Miss Addams on Current Legislation for Working Women," *Ladies Home Journal* 30 (March 1913), 27.

38. Addams, *A New Conscience,* 73.

39. Polacheck, *I Came a Stranger,* 97 and 183.

40. Jane Addams, *A New Conscience,* 28.

41. Interview with Philoine Fried, December 29, 1996.

42. The Statue of Liberty–Ellis Island Foundation, "Ellis Island Passenger Arrivals: American Family Immigration History Center," www.ellisisland.org, history@ellisisland.org.

43. Jane Addams, "The Objective Value of a Social Settlement," *Philanthropy and Social Progress,* 29.

44. Davis, *And Crown Thy Good,* 86–88.

45. Karen Pastorello, "How Did Cross-Class Alliances Shape the 1910 Chicago Garment Workers' Strike?" Women and Social Movements in the United States, 1600–2000. www.alexanderstreet6.com.

46. Bessie Hillman, Speech on Jane Addams (March 1960), ACWA Papers, Box 228, Folder 4.

47. Jane Addams, "An Industrial Union with a Social Vision," undated, n.p., Amalgamated Clothing Workers of America (ACWA) Papers, Folder 229, Box 4, Martin P. Catherwood Library, Kheel Center for Labor-Management Documentation and Archives, School of Industrial and Labor Relations, Cornell University, Ithaca, N.Y., hereafter ACWA papers.

48. Commission on Industrial Relations, *Final Report and Testimony,* 64th Congress, 1st Session, Senate Document #415 (Washington, D.C.: Government Printing Office, 1916), 564.

49. Jane Addams, "The Reaction of Simple Women to Trade Union Propaganda," *Survey* 36 (July 1, 1916): 364–66. For Addams's part in the strike, see Davis, *American Heroine,* 106 and 114–15; and Linn, *Jane Addams,* 240–41.

50. Davis, *American Heroine,* 149–56.

51. Brown, *The Education of Jane Addams,* 52. In the years following the 1910 strike, Robins personally paid Abramowitz six dollars a week so that she could quit her job and become a full-time organizer.

52. Bessie Abramowitz Hillman, "Speech on Jane Addams," March 1960, ACWA Papers, Box 228, Folder 6; and interview with Philoine Fried, March 15, 2002. Hilda Satt Polacheck, a young Polish immigrant who was a regular visitor at Hull-House, also documented Addams's maternal behavior. See Polacheck, *I Came a Stranger,* 103.

53. John E. Williams, "The Russian Jew in American Industry," originally published in the *Streator Independent Times,* June 28, 1913. Reprinted in *Survey,* August 23, 1913, ACWA Papers, Box 228, Folder 4.

54. On the part Addams's spirituality played in her philosophical development, see Brown, *The Education of Jane Addams,* 195–200.

55. Addams, *Twenty Years,* 123–24.

56. Joyce Antler, *The Journey Home: Jewish Women and the American Century* (New York: Free Press, 1997), 59.

57. Jane Addams, "Why Women Should Vote," *Ladies Home Journal* (January 1910), 22–23; Letter from Jane Addams to the General Federation of Women's Clubs," ca. July 7, 1906, *Woman's Journal* 37 (July 7, 1906), 108.

58. Jane Addams, "The Working Woman and the Ballot," *Women's Home Companion* (April 1908), 19.

59. Jane Addams, "Why Women Should Vote," 22–23; Letter from Jane Addams to the General Federation of Women's Clubs," ca. July 7, 1906; and Addams, *A New Conscience,* 192.

60. Orleck, *Common Sense,* 88–89; Schofield, *"To do and to be,"* 13; and Dorothy Sue Cobble, *The Other Women's Movement: Workplace Justice and Social Rights in*

Modern America (Princeton, N.J.: Princeton University Press, 2004), 4 and 56. For an extended discussion of Addams and citizenship, see Carol Nackenoff, "New Politics for New Selves: Jane Addams's Legacy for Democratic Citizenship in the Twenty-First Century," in this volume.

61. Cobble, *The Other Women's Movement,* 56.

62. Only an announcement of the speech has survived in ACWA papers, November 15, 1913. For more on speeches of working-class suffragists, see Carol Nackenoff, "Cross-Class Collaboration in the Progressive Era Women's Movement and its Potential to Expand and Transform the Meaning of Citizenship," unpublished paper presented at Feminism and Legal Theory Workshop on Gender and Citizenship, Cornell Law School, April 2002, 25.

63. Stephan Skala, "The Great Chicago Organizing Campaign," *Advance,* May 5, 1922, 5–6; Sidney Hillman's speech at dual celebration of Jane Addams's seventy-fifth birthday and the twentieth anniversary of the Women's International League for Peace and Freedom, ACWA Papers, Box 228, Folder 6; and Bessie Hillman, "Speech on Jane Addams," March 1960, ACWA Papers, Box 228, Folder 6.

64. Brown, *The Education of Jane Addams,* 3–4.

65. Polacheck, *I Came a Stranger,* xvi and 99; and Davis, *American Heroine,* 291.

66. Linn, *Jane Addams,* 250; Polacheck, *I Came a Stranger,* 74–75; and Jean Bethke Elshtain, *Jane Addams and the Dream of American Democracy* (New York: Basic Books, 2002), 9–11.

67. Addams, *Democracy and Social Ethics,* 12 and 192–213; Addams, "An Industrial Union with a Social Vision," n.p.; and Schofield, *"To do and to be,"* 37–38 and 156, note 44.

68. Bessie Abramowitz Hillman, "A Life for the Workers," 1952 Speech, Private Collection of Philoine Fried; and Addams, "An Industrial Union with a Social Vision," n.p.

69. Bessie Hillman, "Gifted Women in Trade Unions," in *American Women: The Changing Image,* ed. Beverly Benner Cassara (Boston: Beacon Press, 1962); Jane Addams, "The Immigrant and Social Unrest," National Conference of Social Work, *Proceedings* (1920): 59–62; and Jane Addams, "Immigrants Under the Quota," *Survey* 63 (November 1, 1929): 135–39.

70. Karen Pastorello, "A Power Among Them: Bessie Abramowitz Hillman and the Amalgamated Clothing Workers of Chicago" (PhD diss., Binghamton University, 2001), 181–83.

71. Addams, *Democracy and Social Ethics,* 11; and quoted in Robert H. Bremner, *American Philanthropy* (Chicago: University of Chicago Press, 1960), 114–15.

72. Addams, "An Industrial Union with a Social Vision," n.p.

6

New Politics for New Selves

Jane Addams's Legacy for Democratic Citizenship in the Twenty-First Century

CAROL NACKENOFF

Feminist arguments for an ethic of care and at least some strains in the recent civic engagement debate in the United States share the premise that meaningful democratic politics requires transcending notions of the autonomous individual whose self-interest is an adequate expression of citizenship. These current scholarly deliberations have yet to fully engage an earlier twentieth-century predecessor who had an expanded and deeper conception of citizenship and a wider definition of the political than we routinely encounter in American politics. Jane Addams's broad vision of the political, her concern that democratic processes heed the voices and expressed wishes of a wide array of humanity, and her respect for differences still pose a challenge to current civic engagement scholarship. Though ethic of care feminists have addressed some of the weaknesses in the liberal debate over how to make democracy more robust, serious attention to Addams would be instructive for these scholars as well. If would-be reformers were to look to a usable past in order to craft a persuasive model for twenty-first-century democratic selves, they would gain a great deal by drawing upon the wisdom, vision, and activism of Jane Addams.

In the past few years, there has been increased recognition of the potency of narratives in politics. Through narratives, we construct stories about who we are—and link visions of our past and present to conceivable, viable futures. New visions, woven into narratives, offer an explanation for what is immediately and seriously defective about the current political order and help us embark on a voyage to remake some parts of it. According to political scientist Deborah Stone, "much political activity is an effort to control interpretations";

stories become means by which citizens understand the causes of problems, construct perpetrators and victims, and identify likely solutions.[1] At certain political moments, opportunities present themselves for transforming politics via the replacement of causal stories, leading to new policy options. The catalyst need not be a crisis. Leaders and activists armed with new narratives may be able to prevail at a time when the predominant causal stories seem less powerful and when political leaders promoting old stories seem less able to solve highly salient, identifiable problems. Because "incremental drift" so often characterizes American politics, narrative and its capacity to mobilize can be an important way to understand political change.

There are opportunities in our time for new narratives of engaged democratic citizenship. The mid-1950s Hartzian paradigm of a uniform and static liberal tradition in American politics and political thought inhibited a generation of social scientists and historians from exploring adequately the potential of new worldviews and narratives in American politics. New narratives are central to forging new democratic selves, but narratives work best when they draw convincingly upon a useable past. Jane Addams's practice and thought can help forge this link.

Jane Addams and the Liberal Tradition

Jane Addams is not readily encompassed inside the predominant American liberal, state-fearing, rights-based discourse that Louis Hartz depicted in *The Liberal Tradition in America.*[2] She did not speak for what political theorist Benjamin Barber terms the "minimalist disposition in liberal democracy," a form of radical individualism that "proscribes but rarely prescribes action" and "discovers in the limits of power not an opening to more creative forms of politics but merely the limits of politics . . ."[3] Addams maintained there was a political obligation to provide everyone with the opportunity to develop their intellectual, moral, and cultural capacities.[4] Addams, like John Dewey, viewed human beings as inherently social and as having organic interconnections.[5] Dewey and Addams both understood citizenship as active and involved. Democratic men and women are educable and capable of self-transformation.

The narratives of political engagement and visions of politics that Addams and her contemporaries helped construct have contributed to shaping a modern generation of liberal democratic theorists, yet these scholars rarely embrace Addams. They fail to fully appreciate her insights, sometimes make mistakes she had learned to avoid, and generally fail to find in her particular fusion of theory and practice a usable American past. As they look to particular moments, sites of political engagement, or institutions from the past in seeking to revitalize American politics, they would be well served to examine the positive lessons Addams can offer. Rediscovering Addams can also yield important reflections about what can, cannot, and perhaps even should not be recovered from the past to build a stronger democratic future.

Many current democratic theorists argue that democratic citizenship requires consideration of others; it requires the ability to see, understand, and even adopt the standpoint of others. A number of them retain a belief that active and engaged citizens can forge a community of interests and a common agenda. Others recognize that differences in values and goals may not disappear with deliberation and interaction, but that these activities can maximize consideration for the preferences of others. Democracy, then, either requires discussion, deliberation, and collaboration in the forging of common purposes, or it requires, at minimum, the development of compromises and accommodations that respect, as far as possible, the values, views, and needs of other citizens. Discussion and interaction with others helps citizens "to see that their interests are partly identified with those of a larger community of which they are members."[6]

The more Rousseauean and communitarian of these contemporary theorists expect that only by taking care of public business alongside others in the assembly can citizens set aside private interests and discover the general will—indeed, they can only be thought of as citizens as opposed to slaves when they engage in this process.[7] Citizenship that transcends parochialism and mere self-interest has to be constructed; it is not found. Through democratic participation, citizens are transformed. Their faculties are stimulated and developed, their ideas extended, their feelings ennobled, and their whole souls uplifted.[8] Rousseau's citizens—all male and all relatively culturally and linguistically homogeneous—forge a common perspective through their common efforts. They seek and expect to find consensus. Following Rousseau, Benjamin Barber argues that "civic activity educates individuals how to think publicly as citizens even as citizenship informs civic activity with the required sense of publicness and justice"; every citizen must encounter the "other" directly in the political arena. "The citizen is by definition a we-thinker, and to think of the we is always to transform how interests are perceived and goods defined."[9] Democracy improves upon nature by making possible "cooperation and an approximation of concord where they do not exist by nature."[10] For Barber, hallmarks of strong democracy include common deliberation, decision, and work.[11] A period of mandatory universal service for the young is part of his recipe for forging public thinking.[12] "The stress on transformation is at the heart of the strong democratic conception of politics."[13]

In the civic republican tradition, then, citizenship is a practice, not simply a status.[14] To assert that citizenship is active and public suggests that citizenship grows and develops from the ground up; it is not fixed or controlled.

For those civic engagement scholars who romance a communal past with less intrusive national government, democratic revitalization hinges on political association at the neighborhood level, with maximal face-to-face interaction and grassroots activity. Robert Putnam, who seems to have a place among these scholars, terms "social capital" those features of social organization—networks, norms, and trust—"that facilitate coordination and cooperation for mutual benefit,"[15] and he finds these disappearing in contemporary American life. For Putnam, whose work triggered much of the recent interest in civic engagement, civic solidarity and civic participation go hand in hand and "networks of civic engagement foster sturdy norms of generalized reciprocity."[16]

Putnam does acknowledge Addams but appreciates only part of her legacy. He yearns for the heyday of social settlements. Settlement houses embodied community, not simply charity; they nurtured both sewing clubs and civic engagement.[17] For Putnam, many of the community-based associations that developed and sustained social capital had little to do with politics; many of these associations simply linked neighbors who socialized together and who were similarly situated—like bowling in the 1950s. However, Putnam generally ignores the extensive and sustained political engagement of Hull-House residents and neighbors.[18] Efforts to reform public health and sanitation, factory safety, city government, juvenile justice, and child labor, and to support striking workers and press for women's suffrage were surely central to Hull-House denizens and neighbors alongside sewing circles and drama groups. When Putnam envisions the past, he sees dense social networks, but he does not speak to the importance of, or opportunities for trying to replicate, the cross-class, multiethnic, and even cosmopolitan character of the Hull-House networks today.

Though those who yearn for consensus often look to small-scale and local communities for forging democratic social capital, other scholars such as Theda Skocpol and Morris Fiorina maintain that conflict has been and must remain central to democratic development and look elsewhere to nurture civic engagement.[19] Social movements have played a crucial role in extending citizenship rights and in expanding the meaning of citizenship itself.[20] For Skocpol, the mass-membership organizations that flourished between the Civil War and World War II that had chapters across the nation, were federative in structure, and fostered cross-class participation were the kinds of political organizations that best developed social capital and political learning.

For Skocpol, the ways in which governmental policies were formulated encouraged these mass-membership organizations in the past, and government policies could do much more to revive civic engagement at present. Modern mailing list organizations are not engaging citizens or socializing them to public-mindedness in the way that earlier nineteenth- and early twentieth-century mass-membership organizations did. A consequence of the decline of these mass-membership organizations is that support for and participation in national public life is waning.[21]

Jane Addams wrote and worked during the time when mass-membership organizations were practically exploding. Arthur Bentley's classic and formative *The Process of Government* appeared in 1908, arguing that ideas and feelings were social: "[T]he individual as a definite, firm, positive, foundation for individualized feelings and ideas, is a highly abstract social idea himself, and in the way in which he is put to use, fictitious."[22] Bentley pictured the nation "as made up of groups of men, each group cutting across many others, each individual man a component part of very many groups."[23] With all the group activity swirling about him, Bentley argued that the groups directly and indirectly interested in a policy—not self-interested individuals—were the raw materials of political life.[24] Both Addams and Bentley saw politics transcending individuals and engaging social feelings.

Addams encouraged face-to-face interactions in the neighborhood around Hull-House, and she was also an important actor in large-membership organizations, working to organize women municipally, nationally, and internationally. As vice president of the National American Woman Suffrage Association, Addams organized and gave testimony before Congress on suffrage. She participated actively in political campaigns and served on the platform committee on the newly founded Progressive Party. She was a founding member of the National Association for the Advancement of Colored People and president of the National Conference on Corrections and Charities. Addams was a participant in many peace initiatives, cofounder of the Women's Peace Party, and a founder and longtime president of the Women's International League for Peace and Freedom. Jane Addams embodied political activism in an era of remarkable civic activity. She modeled and encouraged both kinds of civic engagement that scholars seek to recover, working both through face-to-face neighborhood interactions and large-scale, mass-membership organizations.

From her perspective of engagement in neighborhood, municipal, national, and international political arenas, Addams would not have endorsed the view of the most committed Rousseaueans that unanimity of thought was the aim of politics. And though she did expected people to voice their differences, she would not have concurred with Skocpol that conflict was inevitable.[25] Addams agreed with the Ethical Culture Society's slogan, "Diversity in creed, unity in deed."[26] Her experiences in the Hull-House neighborhood demonstrated that social cooperation was possible, and collaboration among people who were varied in their backgrounds, experiences, and interests could occur if social intercourse connected them.[27] Cooperation did not require homogenization of interests or cultures. Addams was generally respectful of differences, but like John Stuart Mill, she believed that democratic citizens could learn increasingly to associate their own feelings of happiness with the good of others. Mill argued that as civilization advances, a citizen "comes, as though instinctively, to be conscious of himself as a being who of course pays regard to others."[28] For Addams, this was integral to progress. However, she was far more attentive than was Mill to the interactions and processes necessary to bring about such changes in thinking. Democracy required that the needs and experiences of others be understood and respected, which in turn required contact and collaborative effort.

Addams joined John Dewey in attending to the processes by which a public could be created. There was, in Dewey's estimation, an essential need for the "improvement of the methods and conditions of debate, discussion, and persuasion."[29] Hull-House was a forum for many such discussions. For Dewey, consultation uncovered "social needs and troubles."[30] He asserted that "the public has no hands except those of individual human beings. The essential problem is that of transforming the action of such hands so that it will be animated by regard for social ends."[31] Good citizenship (or civic efficiency) involved a socialization of mind that aids in breaking down barriers of social stratification:

> A democracy is more than a form of government; it is primarily a mode of associated living, of conjoint communicated experience. The extension in space of the number of individuals who participate in an interest so that each has to refer his own action to that of others, and to consider the action of others to give point and direction to his own, is equivalent to the breaking down of those barriers of class, race, and national territory which kept men from perceiving the full import of their activity. These more numerous and more varied points

> of contact denote a greater diversity of stimuli to which an individual has to respond; they consequently put a premium on variation in his action.[32]

Members of the polity had to learn to understand and respect their differences if they were to be constituted as democratic citizens. Jane Addams recognized that appreciation for different perspectives required deliberation inside as well as outside political institutions.[33] For Addams, crafting solutions to social problems was not a matter of mere knowledge, control, or scientific management but rather required experience-based understanding and incorporation of the knowledge and wishes of others.[34] This is all the more reason why deliberative functions could not merely pass to experts nor be monopolized inside governmental institutions.[35]

Though modern social scientists differ in their expectations about what greater civic engagement and democratic deliberation will produce, they all contend that it is essential to a healthy democracy. From the time responses to the fear of mass society flourished in the mid-twentieth century, democratic theorists have maintained that exposure to views different from one's own tends to blunt extremism and encourage tolerance and moderation. Legal scholar Cass Sunstein has more recently expressed concern that increasing technological capacity to filter the kinds of messages citizens read or hear may promote insularity, extremism, and polarization in politics.[36] In much of the civic engagement literature lies a related assumption that participation and deliberation promote openness and sensitivity to others that make us better citizens. Correspondingly, noninvolvement in the larger community breeds disinterest in, distrust of, and disregard for the views and values of others. Engagement is not merely the antidote to political cynicism or alienation; it is about changing how one thinks about the world and about one's relationship to one's fellow citizens. Civic engagement ostensibly creates a different kind of citizen with different thoughts, habits, and political expectations. Though Addams would readily agree that engagement creates a different kind of citizen, she would also argue that the thinking of the relatively privileged needed to be reshaped through engagement. This assertion was at odds with what most thought in her own era, and with what civic engagement scholars may be presuming now.

The task of enhancing democracy was not simply to initiate poor, immigrant, or working-class Americans into processes and modes of thought that were already pronounced among the higher classes. When Tocqueville contended that it was "impossible that the lower orders should take a part in public business without extending the circles of their ideas and quitting the ordinary routines of their thoughts,"[37] the implication seemed to be that the lower orders were the ones who required more socialization and education to think about public interests. In that reading, Tocqueville would be found in the mainstream of much liberal argumentation today. However, for Jane Addams, the relatively privileged needed to learn from the untutored social ethic and sense of interdependence of working-class and immigrant Americans as well.[38]

Addams insisted that a "wider acquaintance with and participation in the life about them" is essential for democratic citizens, "for much of the insensibility and hardness of the world is due to the lack of imagination which prevents a realization of the experiences of other people."[39] Wider experience could combat insularity and individualism, build social perspective, and help people comprehend and develop sympathy for each other.[40] Indeed, immigrant neighborhoods and labor unions were particularly cosmopolitan in Addams's view; in each, people from traditionally hostile nations have to make adjustments and find ways of living peacefully together.[41] Addams thought in terms of the reciprocal obligations of rich and poor to learn from each other.[42] Realizing democracy required identification with the common and humble.

For Addams, voice, agency, and dignity were aspects of citizenship. The poor were deliberative agents capable of forming and articulating their own projects. She was acutely conscious of the deficiencies of a "doing for" approach to poor and immigrant Americans. Experience was the basis of social scientific knowledge, and knowledge was an iterative, error-reducing process.[43] Therefore, young middle-class women who left their parental homes and worked among the poor would accomplish little unless they listened to and learned from those with whom they interacted. And there was much to be learned from immigrant communities.

The far too common approach among reformers tended to breed relations of subordination, where elite and bourgeois women merely spoke for and on behalf of what they perceived as the interests of their charges.[44] As Dewey noted, "What is sometimes called a benevolent interest in others may be but an unwitting mask for an attempt to dictate to them what their good shall be, instead of an endeavor to free them so that they may seek and find the good of their own choice."[45] Respect for variation was essential. Addams commented that "All the members of the community are equally stupid in throwing away the immigrant revelation of social customs and inherited energy."[46]

If current civic engagement scholars paid somewhat more attention to Addams and learned from her, they might look more broadly, discovering more modes of activism and engagement in communities and in the larger polity. They might more fully consider ways in which gender, race, class, and ethnicity shape perspectives and understandings of the political. Putnam, Barber, and even Skocpol all have particular romances for past political practices that pertained to a different world than the one in which we now live. If they confronted the historical Addams, they might consider the limits of such a romance but might also discover an even bolder vision of democracy. Though admirable in seeking a more vibrant democracy, civic engagement scholars seem most passionate about promoting a vigorous but nonetheless comfortable, unthreatening, middle-class vision of the political in a twenty-first-century world. They seem less willing to learn from the experiences of others or to consider their ways of seeing, and more reluctant than Addams to leave safe places.[47] This remains a challenge for liberal theory.

Addams's vision of pluralism is arguably compatible with postmodernism's concern for "the dehierarchization of cultural systems (and hence the conditions for a partial democratization of culture)."[48] As illustrated by Hull-House's embrace of immigrant arts and crafts, Addams at least partially confronted the hierarchical differentiation between high and low culture. Because one aspect of postmodernism is taken to be "the celebration of the idea of difference and heterogeneity (against sameness and standardization) as minimal normative guidelines in politics and morality,"[49] Addams was in this sense an early spokesperson for a perspective that did not find a wide audience for at least another half-century.

Jane Addams and Feminist Theory

A long tradition in Western scholarship has linked the public realm with freedom and human realization and the private realm with necessity, where noncitizens minister to bodies and needs. The citizen in liberal democratic theory comes to the public sphere as an autonomous individual who is not dependent on others. Although male workers were enfranchised as individuals in the United States by the mid-nineteenth century, a suspicion remained that those who were dependent upon others for their sustenance were too easily influenced and were not their "own men."[50] Women's nurturing, economic dependence, perceived weakness and timidity, and purity, all considered as part of their nature, excluded them from formal participation in the public sphere. When early twentieth-century feminists such as Addams challenged their exclusion in terms that sought to valorize what women do, they were also entering the thicket—whether wittingly or not—of the relationship between work that provided for the needs of others and full citizenship in the polity.[51] This issue remains contentious in the early twenty-first century.

In modern liberalism, the "tasks" of ministering to others, showing empathy and concern, and providing for the next generation are not only relegated to the private sphere but are often segregated on the basis of gender, race, and class. In recent years, feminist scholars have again been at the forefront of incorporating into the public sphere many of the ethical concerns that liberal theory had relegated to the private sphere. These scholars theorize the relationship between needs, dependence, and democratic politics, arguing that responsibility for and sensitivity to others are public and not merely private concerns. Everyone, whether during specific stages of the life cycle or sporadically during the years considered the most competent ones, requires care; it is part of what citizens are. Thus, care and the assignment of tasks to caregivers must become an explicit object of politics.[52] When feminists stress connectedness and interdependence as important components of democratic citizenship and work to extend the boundaries of the public, they, too, are working alongside Addams.

A frequent theme in the democratic revitalization literature is that democratic citizenship means leaving one's "home," one's sheltered existence, and one's privatized leisure pursuits in order to interact with others. Robert Putnam is noted for the argument that contemporary citizens need to leave their homes, televisions, and computers if they are to develop the social trust and community networks that sustain democracy.[53] Though leaving home could be understood quite literally, many feminists have understood it to mean and demand more, including "questioning of conventional notions of experience" and "unsettling of boundaries and identities."[54] Leaving home means a willingness to define oneself anew in relation to the others one meets.[55] It means creating new forms of community beyond those comfortable, secure, and homogeneous places people know best. It means expanding experience. Feminist scholarship at its best has worked toward this goal. Leaving "home" and reimagining it in the process is part of a narrative altering the meaning of public and private, and altering the boundaries between them.

Jane Addams had walked this path. She and many of her contemporaries brought women's concerns into the state, actively reimagining "home" so as to reorder politics.[56] They saw government as housekeeping on a larger scale and took their domesticity outdoors. For Addams, women had to confront the insularity of the home if they were to take care of what had traditionally interested them. Assuring safe drinking water, disposing of garbage, safeguarding food, protecting and educating children, promoting health and safety, and many other concerns that used to be handled in the domestic sphere were now handled in the urban public sphere.[57] Addams emphasized "the futility of the individual conscience when woman insists upon isolating her family from the rest of the community and its interests."[58] To expand experience beyond "home" was to enhance democracy and create better citizens. This meant questioning public/private boundaries and questioning the exclusion of morality from the public sphere. The narrative of social housekeeping helped early twentieth-century women revision the state and their place in it. The current feminist emphasis on care work can likewise help early twenty-first-century women in their attempt to revision political space and political values.

The notion that all selves are of necessity connected to others, interdependent and sometimes even dependent on others, stands in marked contrast to prevailing individualist expectations of autonomy. Ethic of care theorists Joan Tronto and Selma Sevenhuijsen write of a civic responsibility to respond to others. As Tronto argues in *Moral Boundaries,* care emphasizes human interdependence rather than autonomy; caring about as well as caring for are part of citizenship.[59]

For feminist ethic of care proponents, care is a wedge issue that insinuates itself into the public/private split, reintroduces moral arguments into liberal politics, gives needs new currency, and renders politically visible and valuable the work frequently done by women, but especially by working women of color and the poor.[60] Linking justice and care assaults the primary dualisms that are so constitutive of the central discursive mechanisms of Western thought and so integral to the procedures of Western political practice; this, in turn, requires a different conception of identity and selfhood.[61] Care stands to revalorize what women, servants, domestic workers, and many service workers do.[62]

Care purports not only to give needs new political currency but also offers the possibility of alliances between those who care for and those who care about. As a feminist issue, it potentially unites women and care workers across lines of race and class, much as Progressive Era women tended to forge some cross-class (if not often cross-race) linkages around labor and social welfare legislation. Jane Addams came much earlier than many activists to the causes of workers, including unemployment, sweatshop work, maximum hours, workplace safety, child labor, arbitration, and unionizing. When Hull-House residents stood on picket lines, this was simply one way they demonstrated their desire to transform interpersonal service from an activity performed by subordinates to one involving equals.[63]

Addams's insistence on a richer and deeper conception of citizenship and on the role of the social ethic in politics would seem to have found new resonance. Quite a few contemporary voices argue that politics is impoverished when ethical considerations and deliberations are segregated from the liberal public sphere, leaving masked the exclusionary dimensions structured into liberal citizenship.[64] Even the Green movement could find a model ancestor in Addams, for the movement has a complementary concept of ecological citizenship that extends well beyond geographically and temporally bounded groups and requires a globalized sense of community. Caring entails caring for and responsibility toward animals, nature, and future generations.[65] In this sense, "participation refers to 'being part of' as well as to being active in and fully responsible for."[66]

On Reappropriating Jane Addams

There are many reasons to return to Jane Addams and to find inspiration in her writing and activism. Her visions and hopes for democracy can help us construct narratives that lend themselves to contemporary, progressive political projects. However, there are reasons why reappropriation of Addams must be approached with caution. Not only are there lessons to be learned from the limits of Addams's success, but many developments since the early twentieth century have affected the way we must think about her visions.

Ethic of care scholars, civic engagement scholars, and many proponents of enhanced conceptions of democracy have not rushed to rediscover or embrace Addams. Some who think of her at all have unfortunately viewed Addams as a mere footnote to Dewey.[67] For others, her era's unshakeable belief in progress and fellow-feeling seems antiquated for generations living in the shadow of the Holocaust, nuclear warfare, terrorism, religious and ethnic violence, and potential environmental destruction. For a number of scholars, Progressive Era reformers have all been tarnished by charges that their projects were in fact more coercive than rights enhancing and that, despite Dewey and Addams, they privileged expertise and state building over democratic deliberation.[68] But there is one minefield that certain feminist scholars seek to avoid, and in order to avoid, have been reluctant to appropriate Addams.

Some political scientists and historians have faulted Progressive Era feminists for employing maternalist arguments. It has become almost commonplace in the literature that maternalism, or "difference feminism," was responsible for social policies that engendered a second-class citizenship for working women and women of color during the 1920s and 1930s, and that had continuing impact in the welfare state.[69] For Wendy Mink, the social policies advanced by maternalist reformers withheld "the tools of independent citizenship from most poor women."[70] Eileen McDonagh has argued that by enfranchising women as mothers, the state ended up "privileging women's private maternal roles as benefiting political society rather than women's formal political roles."[71] Julie Novkov maintains that when the Supreme Court accepted the notion that all workers could be protected in *West Coast Hotel,* building on the *Muller*-era maternalist vision that female laborers warranted protection, it was anything but a victory for workers.[72] Many maternalists defined "women" in such a way that they were classed and raced. For many who extended maternal or housekeeping imagery into the public sphere, there was a logic linking their agendas to policies and political processes in which responsible agents took care of dependents, rather than where equal citizens forged solutions to problems.[73] It is undoubtedly true that women's activism of the era sometimes contributed to policy outcomes that privileged white, middle-class interests.

Addams herself rooted the power of women's voices in their distinctive experiences rather than in their nature, but she used the language of housekeeping and maternalism.[74] Few of her contemporaries were committed to active democracy as a method for broadening gendered experiences. Although Nel Noddings remains an exception, current ethic of care scholars tend to be far more careful than many Progressive Era feminists had been not to essentialize women's nurturing.[75] Politicizing care would not mean arguing for the insertion of a "female" morality or a "moral motherhood" in politics.[76]

Ethic of care proponent Joan Tronto believes Jane Addams's arguments for peace, forged from a groundwork of "women's morality," earned her vilification in the World War I era and its immediate aftermath because the operative political morality dictated that morality had no place in the nasty world of politics. Morality's place was thought to be in the home or the church.[77] In this account, Addams's plummeting popularity was an indication that, at that time, she could not break through the dichotomization of morality and politics; Addams could not speak authoritatively.[78]

A lesson that Tronto takes from Addams's experience with the language of maternalism is that political context and existing power relations affect the acceptability of particular moral arguments.[79] Tronto implies that moral/political boundary transgressions were unacceptably formulated and offered up in Addams's time but that the time might now be riper for such transgressions to succeed. An answer to the question whether Progressive Era feminists who embraced caregiving and nurturing as political virtues were unwise to have played upon gender and to have strayed some distance from the less dangerous language of rights would seem to have bearing both on the potential and possible limits of an ethic of care approach to expanding democratic values now.

Different kinds of concerns about reappropriating Addams confront those who seek to extend engaged, participatory citizenship beyond nation-state boundaries.[80] As a feminist who reached out to organized women and peace activists across the globe, Addams embraced a concept of citizenship that included growing human interconnectedness. Addams was party to the birth of a number of cross-national organizations, and along with new international institutions, global perspectives began to develop. In a world that is rapidly globalizing and where some barriers—distance, time, and even language—are disappearing, other barriers seem ever more formidable today.

Globalizing Western enlightenment projects—including democracy—are meeting increased resistance in the name of religion, culture, and tradition. In addition, few contemporary political activists hold to the illusion that global integration even promotes justice, equity, or democracy. And yet globalization has made possible the flourishing of transnational political movements for social or economic justice. These are often indigenous movements that seek strength from global activist networks.[81] One can only presume that a modern Addams would have cast her lot with some of the transnational social movements that combat these very international organizations and institutions and their global agendas.

For those who look to revitalize civic engagement nationally and locally, reappropriating Addams has its problems as well. In the United States, gated communities, residential segregation, cities where the overwhelming majority are people of color, and suburban and exurban sprawl make interaction of the sort Addams envisioned even more difficult. Because many Americans experience a high degree of insulation from those of other classes or ethnicities, how can they forge the sympathies and understanding in which Addams had so much faith? (Conversely, some recent findings even suggest that increasing levels of racial and ethnic diversity within communities tends to lower certain measures of civic engagement, and that in general, civic engagement is lower in more heterogeneous communities.)[82] Where and how can deliberation, discussion, collaboration, compromise, and accommodation best be encouraged in a contemporary polity that sometimes seems to be increasingly segmented and divided, and where participation and civic engagement have, at a minimum, changed substantially since the time of Addams?

In insisting that civic life is deteriorating in America, Putnam and Skocpol look to forms of organization and association that are no longer as vibrant as they once were. However, there are grounds for encouragement. Civic engagement may be more episodic and ad hoc than a century ago, but there is evidence that, if one defines civic engagement generously enough, there is a great deal of civic energy afoot, and a strong impulse to get involved.

There is at least some evidence of yearning for the more active and public conception of citizenship in the United States. There is hunger to engage and be involved in times of crisis that goes beyond responding to appeals for funds or appeals by the president to go shopping in New York in the aftermath of the 2001 terrorist attacks. Volunteers went immediately to Ground Zero to provide nourishment and support to rescue workers, and blood donations skyrocketed. On their own initiative, or through voluntary organizations and churches, citizens drove supplies to disaster zones or worked to rebuild the homes and lives of strangers with whom they could identify and empathize in the aftermath of Hurricane Katrina. They were dissatisfied with how little was being asked of them as citizens. Though it is not obvious that politicians would like to see that kind of engagement mobilized into the political sphere, leading as it does to less manageable and predictable political outcomes, the sentiment and concern that Addams saw constituting the building blocks of a more ethical, engaged citizenship can be seen around us.

Public space is, in many ways, different from what it was in Addams's era. Conventional opportunities shrink but new ones may emerge. There is increased evidence that the electronic information era offers new opportunities for coordinated efforts on the ground. Cooperation and concerted action can increasingly be organized in cyberspace and across thousands of miles. French immigrant youth organized near-simultaneous uprisings across the country in early 2006 via text messaging (though this is not what either Putnam or Skocpol would regard as constructive engagement).[83] Environmental activists make policy research, data, experts, consultants, organizations, lobbying, publicity, and pressure available in cyberspace. Though it is fairly clear that these examples are not what either Putnam or Skocpol would readily regard as enhanced civic engagement, would they have embraced some of the political work that Addams and her contemporaries did on the street (for example, joining picket lines) as civic engagement?

There is also the issue of how to understand political change. Addams lived and wrote during a heady time when there was a passion for reform, when she and those around her saw the possibilities of politics. There was widespread faith that proper methods could solve social problems. Though Addams recognized that progress and human improvement were not mechanistic, she believed that increasingly enlightened politics and increasing success in the identification of shared interests deriving from the experiential method were not only possible but likely.

Despite the belief of many Progressive Era activists, there is no single liberal or progressive trajectory in our political history. Liberal and illiberal ideals alike are available for appropriation in American politics,[84] and no direction of change is assured.

Though new narratives can open politics up to change, the direction and extent of that change remains contingent upon political forces and institutional responses that are themselves shifting. Other narratives also drove and confronted reformers of Addams's era.[85] Creating the kind of *we* in political discourse that Addams hoped for involves struggle and contingency. Formulating new visions of *we* is bound to be conflictual, because old identities and interests have stakes in existing power relationships and definitions of citizenship. A new *we* can be more inclusive or it can be less so.

If ethic of care proponents and other feminist scholars want to transcend the public/private divide, it should be noted that the boundary between morality and politics has certainly been breached in contemporary American politics, but the dynamic forces of change in the recent past have been socially conservative. An attempt to foreground care, nurture, and relations of dependence as political concerns might play into the hands of activists of America's religious right, who would gladly assign the state a larger role in promoting and policing virtue, which in their view is based in a gendered division of labor. Though a more progressive narrative can be constructed, it is not obvious what power it has in the world unless there is a social movement behind it.

It is often presumed that democratic deliberation produces outcomes that make everyone better off—at least in the sense that citizens feel membership in the community that made the decisions. These benefits are not automatic, and it depends on what subjects are—and are not—permitted on the table. It may not be true under current rules for aggregation of preferences, even if enhanced deliberation takes place. Simple aggregation of preferences under majority rule may well result in a situation in which some citizens feel as if their interests and preferences are never taken into account because they cannot constitute a majority.[86] The nature of decisions to be made and resources available to be allocated will also impact interactions and perceptions of interests. When important resources are scarce (or perceived to be so because certain prior decisions are considered fixed) or when it is necessary to impose costs or losses in order to restore economic prosperity, it is not obvious that democratic deliberation will deal adequately and fairly with zero-sum or negative-sum allocations.[87] It is essential that no members or groups in the polity be permanent losers in establishing goals and priorities. Otherwise, "accommodation" will tend to be on the terms most comfortable to and least disturbing to those whose voices and power have been most pronounced.[88] Those benefiting from current distributions of power tend to see the language and values of politics as both objective and neutral. The terrain on which accommodations are forged cannot simply be that held by dominant interests. Addams's hope and belief would be that new kinds of citizens will be forged in the crucible of enriched democratic engagement and that these new citizens will see and solve such problems more equitably than now.

Despite these concerns and difficulties, citizenship remains a promising and dynamic concept for those who want to take inspiration and guidance from Jane Addams. The meaning of citizenship is not given but rather highly contested, if at some times more vigorously than at others. "It is contested at every level from its very meaning to its political application, with implications for the kind of society to which we aspire."[89] In recent years, feminists and progressive scholars have been busy unpeeling the veneer of impartiality and gender neutrality from the concept of citizenship and seeking to reappropriate the concept. Historians and political scientists have been examining how neutral language accompanied raced, gendered, and classed practices. Women of the Gilded Age and Progressive Era were repeatedly assured that they were citizens, while access to the ballot, to the workplace, and to military service—all arguably markers of full membership in the realm—was denied.[90] They used understandings of gender to challenge a guise of neutrality in political discourse. Though women effectively challenged their formal exclusion from the ballot in this era, for Addams, transforming citizenship was about much more.

Addams joined other feminists of the Progressive Era in challenging the moral authority of the independence/autonomy formulation of citizenship. She insisted that politics needed to be informed by a new kind of morality, and challenged traditional notions of "home" and the boundary between public and private realms. This was a substantial challenge.[91] There was, with Addams, something quite different at work in American political discourse. If we grant that Addams and a number of her coworkers expanded understandings of citizenship, reenvisioned the nature of public business (so that social welfare was on the state's agenda), reformulated boundaries between public and private spheres, placed a "social ethic" on the public table for discussion, and engaged in a significant amount of cross-class collaboration, there was radical potential in the work going on and the visions being forged.

We can and should understand the vision of American citizenship that Addams and a number of her collaborators forged as an alternative political narrative that had an important power in early twentieth-century politics. They proposed a social ethic engaged in discursive processes that offered new constructions of political identity and self-interest; wove women's experiences into this new vision; reconstructed stories of how our (rewoven) core American values shaped our past, present, and stood to shape our future; and offered to redefine the terms on which politics would take place. Addams and a number of her feminist colleagues offered ways of rethinking American traditions and values that were transformative and opened up more new political possibilities than were ultimately realized.

Publicly engaged scholars who call for the revitalization of democracy, redefinition of citizenship, and expansion of the meaning of politics to incorporate care would do well to consult Addams as they work toward new political narratives, new politics, and new policies. Addams knew that democracy does not work if citizens feel powerless and distrustful, divided from each other and without a sense of common bonds. If we do not possess the heady optimism of Addams and many of her fellow progressives, we may still, if we grasp how to learn from the past without trying merely to recapture it, at least hope to make democracy much healthier.

Notes

The author would like to thank Marilyn Fischer, Cynthia Halpern, Caitlin Markowitz, and James L. Greer for their extremely helpful comments and suggestions on this manuscript.

1. Deborah Stone, *Policy Paradox: The Art of Political Decision-Making* (New York: W.W. Norton, 1997), 28 (quote).

2. Louis Hartz, *The Liberal Tradition in America* (New York: Harcourt, Brace & World, 1955).

3. Benjamin R. Barber, *Strong Democracy: Participatory Politics for a New Age* (Berkeley: University of California Press, 1984), 15, 19.

4. J. David Greenstone, "Dorothea Dix and Jane Addams: From Transcendentalism to Pragmatism in American Social Reform," *Social Service Review* 53 (December 1979): 527–59. Greenstone classified Addams as a Yankee Protestant liberal, belonging to a different strain of a bipolar American liberal tradition than the radical individualistic, minimalist state liberals.

5. Marilyn Fischer, "Jane Addams's Critique of Capitalism as Patriarchal," in *Feminist Interpretations of John Dewey*, ed. Charlene Haddock Seigfried, 281 (University Park: Pennsylvania State University Press, 2002).

6. Dennis F. Thompson, *The Democratic Citizen: Social Science and Democratic Theory in the Twentieth Century* (London: Cambridge University Press, 1970), 99 (quote), 86.

7. Jean Jacques Rousseau, *The Social Contract* in *The Social Contract and Discourses,* translated and with an introduction by G. D. H. Cole. (New York: E.P. Dutton, 1950), book III, chapter 15, pp. 93–96.

8. Rousseau, *The Social Contract,* book I, chapter 8, p. 18.

9. Barber, *Strong Democracy,* 152–53.

10. Ibid., 118–19.

11. Ibid., 133.

12. Ibid., 297–303; Benjamin R. Barber and Richard Battistoni, "A Season of Service: Introducing Service Learning into the Liberal Arts Curriculum," *PS: Political Science and Politics* 26 (June 1993): 235–40.

13. Barber, *Strong Democracy,* 119.

14. Ruth Lister, *Citizenship: Feminist Perspectives* (New York: New York University Press, 1997), 13–33, 196; Adrian Oldfield, *Citizenship and Community, Civic Republicanism and the Modern World* (London: Routledge, 1990). See also Bryan S. Turner, "Outline of a Theory of Citizenship," *Sociology* 24 (May 1990): 206–9 for the contrast between citizenship as status and citizenship as practice.

15. Robert D. Putnam, "The Prosperous Community: Social Capital and Public Life," *American Prospect* 13 (Spring 1993): 35. See also Putnam, *Bowling Alone: The Collapse and Revival of American Community* (New York: Simon & Schuster, 2000).

16. Putnam, "Prosperous Community," 37.

17. Ibid., 40.

18. See ibid., 41.

19. Theda Skocpol and Morris P. Fiorina, "Making Sense of the Civic Engagement Debate," in *Civic Engagement in American Democracy,* ed. Theda Skocpol and Morris Fiorina (Washington, D.C.: The Brookings Institution Press and the Russell Sage Foundation, 1999), 1–23 (see especially 13–14).

20. On at least the first part of this claim, see Bart van Steenbergen, "Towards a Global Ecological Citizen," in *The Condition of Citizenship,* ed. Bart van Steenbergen, 143, citing Bryan S. Turner's *Citizenship and Capitalism* (London, Thousand Oaks, Calif., and New Delhi: Sage, 1994). Drawing on T. H. Marshall, van Steenbergen elaborates on the second element in this claim.

21. Theda Skocpol, *Diminished Democracy: From Membership to Management in American Civic Life,* vol. 8, Julian J. Rothbaum Distinguished Lecture Series (Norman: University of Oklahoma Press, 2003); Skocpol, "The Narrowing of Civic Life," *The American Prospect* 15 (June 2004): A5–7. See also Skocpol, *Protecting Soldiers and Mothers: The Political Origins of Social Policy in the United States* (Cambridge, Mass.: Belknap Press of Harvard University Press, 1992).

22. Arthur Bentley, *The Process of Government* (1908, 1935), with an introduction by H. T. Davis (Evanston: Principia Press of Illinois, 1949), 170.

23. Bentley, *The Process of Government,* 204.

24. Ibid.

25. For a discussion of Addams's claim that antagonism is unnecessary, see Louis Menand's account of Addams and Dewey's conversations during the Chicago' Pullman Strike. Louis Menand, *The Metaphysical Club* (New York: Farrar, Straus and Giroux, 2001), 310–16.

26. The slogan "Diversity in creed, unity in deed" is from a speech Felix Adler gave in 1876. Thanks to Marilyn Fisher for this reference.

27. See Louise W. Knight, "Jane Addams's Theory of Cooperation," in this volume; Jane Addams, *Twenty Years at Hull-House* (1910) (New York: Macmillan, 1925), chapter XIV.

28. John Stuart Mill, *Utilitarianism* (1863, 1871), in *Essential Works of John Stuart Mill,* edited and with an introduction by Max Lerner (New York: Bantam, 1961), 217–18.

29. John Dewey, *The Public and Its Problems* (New York: Henry Holt and Company, 1927, renewed 1954 by Mrs. John Dewey), 208.

30. Ibid., 206.

31. Ibid., 82.

32. John Dewey, *Democracy and Education* (New York: Macmillan, [1916] 1920), 140–41; quote 101.

33. See Camilla Stivers, *Bureau Men Settlement Women: Constructing Public Administration in the Progressive Era* (Lawrence: University Press of Kansas, 2000); and Stivers, "A Civic Machinery for Democratic Expression: Jane Addams on Public Administration," in this volume. See also Wendy Sarvasy, "Social Citizenship from a Feminist Perspective," *Hypatia* 12:1 (1997): 54–74.

34. See Stivers, "A Civic Machinery for Democratic Expression."

35. See Amy Gutmann and Dennis Thompson, *Democracy and Disagreement* (Cambridge, Mass.: Belknap Press of Harvard University Press), 358–59.

36. For a recent exposition of the argument that the Internet could blunt extremism and political polarization by directing news watchers to linked sources of opinion that contrast with their own proclivities, see Cass Sunstein, *Republic.com* (Princeton, N.J.: Princeton University Press, 2001). For an example of the earlier argument, see Seymour Martin Lipset, *Political Man* (Garden City, N.Y.: Doubleday, 1960).

37. Alexis de Tocqueville, *Democracy in America* (1835), ed. J. P Mayer, trans. George Lawrence (Garden City, N.Y.: Doubleday, 1969), vol. 1, 252.

38. Jane Addams, *Democracy and Social Ethics* (1902), edited and with an introduction by Anne Firor Scott (Cambridge, Mass.: Belknap Press of Harvard University Press, 1964) 143–49, 158–59, 214 for some examples.

39. Addams, *Democracy and Social Ethics,* 5, 9.

40. Carol Nackenoff, "Gendered Citizenship: Alternative Narratives of Political Incorporation in the United States, 1875–1925," in *The Liberal Tradition in American*

Politics, ed. David F. Ericson and Louisa Bertch Green, 137–69 (New York: Routledge, 1999), 150–51.

41. Marilyn Fischer, *On Addams* (Belmont, Calif.: Wadsworth, 2004), 81–83.

42. See ibid., 26, 42–43, 44, 52–53. It is important to note that, though experience borne of travel would create broader views, there is a certain luxury to such experience. Those who have such opportunities are likely to be those who are already advantaged. It may make elites more liberal but do nothing to tune their ears to the actions and needs of those of other classes with whom they are still unlikely to come willingly into contact except as spectators or reformers. For Addams, the poor were "cosmopolitan" and so were labor unions.

43. Addams, *Democracy and Social Ethics,* introduction and chapter 2, also 274, 176–77. See also Greenstone, "Dorothea Dix and Jane Addams."

44. On this theme, see Peggy Pascoe, *Relations of Rescue: The Search for Female Moral Authority in the American West, 1874–1939* (New York: Oxford University Press, 1990).

45. Dewey, *Democracy and Education,* 141.

46. Fischer, *On Addams,* 26–44. Addams, *Newer Ideals of Peace* (1906), in Marilyn Fischer and Judy D. Whipps, eds., *Jane Addams's Writings on Peace* (Bristol, U.K.: Thoemmes Press, 2003), vol. 1, 64 (quote).

47. See Wendy Sarvasy, "A Global 'Common Table': Jane Addams's Theory of Democratic Cosmopolitanism and World Social Citizenship," in this volume.

48. Turner, "Postmodern Culture/Modern Citizens," in *The Condition of Citizenship,* ed. Bart van Steenbergen (London, Thousand Oaks, Calif., and New Delhi: Sage, 1994), 155.

49. Turner, "Postmodern Culture/Modern Citizens," 154.

50. Carol Nackenoff, *The Fictional Republic: Horatio Alger and American Political Discourse* (New York: Oxford, 1994), especially chapters 5–8.

51. The fact that a particular type of politicized feminist vision stressing what women as potential voters had in common beyond their exclusion gained prominence at the same time as working men and women were seeking their collective political voices as workers (rather than as individuals) may then be no accident. The fact that middle-class and elite female activists seeking suffrage and social welfare legislation in this era increasingly turned their attention to working-class women and interacted with them becomes highly interesting in the context of this theoretical juncture. With different alliances and policy collaborations came creative opportunities.

52. Joan Tronto, *Moral Boundaries: A Political Argument for an Ethic of Care* (New York: Routledge, 1993).

53. Robert D. Putnam, "The Strange Disappearance of Civic America," *American Prospect* 24 (Winter 1996), 46–48 on the role of television. Putnam tends to believe computers follow by extension, despite the existence of opportunities for network-

ing, organizing, talking, and fund-raising online. For an alternate perspective, see Eric M. Uslaner, "Social Capital, Television and the 'Mean World': Trust, Optimism, and Civic Participation," *Political Psychology* 19, no. 3 (1998): 441–67.

54. Biddy Martin and Chandra Talpade Mohanty, "Feminist Politics: What's Home Got to Do With It?" in *Feminist Studies/Critical Studies,* ed. Teresa de Lauretis (Bloomington: Indiana University Press, 1986), 191–212.

55. Martin and Mohanty, "Feminist Politics: What's Home Got to Do With It?" 199. See also Bernice Johnson Reagon, "Coalition Politics," in *Home Girls: A Black Feminist Anthology,* ed. Barbara Smith (New York: Kitchen Table Press, 1983), 356–68 and especially 357–59.

56. See Shannon Jackson's excellent and provocative contribution to this volume, "Toward a Queer Social Welfare Studies: Unsettling Jane Addams," which includes a discussion of Addams's response to maternalist assumptions.

57. For further discussion of this theme, see Carol Nackenoff, "Gendered Citizenship."

58. Jane Addams, "Why Women Should Vote" (New York: National American Woman Suffrage Association, 1912), 4–5.

59. Tronto, *Moral Boundaries.*

60. Ibid.

61. Selma Sevenhuijsen, *Citizenship and the Ethics of Care: Feminist Considerations on Justice, Morality and Politics* (London and New York: Routledge, 1998), 48, 55.

62. Tronto, *Moral Boundaries.*

63. Sarvasy, "Social Citizenship from a Feminist Perspective," 60.

64. Turner, "Postmodern Culture/Modern Citizens."

65. See, for example, van Steenbergen, "Towards a Global Ecological Citizen," 141–52.

66. van Steenbergen, "Towards a Global Ecological Citizen."

67. For an account of Addams's influence on Dewey, see Menand, *Metaphysical Club,* 310–16; and Charlene Haddock Seigfried, *Pragmatism and Feminism* (Chicago: University of Chicago Press, 1996), 29–30, 45, 48–49, 58–59, 73–78.

68. For a few of these, see Stephen Skowronek, *Building a New American State* (Cambridge, U.K., New York, and Melbourne: Cambridge University Press, 1982); Michael E. McGerr, *The Decline of Popular Politics: The American North, 1865–1928* (New York: Oxford University Press, 1986); Daniel J. Tichenor, *Dividing Lines: The Politics of Immigration Control in America* (Princeton, N.J. and Oxford: Princeton University Press, 2002); and Ken I. Kersch, *Constructing Civil Liberties: Discontinuities in the Development of American Constitutional Law* (New York and Cambridge, U.K.: Cambridge University Press, 2004).

69. See Gwendolyn Mink, *The Wages of Motherhood: Inequality in the Welfare State, 1917–1942* (Ithaca, N.Y.: Cornell University Press, 1995).

70. Mink, *The Wages of Motherhood,* 8.

71. Eileen McDonagh, "Race, Class, and Gender in the Progressive Era," in *Pro-*

gressivism and the New Democracy, ed. Sidney M. Milkis and Jerome M. Mileur (Amherst: University of Massachusetts Press, 1999), 167.

72. Julie Novkov, *Constituting Workers, Protecting Women: Gender, Law, and Labor in the Progressive and New Deal Years* (Ann Arbor: University of Michigan Press, 2001), chapter 6. *Muller v. Oregon* 208 U.S. 412 (1908); *West Coast Hotel v. Parrish* 300 U.S. 379 (1937).

73. Nackenoff, "Gendered Citizenship," 165.

74. For a discussion of Addams's use of maternalist rhetoric in her peace speeches and writings, see Marilyn Fischer, "Addams's Internationalist Pacifism and the Rhetoric of Maternalism," *National Women's Studies Association Journal* 18, no. 3 (Fall 2006): 1–19.

75. Nel Noddings, *Caring: A Feminine Approach to Ethics and Moral Education* (Berkeley: University of California Press, 1984).

76. Sevenhuijsen, *Citizenship and the Ethics of Care,* 13.

77. Tronto, *Moral Boundaries,* 5–6.

78. Ibid., 8–9.

79. Ibid., 5.

80. For a contemporary expression on global citizenship, Bryan S. Turner writes, "The traditional language of nation-state citizenship is confronted by the alternative discourse of human rights and humanity as the normatively superior paradigm of political loyalty." Turner, "Postmodern Culture/Modern Citizens," 157.

81. See, for example, Ken Conca, *Governing Water* (Cambridge, Mass.: M.I.T Press, 2006); Oscar Olivera in collaboration with Tom Lewis, *¡Cochabamba! Water War in Bolivia* (Cambridge, Mass.: South End Press, 2004); works by Vandana Shiva including *Stolen Harvest* (Boston: South End Press, 2000) and "Earth Democracy" (Boulder, Colo.: Alternative Radio, 2004); and David Schlosberg, "Reconceiving Environmental Justice: Global Movements and Political Theory," *Environmental Politics* 13 (Autumn 2004): 517–40.

82. Dora L. Costa and Matthew E. Kahn, "Civic Engagement and Community Heterogeneity: An Economist's Perspective," Symposium on Social Capital and Diversity, *Perspectives on Politics* 1 (March 2003): 103–11; Robert D. Putnam, "*E Pluribus Unum*: Diversity and Community in the Twenty-first Century. The 2006 Johan Skytte Prize Lecture," *Scandinavian Political Studies* 30, no. 2 (2007), 142–59.

83. Holloway Sparks, "Dissident Citizenship: Democratic Theory, Political Courage, and Activist Women," in *Theorizing Feminism,* 2nd ed., ed. Anne C. Hermann and Abigail J. Stewart (Boulder, Colo.: Westview Press, 2001).

84. Rogers Smith, *Civic Ideals: Conflicting Visions of Citizenship in U.S. History* (New Haven, Conn. and London: Yale University Press, 1997).

85. See Robert Post, "Defending the Lifeworld: Substantive Due Process in the Taft Court Era," 78 *Boston University Law Review* 1489 (1998). The postwar red scare and reaction against the expansion of the Progressive Era nation-state and its enhanced role in management and direction of the wartime economy were part of the "return

to normalcy" that countervailing political forces were able to place on the political agenda.

86. Lani Guinier, *The Tyranny of the Majority: Fundamental Fairness in Representative Democracy* (New York: The Free Press, 1994).

87. See Lester C. Thurow, *The Zero-Sum Society: Distribution and the Possibilities for Economic Change* (New York: Basic Books, 1980).

88. The importance to democracy of assuring that there is no permanent minority was recognized by Robert A. Dahl, *Democracy and Its Critics* (New Haven, Conn.: Yale University Press, 1989). On agenda setting, problem definition, and power, see Catharine A. MacKinnon, *Feminism Unmodified.* (Cambridge, Mass.: Harvard University Press, 1989). See also Mari Matsuda et al., *Words That Wound* (Boulder, Colo.: Westview Press, 1993).

89. Lister, *Citizenship: Feminist Perspectives,* 3.

90. See, for example, Judith N. Shklar, *American Citizenship: The Quest for Inclusion* (Cambridge, Mass.: Harvard University Press, 1991).

91. Nackenoff, "Gendered Citizenship," 140.

7

Toward a Queer Social Welfare Studies

Unsettling Jane Addams

SHANNON JACKSON

Just when our affection becomes large enough to care for the unworthy among the poor as we would care for the unworthy among our kin, is certainly a perplexing question.[1]

If we understand kinship to be a set of practices that institutes relationships of various kinds that negotiate the reproduction of life and the demands of death, then kinship practices will be those that emerge to address fundamental forms of human dependency.[2]

My task in this essay, located as it is in a volume that explores Jane Addams's relationship to contemporary theory, is to imagine a relationship between the legacies of Hull-House and a body of thought that consolidated in the 1990s under the rubric of post-structuralist queer theory. To argue for that relationship is, to some degree, an improbable task. Many historians of social welfare place Jane Addams's Hull-House settlement as an origin point in the invention of state welfare in the United States; meanwhile, many post-structuralist critics of sexual identity invoke the operations of state welfare as an insidiously dangerous source of social normalization. Similarly, many historians of the family position Addams's Hull-House settlement as a central locus and activator of maternalist politics; meanwhile, many critics of gender and sexuality cite the rhetoric of the family and motherhood as an instantiator of gender and heteronormative inequity. Given the critical suspicion of the "maternal" "state" with which she has been allied, how could it be possible for Jane Addams and Hull-House to converse transhistorically with contemporary theoretical paradigms? I will say at the outset of this short essay that any conversation will require a more heterogeneous view of the concept of state welfare and a more heterogeneous view of Hull-House as a place of operation. As Licia Fiol-Matta demonstrates in her study of Latin American leader Gabriela Mistral in *A Queer Mother for the Nation*, the public and private practices of maternalism, sexuality, and the nation-state can intersect in complex and ambiguous ways.[3] It is only by recognizing the challenge of both state welfare and of Hull-House to conventions of private and public that we can find an alternate way of connecting the dots between them. Indeed, whatever the limits of both of these spheres, I want to foreground the capacity of both state welfare and Hull-House to imagine a sphere of obligation and kinship that exceeds biological ties, undoing conventions of publicity and privacy along the way. It is only with such an alternate emphasis that we can begin to conceptualize the legacy of Jane Addams and Hull-House for post-structuralist critiques of sexual identity and social belonging. And it is only with such an alternate emphasis that we can begin to see queer politics as having something to do with the domestic politics that is state welfare.

In an earlier book on Hull-House reform called *Lines of Activity*, I analyzed a variety of politically volatile Hull-House performance spaces—social clubs, festivals, athletics, gymnastics, theater, living history museums, dance, and folklore—in connection to larger issues of immigration, juvenile justice, and urbanization.[4] Here, I want to develop the historiographic implications of another strain of settlement performance, specifically the everyday performances of "home," "family," "kinship," and "domesticity" developed by reformers themselves. My goal is to argue for a connection between what I called Hull-House's "queer domesticity" and several contemporary concerns. Those concerns are various but related. At a time when theorists of sexuality are attempting to map a relation between the psychic and the social, that is, between the most intimate and the most abstract structures of social life, the discourse of and around Jane Addams offers a useful case study. Conversely, queer studies offers a particular opportunity for staging an investigation of Jane Addams. Queer theory's emergence within the discontinuous field of "gender studies" has revised feminisms of all varieties while also countering sexual essentialisms and sexual positivisms in gay and lesbian historiography; hence, queer theory also provides a way of reevaluating some of the ways historians of gender and sexuality have made use of Jane Addams. More important, I want to use Jane Addams and Hull-House to argue for a more considered and mutually galvanizing relationship between the field of feminist welfare studies and the field of queer theory. It is my sense that both of these domains possess reductive conceptions of the other, casting the first as unreflecting state functionalism and the second as an abstract form of groundless theoretical musing. To me, each of these domains only fits these stereotypes in their habits of stereotyping the other. And when that happens, the potential for creating a rigorous and mutually transforming interdisciplinary project goes unrealized, as does the possibility for a vibrant, if internally bracing, political alliance.

Central to a concept of queer welfare studies is my interest in imagining a kind of progressive model of extended kinship in the state's attempt to encourage its members to "care" for those who are not biological kin. My hope is to argue for a connection between the necessity of reorganizing what Judith Butler calls "fundamental forms of human dependency" and Jane Addams's question—posed in the language of her time—about what it takes to care for all human beings as "we would the unworthy amongst our kin." I will want to suggest that Jane Addams's pursuit of social welfare within the context of state government is, along with its limits and unintended consequences, a queer imagining. Such a connection means reanimating another, older, leftist image of the state. It means figuring the state, not only as an insidious propeller of gender normalization, but also as a vehicle for instantiating and supporting publicly diffused forms of human attachment and obligation. Indeed, it is with such an emphasis that a notion of "queer welfare studies" can be conceived as a useful rather than oxymoronic phrase. The state, it is important to remember, has a history of being figured not only as the seat of paternal, disciplinary, or capitalist authority but also as the vehicle for actualizing a social contract based in human interdependency. Like the effort to imagine queer kinship in our contemporary moment, such a model of the state is also important for the as-yet unrealized possibility of imagining human interdependency as something that exceeds biological ties and that surpasses the obligatory network of the private nuclear family. Intriguingly, and to some perversely, it is in this imagined network of nonbiological obligation and extrafamilial connection that the social impulses of state welfare can start to look provocatively, and progressively, queer.

We cannot resituate the state's pursuit (or the pursuit of the state), however, unless we also contend with the essentializing effects of the maternal politics with which Addams has been aligned in certain strains of feminism, as well as with the normalizing effects of the state criticized by liberal, feminist, conservative, libertarian, queer radical, and radically right thinkers alike. To do so, I focus my attention on Jean Bethke Elshtain's recent book on Jane Addams, particularly as I see it refracted through Elshtain's earlier feminist scholarship in *Public Man, Private Woman.*[5] My interest here is to consider feminism's ability to foreground the intensely contingent, micro, affective, and (after Charlene Haddock Seigfried) "pragmatic" domains with which kinship and domestic knowledge is traditionally associated.[6] However, I am equally concerned to address the untoward consequences of certain deployments of categories such as "woman" or "family" or "mother" and to resist prescriptive assessments of how domestic lives, familial lives, parental lives, or women's lives should be instituted. In returning this doubled approach back to issues of the state, I will argue for a more situated understanding of state welfare, questioning liberal, conservative, and feminist critiques of its heartless institutionalization and anti-essentialist critiques of its gendered normalization. Again, I think that an unsettled interpretation of Jane Addams's unsettled life elicits reflection on these conundra, central as they are to the articulation of a relationship among queer theory, the legacies of feminism, and the socialized operations of public welfare.

Earlier, I suggested the need to reanimate an older leftist model of the state; however, the suggestion bears reflection about exactly why that model is less than animate in our contemporary moment. The suspiciousness of state involvement in matters of family and childhood are well known in a contemporary U.S. context where constituencies affiliated with the right argue against the intervention of "big government" in private matters. That critique is largely expressed as a concern for "taxpayers' money" and for what in the 1990s was called the "culture of dependency" that such programs ostensibly produce.

The critique of state intrusion is not only a habit of the right, however, for other left-allied thinkers are also suspicious of state operations, though on quite different grounds. Feminist historians and theorists such as Mimi Abramovitz, Nancy Fraser, Linda Gordon, Wendy Brown, and Kathy Ferguson have been concerned with the way in which the inherited liberal, capitalist, paternalist, and bureaucratic dimensions of the state carried gendered assumptions that actually hampered rather than enabled gender equity.[7] Whether by naturalizing the concept of the private family, by instituting family wage policies that reinforce the notion of the male breadwinner, by construing reproductive labor as something other than productive, or by feminizing the bureaucratic implementations of state power, these and other scholars have argued that what Brown calls the "man in the state" could directly and indirectly neutralize the feminist possibilities of federal redress.[8]

While the work of Michel Foucault has influenced a number of these feminist critiques, his intellectual histories have also galvanized the equally strong if somewhat differently inflected suspicions of the state that appear in post-structuralist queer theory. Spurred by Foucault's excavations of the state and prison apparatus, by his historical critiques of sexual normalization, and by his identification of the network of nonstate public operations he called "governmentality," a variety of critical theorists in the humanities and social sciences have become concerned with the "productive" effects of power. Scholars such as Michael Warner, Lauren Berlant, Lee Edelman, and Judith Butler particularly seek to understand the paradoxical ways that juridical and governmental systems can have the effect of standardizing the persons and experiences that they "help," requiring normative and normalizing discourses that define and delimit human categories in order to recognize, provide for, and evaluate them.[9]

Wendy Brown, one of the figures whose work crosses the domains of both feminist political theory and queer theory, cowrote an introduction to *Left Legalism/Left Critique* with Janet Halley that outlines the Foucaultian concern succinctly: "Whereas 'liberals' treat identities as mechanisms for voicing injustice that the state must recognize and repair, from [our] left perspective, identities are double-edged: they can be crucial sites of belonging and political mobilization, but they can also be important vehicles of domination through regulation."[10] This tacit and insidious form of domination, so central to a Foucaultian understanding of power, has been fundamental to a left-allied, post-structuralist critique of sexuality. In the strains of queer theory that have been particularly concerned with this question, the state is largely figured as a diffuse but pervasive force in sexual normalization. Its operations, therefore, should be resisted. In Judith Butler's discussion of kinship (reprinted also in Brown and Halley's collection), for example, she offers a strong argument in favor of this resistance by using the example of "gay marriage." Butler's concern is that gays and lesbians who seek state sanction for same-sex partnership under the marriage law are at risk of becoming newly vulnerable to the state's regulatory operations:

> The petition for marriage rights seeks to solicit state recognition for non-heterosexual unions, and so configures the state as withholding an entitlement that it really should distribute in a nondiscriminatory way, regardless of sexual orientation. That the state's offer might result in the intensification of normalization is not widely recognized as a problem, typified by the Human Rights Campaign. The normalizing powers of the state are made especially clear, however, when we consider how continuing quandaries about kinship both condition and limit the marriage debates. . . . Variations on kinship that depart from normative, dyadic heterosexually based family forms secured through the marriage vow are figured not only as dangerous for the child,

> but perilous to the putative natural and cultural laws said to sustain human intelligibility.[11]

The danger here is that the privileges and recognition that might come from the state's involvement in same-sex marriage in turn come with varieties of prescription and standardization. A moment that might seem to open up conventional definitions of attachment and belonging will in fact enforce more conventions—based in "dyadic heterosexually based family forms"—into this space of alternate imagining.

Nearly one hundred years ago, Jane Addams and her coterie of Hull-House activists began what contemporary theorists might retroactively construe as a similarly dangerous bargain with the state. Having worked to give discursive and structural power to a number of issues that pressed heavily on the lives of their neighbors—particularly those involving issues of immigration, labor, and women's rights—Hull-House residents worked continuously on a number of overlapping fronts that affected the so-called private lives of children and their parents. From juvenile justice to public health to public child care, these activists sought ways of alleviating the stresses, economic deprivations, and health dangers that affected the lives of working parents and their children. The difficulty of addressing such issues in the United States, then as now, revolved around the appropriateness of governmental involvement in matters deemed "private." Jane Addams remembered with frustration the ideological resistances to federalization:

> It became clear that the Federal Government could interest itself in agriculture and fisheries, but not in childhood. There was evidently confusion in the minds of many of our fellow countrymen between self-government and local government. Americans have thought for a long time—perhaps the idea is inherited from town meetings—that unless government is localized they do not exercise self-government at all. Such a conception, if persisted in, must narrow our notion of government and circumscribe our national life. We forget that politics are largely a matter of adjusted human relations through any unit of government which best serves the purpose. More and more, social workers, with thousands of other persons throughout the nation had increasingly felt the need . . . [to] . . . make social reform a political issue of national dimensions.[12]

It was the strong belief of many of these reformers that matters of childhood in all their variety warranted the "adjusted human relations" that governmental interest could provide. Many of these activists were in fact not biological mothers but deployed an expediently "maternalist" discourse, one that would sound essentialist a century later. Indeed, discourses of "city housekeeping" and "mother's politics" propelled various efforts in domestic democracy where activists sought recognition and aid to support the social labor of women. With such hopes in mind, reformers and researchers endeavored to reach state and federal levels of influence on a number of fronts. It was with no small degree of pride that Hull-House resident Julia Lathrop completed a study of and recommendations for addressing maternity health and compensation, introducing the plan with the sardonic humor of an ironic progressive: "This document has been compiled in the hope that the information might prove useful to the people of one of the few great countries which as yet have no system of State or national assistance in maternity—the United States."[13] Lathrop herself was, by this point, the first director of the Children's Bureau, saddled with the task of creating a federal social service network that would provide the care necessary for the health and welfare of children and working families.

Of course, it has become clear to a variety of historians of social welfare—and clear, from a different perspective, to a variety of post-Foucaultian theorists of identity—that the bargain struck by Jane Addams, Julia Lathrop, and so many other domestically inspired reformers was, to echo Brown and Halley, "double-edged." To some, the federal government's "interest" in childhood became a means of disseminating prescriptions and censorships about what proper childhood entailed. Similarly, the "adjusted human relations" provided by a governmental interest in maternity came with new ideals and normalizations about how the maternal should be performed. In many cases and from several vantage points, the governmental interest in caring for families came with the price of instituting bounded familial models, those dyadic forms whose restriction Judith Butler would critique at the end of the twentieth century. Brown and Halley turn to a familiar figure to dramatize the argument:

> Although Foucault helpfully drew our attention to the ways that powers of regulation operate and regulate in extralegal or legal domains, he may have underestimated the degree to which the modern liberal state itself can operate as micropower . . . "the law" . . . has incorporated the managerial, normativizing, regularizing biopoweristic forms that he proposed were distinguishable from the juridical form . . . now also [taking] the form of the Department of Youth Services worker who inspects your personal life in minute detail to decide whether you are a fit person to adopt your lover's child. This underpaid and overworked functionary, laden with forms that standardize good parenting, has his or her effects on you and on parenting more broadly not through rules about it but through mobile, shifting, highly momentary assessments.[14]

The biopoweristic form of the Youth Services worker serves as an emblem of the indiscrete invasion of the state, one where even well-intentioned adoption laws create the grounds for uncomfortable assessments of sexuality, parenting, and kinship performance. The encounter with what is now the state's "underpaid and overworked functionary" may sound quite familiar to readers of Jane Addams, for the kind of untoward scrutiny Brown and Halley find in the state's practice is quite similar to the one Addams criticized in charity practice. Indeed, Addams's potent dramatization of the politics of "friendly visiting" of poor families—and the conflicted mindset of the "friendly visitor"—is one of her most quoted:

> The daintily clad charity visitor who steps into the little house made untidy by the vigorous efforts of her hostess, the washerwomen is no longer sure of her superiority to the latter . . . she is often embarrassed to find herself obliged to lay all the stress of her teaching and advice upon the industrial virtues. . . . She insists that they must work and be self-supporting, that the most dangerous of all situations is idleness, that seeking one's pleasure, while ignoring claims and responsibilities, is the most ignoble of actions. . . . As she daily holds up these standards, it often occurs to the mind of the sensitive visitor, whose conscience has been made tender by much talk of brotherhood and equality, that she has no right to say these things; that her untrained hands are no more fitted to cope with actual conditions than those of her broken-down family.[15]

Even as a contemporary reader might be chagrined to find similar practices of assessment and judgment—whether of work ethic or of sexual normativity—across these historical moments, it is worth noting that Addams's involvement with Hull-House was in part an attempt to take relations of "care" out of this kind of charity model. Hull-House and the settlement movement were attempts to create a more reciprocal sphere of interpersonal engagement across class lines, one where life instruction and personal transformation happened in more than one direction. Addams and fellow settlers, however, soon felt that they needed to turn to civic and state power in order to actualize this goal, for settlers found that a highly local focus on interpersonal ethics could not compensate for systemic inequities of gender, ethnicity, age, and class. Addams's quest for a redefinition of government was thus based on the desire to institute provisions for all citizens and to do so without recourse to what she and others found to be the undemocratic "relation which obtains between benefactor and beneficiary." The turn to government occurred after she and fellow settlers realized that such "adjusted human relations" required intervention at the macro level of federal structure as much as at the micro level of private ethics. Indeed, the effects of poverty, prejudice, and gendered labor practices demonstrated again and again that so-called macro and micro spheres, so-called public and private realms, were intimately entangled with each other. The contemporary paradox now is that such a well-intentioned progressive vision of the state has morphed to justify the insidious appearance of the "Youth Services worker" in the present. Is that appearance a sign of what remains of the U.S. welfare state's progressive social contract? Or is that appearance of the "State at Your Door" a sign of state normalization in Halley and Brown's terms?

In the different answers to these questions, we have an exemplary instance of mutual distrust between the domain of social welfare studies and the thought structures of post-structuralist queer theory. Hence, it is at such a moment that I want to suggest an alternate remembering is in order. Without endorsing the practices of assessment or the standards used by this invasive state functionary, I think that it is equally important for left-allied thinkers in queer theory and post-structuralist political theory more generally to remember the broader systemic impulses that brought the Youth Services worker to our door, as well as the feminist critique of public and private that she has the potential still to supply. A more capacious understanding of social welfare and domestic democracy is central to imagining a relational model of subjectivity and extended kinship for both critical welfare studies and queer theory; it is also central to countering the hyper-individualist impulses that currently and oddly appear in both right and left critiques of governmental intrusion.

I would like now to take this kind of reflection back to the historiography on Jane Addams and Hull-House in order to see how an orientation toward queer welfare studies adjusts our view of Addams as well as certain habits of critical reflection in feminism, welfare history, and queer theory. Questions of history, theory, publicity, gender, and sexuality are at issue in the attempt to train one's attention on domestic life at Hull-House, as Jane Addams indirectly elaborated in her own writing but also as practiced in the highly encumbered, embodied, and spatially innovative life of the settlement. As most readers of this volume know, the settlement endeavor differed in method from other philanthropic efforts of the time in that its reformers moved into the neighborhoods they sought to help. Hull-House residents and their colleagues throughout the nation followed an ethic of radical locality, choosing to spend all hours of work, living, and leisure within the spaces they sought to change. I think there is a certain kind of theoretical opportunity—particularly an opportunity for theories of sexuality—in the attempt to analyze the settling processes of the settlement.

Though earlier sexual historiographical questions might have focused on "whether Jane Addams was a lesbian," recent scholarship on queer theory has focused its lens less on recovering bounded instances of gay and lesbian identity; instead, it investigates the structures by which subjectivity is provisionally constituted in order to isolate the instabilities of apparently "normal" and normalizing social spheres. Such a sensibility provides a useful starting point for interrogating Hull-House practice, asking us to think about how what Beatrice Webb called its "higgledy-piggledy" social life created an alternate kind of social sphere.[16] As I have argued elsewhere, settling at Hull-House was a daily lesson in undoing gendered and classed conventions of privacy and publicity, providing a material plane that actuated and was actuated by the movement of people who patently and tacitly redefined their lives. It is here that a queer theoretical approach to Hull-House space proves useful, asking us to see something conceptually generative in its contradictions and its movement. Hull-House's queer domesticity, fragile and provisional as it was, finds a suitably complicated analytic in the kind of frame Judith Butler offers for the study of queer kinship and its less than intelligible manifestations:

> Even within the field of intelligible sexuality, one finds that the binaries that anchor its operations permit for middle zones. . . . These are not precisely places where one can choose to hang out, subject positions one might opt to occupy. These are nonplaces in which one finds oneself in spite of oneself. . . . They are not sites of enunciation, but shifts in the topography from which a questionably audible claim emerges: the claim of the not-yet-subject and the nearly recognizable. That there are such regions, and that they are not precisely options, suggest that what troubles the distinction between legitimacy and illegitimacy are social practices, specifically sexual practices, that do not appear immediately coherent in the available lexicon of legitimation.[17]

Indeed, the social and domestic practices of Hull-House have not always been "immediately coherent in the available lexicon of legitimation." Contemporaneous outsiders called the settlement "unnatural," worrying that its women were "spinsters" or that its men were "mollycoddles." More recently, contemporary scholars have worked to make sense of the settlement within available normative terms such as home, woman, family, and mother or within available counternormative terms such as commune, feminist, lesbian, or activist. By attending to the nonplace of the settlement as a "shift in the topography" of available subjectivities, however, we come instead to a better sense of the significance of its lived character. Rather than using available terms as critical barometers with which to measure deviation, we can conceive Hull-House space as a generative region, if not exactly a fixed "option," thereby allowing us to see the unsettling of terms such as family, kinship, welfare, and the state, even when such redefinition was not self-consciously foregrounded.

That redefinition, for instance, meant adapting to an alternate spatial style, allowing the inherited formality of the Hull mansion's parlors, dining rooms, and bedrooms to be disrupted by the continual reentry of children, adolescents, working women, immigrants, and varieties of neighbors.[18] Residents learned to write up urban reports in the middle of a house filled with children's social clubs. Bedroom spaces became receiving spaces with an addition of extra chairs; bedroom spaces became storage spaces when the settlement's theater director housed all of her costumes and props in her room. New social rituals were created to facilitate a public household; residents shared the responsibility of waiting at the door to receive expected but mostly unexpected visitors. Hull-House's ongoing social redefinition also meant adapting or retreating when the disruption was too much, when it felt too crowded, or too loud, or, as one resident complained, when "the bell kept ringing." At these and other more discouraging moments, residents worried that the social claims of urban life were too overwhelming or that, as one resident lamented, "we were trying to sweep back the tide with a broom."[19]

That spatial redefinition also supported and was supported by a redefinition of kinship that settling women and men performed in the hallways, kitchens, and gathering spaces of the settlement. Many who opted out of traditional heterosexual marriage formed same-sex bonds of attachment with fellow "sister-settlers" as well as bold, mutually supporting, and only occasionally romantic heterosexual attachments with sibling "brothers."[20] It meant forming bonds of attachment to hundreds of children who were not biological offspring, whether in a children's health clinic, a children's art class, or in the free child care offered in the settlement living room. Settlers argued, shared meals, and distributed household tasks while juggling their commitments as labor leaders, teachers, club leaders, urban analysts, scientists, and policy writers. Indeed, this "plan of living which may be called cooperative," as Jane Addams roundaboutly phrased it, seemed necessary to act on the public mission of Hull-House.[21] Such a realization comes when reckoning with the very public doings of this previously private house, in reading stories and letters of sensory disruption and transformation in the settlement's living rooms, dining rooms, bedrooms, bridges, and relocated front doors. Hull-House's complexly shifting topography not only disrupts the available lexicons of publicity and privacy but threatens to expose the instability of that binary in apparently stable forms of family, home, kinship, and state welfare as well.

To bring this domain of Jane Addams's life back to a critique of feminist and queer studies, I would like now to turn to Jean Bethke Elshtain's recently published study of Jane Addams, *Jane Addams and the Dream of American Democracy: A Life*. Elshtain's work provides a useful place from which to link Jane Addams to debates within gender studies, for Elshtain has been a key figure in feminist political theory more generally. Elshtain's groundbreaking *Private Man, Public Woman* was intent upon articulating a feminist politics that acknowledged the limits placed upon women by their association with the private but took issue with a feminist politics that, in Elshtain's view, was in danger of forfeiting the pleasures and dismissing the importance of maintaining a bounded private sphere. For Elshtain, this was also an epistemological issue. It was about valuing knowledges of the particular and the concrete, rather than the "rational" and the "abstract" that were the traditional orientation of a Western, masculinist intellectual perspective. "Why should a personalized, localized, particular female subject be brought into the more abstract, rationalized, universal mode? . . . [T]he private world also exudes its own values and imperatives in part because it is the theater of particularity and everyday concrete meaning. If that mode were suppressed altogether in favor of the exigencies and demands of abstract personhood and the pull towards rationalization . . . who would tend to the little world, keeping alive its life-redeeming joys and tragedies?"[22] For her, feminist thinkers were in danger of remarginalizing the care of that "little world" in a way that perpetuated rather than challenged the perceptions of their male philosophical forebears. Hence, Simone de Beauvoir received as formidable a critique from Elshtain as did a canon of white male figures culled from the history of Western intellectual thought.

Interestingly, a very similar kind of analytic orientation can be found in Elshtain's 2002 biography of Jane Addams. In Elshtain's chapter titles such as "The Family Claim and the Social Claim," "Compassion Without Condescension," and "Women's Remembering Heart," Addams's vocabulary mixes with Elshtain's earlier concepts to argue for the relevance of the so-called private realm in the upkeep of and reformation of the public. Addams's concepts of city housekeeping are invoked throughout these chapters. Within American feminist history, of course, Addams is recognized for her writings on city housekeeping where she defined women's involvement in public life as an extension rather than as a violation of their traditional domestic roles. This was Addams's strategic, and rhetorically deferential, contribution to the suffrage movement and to a longer tradition of domestic democracy, arguing for the vote as a means for women to sustain rather than to violate their traditional roles as nurturers of the health and cleanliness of the community. Indeed, along with her study of charity workers cited above, Addams's stories of the role of women in reforming the inequities of garbage collection, of contaminated milk supplies, and of unsanitary housing are some of her most memorable.

Addams deploys such stories in her arguments for city housekeeping to rationalize women's public participation on behalf of issues that, because of their systemic dependence upon governmental operations, were improperly understood as stably private. Elshtain rechronicles many of these stories as well, though she is more interested in using those stories to celebrate the "private" world than she is in unsettling divisions between public and private. What is, I think, more uncertain is where Elshtain locates the discursive origin of Addams's thoughts on the relation between private and public. "What Addams insists upon is that the female body—most important, the maternal female body—is the central image of social generativity and fecundity. Clearly, one need not be a mother in the biological sense—although she found this the most vital of human activities—in order to locate oneself with this image."[23] This image, Elshtain argues, served as the foundation for Addams's imagining of a new body politic, a society of what Elshtain calls, quoting John O'Neill, "familied contexts" that held up the maternal body as the basis for their own social generativity. If there is a fixation on the maternal body in all its corporeality and "fecundity" in Addams's writing, Elshtain's book does not offer a quotation. The fact that this biography included no such quotations testifies, I think, to a slip in an argument that wants to foreground the world of contingency but ends up essentializing the bodies of the female figures who historically have managed it.

In part, my concern with this move is that Elshtain's argument ignores the rhetorical expediency of "city housekeeping" as an expediently self-deferential argument; by telling citizens that female publicity could be a continuation rather than a violation of gendered roles, city housekeepers made use of a strategic essentialism whose public incarnation actually involved behaviors that were far from traditional and that kept them outside the walls of the "house." There is a related concern, however, that to me is more urgent for my argument. I am concerned about the way that Elshtain's valuation of the private ends up fortifying its boundaries, indirectly normalizing its contents, and, moreover, standardizing proper conceptions of the feminine, the family, and the maternal along with it.

Indeed, it seems that this is a place where Elshtain's analysis of Jane Addams bears the burden of reinforcing her earlier arguments in *Public Man, Private Woman*. That burden in turn produces blind spots around her analysis of Hull-House's own domestic practices on the micro scale as well as the involvement of Hull-House in social welfare on the macro scale. Elshtain's caveat that one "need not be a biological mother" too cavalierly bypasses the limits placed on some people's full identification with this image. Indeed, a psychoanalytic frame joined to a social analysis would foreground the partiality of anyone's complete identification with such an image, note the politics of that partiality, and elaborate the dangers of its disavowal. Although I would not suggest that queer theory has a purchase on this kind of analytic, I would suggest that it is that kind of question theorists of sexuality would want to ask. Because Jane Addams was not a biological mother who simultaneously made use of a kind of maternal rhetoric, the partiality of her alignment seems particularly important. It is in that space between the regulating image and the daily practices of individuals—a "shift in the topography" that does "not appear immediately coherent in the available lexicon of legitimation"—that alternate conceptions of parenthood, family, and social formation can be gleaned, if not exactly legitimated. Indeed, Elshtain's invocation of the "maternal body" in Addams's thought (without a citation of the maternal body in Addams's thought) seems an exemplary instance of an "available lexicon" being imposed upon a practice and a person whose place in the topography of family and sexual politics is not as easily fixed.

It is with this sense of possibility in mind that we might return to the everyday practices of the settlement; here, Hull-House's daily performances of domesticity become not only methodologically interesting but also politically weighted. To examine the internals of Hull-House is to see the spaces of public and private redefined in several directions and on different scales. As my brief account of the redefinition of spatial styles and cooperative living suggests, the "settling" process of the settlement reflected the need not simply for an extension beyond the domestic sphere (for example, garbage collecting and suffrage) but also a reciprocal undoing of the domestic sphere (for example, household duties and kinship bonding). That is, the externalized maternality of city housekeeping simultaneously required an internalized sociality within the household sphere. This undoing produced a space of everyday life that was intriguingly unsettled, with doors opening, bells ringing, and chairs moving as the push and pull of settlement practice dictated. As noted above, Hull-House settlers cultivated relationships of various kinds—same-sex attachment and identification (Jane Addams and Mary Rozet Smith being the most famous), mixed-sex romantic attachment (among several male and female residents), fictive kinship between metaphoric "sister-settlers" and later "brothers" (who called each other "Sister Kelley, Sister Lathrop, Brother Twose"), and committed attachment between children and nonbiological parental surrogates (Florence Kelley's children being an early example).[24] This kind of everyday life diffused and rerouted intimate attachment onto an alternate familial plane, one that resisted heteronormativity without necessarily falling into the presentist categories of homosexual identity. My interest in the queerness of Hull-House's queer domesticity thus has to do with how nonnormative formations of what was often called a "family" by its inhabitants occurred in a space of varied intimate alignments between and among the sexes and between and among biological and nonbiological parents, children, and siblings.

To incorporate this provocative "region" into a discussion of city housekeeping is thus to expand the reach of the concept. It is to show domesticity as something that is both extended publicly but also reworked privately. It is also to allow the value of the epistemologically particular and concrete (Elshtain's "little world") to be shared by different domains and persons, not always biological mothers and not always women. Though there might be several ways to explain the reluctance of Elshtain's biography to contend with the full history of the settlement, I want to address the oversight by pursuing another tack that further addresses tensions in gender studies. For if, as I suggested, the extension of the domestic sphere also requires its reciprocal undoing, then it is this latter part of the equation that Elshtain's feminist political theory cannot abide. It is precisely the ability of Hull-House reformers to imagine systemic connection and obligation outside blood family ties—that is, social welfare—that her analysis seems unwilling to track.

Let me return to Elshtain's earlier critiques of feminist theorizing in *Public Man, Private Woman* where she writes, "the past fifteen years have seen a number of visions of family-less, asocial existence celebrated. These have taken several forms, including one in which, not having biological nuclear families, all individuals, including children, would be 'free' to look for the best contractual deal in living arrangements."[25] In an argument that defines feminism within a classically liberal distrust of the threat to private autonomy, she criticizes the contemporaneous commune experiments of the sixties and seventies as having a similarly flawed understanding of freedom. Additionally, "institutional" forms of child care—presumably those that occur in social service agencies—receive a blow. Modes of institutional child care that call themselves "familial," Elshtain writes, use only "hollow, sentimentalized repetition of terms for family relations—'brother,' 'sister,' 'family.'"[26]

She continues, "To call some abstract structure, or a loose collection of like-minded, unrelated peers 'families' is to treat our most basic human relationships frivolously."[27] Using the failure and exhaustion of social experiments on the fringes and on the federal level as proof against possible alternatives, she argues, "It is the family that constitutes our 'common humanity.' . . . This makes the family 'the universal basis of human culture. . . . As language constitutes the essence of man as a species, and not reason, so the family and not the social order is the setting that humanizes him.'"[28]

I would not myself want to over-sentimentalize the practices of the like-minded peers who called themselves a family at Hull-House. Nor would I want to ignore the difficulty and exhaustion they endured in the maintenance of this sphere. However, I do think we need a more complex analytic in order to recognize and interpret the fullness of these people's very full lives. I think we need to value the rituals by which biologically unrelated persons formed a relation, and I think we need terms other than "hollow" and "frivolous" to characterize them. Elshtain's rhetoric provides little to help us understand, for instance, the expressions of emotion found in the letters of settlers who tended to children not their biological offspring, an attachment that is as clear in Dr. Alice Hamilton's descriptions of her work with settler and neighborhood children ("He stood the cauterizing in a way that made me feel like crying") as it is in Jane Addams's and Mary Rozet Smith's poignant conversations around a Jane Club resident's decision to give up her child for adoption ("My heart quaked when I first had it definitely fixed in my mind").[29] Nor does it help us account for how the settlement as an institution provided hundreds of children with a sense of kinship. To recognize the affective world of this "institution" would not ignore the partiality—what Elshtain calls the "looseness"—of these relations but rather use that partiality to allow the family, the maternal, and the child to be the basis for our most complicated theorizing rather than the basis for our most unchallenged prescription. That kind of complexity has been a persistent goal in queer studies where, before and after Kath Weston, same-sex partnerships have prompted a necessary investigation of the character, nature, reach, and limits of having "families we choose."[30] As such, it is one place where Jane Addams's life and career can help us reflect more generally on some key debates in the fields of gender studies. The supposed contradictions of her historical example can help us think with more openness and precision about the principles of feminism and sexuality. They also help us imagine a queer welfare studies based in shared systems for promoting an ethics of extended kinship.

A similar kind of blind spot can be turned to opportunity when it comes to Jane Addams's equivocal position in the formation of social welfare. Again, the fact that the precepts of city housekeeping also contributed to a discourse behind the formation of this large, state apparatus is largely ignored in Elshtain's book. Given the tendency in Elshtain's earlier work to criticize such "institutional" formations for their erosion of the family, this is consistent. Once again, however, I think that those contemporary individuals who devote themselves to working within the field of social service—Brown and Halley's "overworked functionaries"—and those scholars who devote themselves to historicizing its predicament need a more complicated and hospitable analytic to make sense of their work. They need something more than accusations of "hollowness" from certain feminists, and they need more than unremarked indifference from the intellectual biography of one of social welfare's most pivotal historical figures. Jane Addams's original interest in the intensely local, micro-practices of neighborly interaction cannot neutralize the fact that Hull-House played a role in the formation of a more diffuse, macro-oriented system of public welfare.

Many of us—and I would include myself—are perhaps more interested and more skilled in interpreting the local and intimate practices of settling than the federal processes of social servicing. Nevertheless, it seems important that our shared paradigms allow a conversation between these scales rather than foster more defensiveness between them. Elshtain's earlier argument against the frivolous, institutional, and loose redefinition of the family only exemplifies Judith Butler's claim that "[v]ariations on kinship that depart from normative, dyadic heterosexually based family forms secured through the marriage vow are figured not only as dangerous for the child, but perilous to the putative natural and cultural laws said to sustain human intelligibility." While Butler's critique is directed at "the normalizing powers of the state," the example of Elshtain's analysis shows that criticism of variation is also possible within certain strains of feminism. Placing them together forces attention on the fact that same-sex partnership might not be the only castigated "variation" but that the operations of public institutions of care—that is, social welfare—often receive similar castigations of abnormality and unnatural violation. Indeed, as much as the state figures in leftist critique and queer theory as an insidious vehicle of familial normalization (as I noted in my opening paragraphs), it is just as likely to receive criticism from the right and from liberal feminists for being a violation of the family as "our most basic human relationship."

It is the prevalence of a strangely similar argument from so many sides of the political spectrum that makes queer welfare studies so hard to sustain. From some quarters, social welfare is a scandalous vehicle of familial denormalization; from others, it is a scandalous vehicle of familial renormalization.

The public institutionalization of care across nonbiological lines—my tax dollars for your children, my psychic allegiance for your regulating society—can not quite get support from anywhere in the United States. Jane Addams and Hull-House, however, occupy an intriguingly liminal position in this overdetermined critical topography. Her example is a reminder that the system of social welfare is part of a complicated genealogy that is associated as much with the denormalization of nuclear family bonding as it is with the family's oppressive renaturalization. By remembering that social welfare and queer studies both promote a model of extended kinship, we have the potential for an interdisciplinary allegiance that can not only do a better job of remembering the radicality of Jane Addams's life, but do a better job of promoting queer welfare studies as a generative space of social imagining.

My thoughts in this essay have focused mostly upon how debates within feminism, sexuality, and queer theory help to unsettle Jane Addams. By way of conclusion, I would like also to reflect further in the reverse direction, that is, on how an unsettled Jane Addams speaks back to these fields. If Hull-House and Jane Addams can elicit methodological innovation from queer theory, then the same goes for queer theory's political significance. What I find particularly significant is an undertheorized connection between Hull-House's queer domesticity and the larger kinds of social unsettling for which it is better known.

The conventional history of social welfare questions the role of such "abnormal" women in the history of social welfare. How could such women—the majority unmarried, and not biological parents—guide a system that attends explicitly to the cultivation of families and of children? A more generous answer to the question could suggest that there is a relation between micro-redefinitions of family and the macro-formation of state welfare. Given that queer theorists such as Lisa Duggan, Judith Butler, Wendy Brown, and others have worked recently to translate the psychoanalytic operations of queer subjectivity to larger public spheres, Hull-House enables links to micro and macro domains. To take this connection seriously, however, would be to resist some convenient prejudices, to be willing to see, for instance, public welfare as something more than "a force of normalization" (from queer theorists) or just another "abstract structure" (from liberal feminists). Indeed, if the practitioners of social welfare are merely "functionaries"—whether "hollow" or "insidious"—in the work of Halley and Brown *and* in the work of Jean Bethke Elshtain, then we have an odd alignment that renders the important philosophical differences among and between these thinkers obscure.

To take the possibility of queer welfare studies seriously would also require a more subtle analysis of what counts as "nonnormative" and a willingness to see it even in women who look, to presentist eyes, somewhat conventional. If queer theory has been somewhat ahistorical in its objects and in its approaches, then Jane Addams and Hull-House offer the challenge of interpreting queer subjectivities that do not always overtly "resist," that rarely cross-dressed, and that spoke sentences that sounded the maternal discourses of their times. That these same individuals argued for care and nonphilanthropic obligation beyond blood ties, that they rarely had biological children but were never "childless," suggests that they occupied one of those less-than-legible topographies to which Judith Butler refers. A cautious approach to the understanding of this zone exposes similarly ambivalent zones within the history of families and the histories of state welfare, both of which are now too quickly bounded for easy celebration or easy vilification from several directions—some conservative, some liberal feminist, and some queer left. Through such methodological and conceptual experiments, however, we might come to a better understanding of a tacit, formative, and undertheorized connection between queer politics and domestic politics, between a queer critique of sexuality and a left imagining of social welfare.

Notes

1. Jane Addams, "The Charitable Effort," in *Democracy and Social Ethics* (New York: Macmillan, 1902), 63.

2. Judith Butler, "Is Kinship Always Already Heterosexual?" in *Left Legalism/Left Critique,* ed. Wendy Brown and Janet Halley (Durham, N.C.: Duke University Press, 2002), 229.

3. Licia Fiol-Matta, *A Queer Mother for the Nation: The State and Gabriela Mistral* (Minneapolis: University of Minnesota Press, 2002).

4. Shannon Jackson, *Lines of Activity: Performance, Historiography, Hull-House Domesticity* (Ann Arbor: University of Michigan Press, 2000).

5. Jean Bethke Elshtain, *Jane Addams and the Dream of American Democracy: A Life* (New York: Basic Books, 2002); Elshtain, *Private Man, Public Woman: Women in Social and Political Thought* (Princeton, N.J.: Princeton University Press, 1981). For additional discussion and critique of Elshtain's presentation of Addams, see Wendy Sarvasy, "'A Global Common Table': Jane Addams's Theory of Democratic Cosmopolitanism and World Social Citizenship," in this volume.

6. Charlene Haddock Seigfried, *Pragmatism and Feminism: Reweaving the Social Fabric* (Chicago: University of Chicago Press, 1996).

7. Mimi Abramovitz, *Regulating the Lives of Women: Social Welfare Policy from Colonial Times to the Present,* rev. ed. (Boston: South End Press, 1996); Nancy Fraser, *Justice Interruptus: Critical Reflections on the "Postsocialist" Condition* (New York:

Routledge, 1997); Linda Gordon and Nancy Fraser, "A Genealogy of Dependency," *Signs* 19 (1994): 309–36; Wendy Brown, *States of Injury: Power and Freedom in Late Modernity* (Princeton, N.J.: Princeton University Press, 1995); Kathy Ferguson, *The Feminist Case Against Bureaucracy* (Philadelphia: Temple University Press, 1984).

8. Brown, *States of Injury*, 166.

9. Judith Butler, *The Psychic Life of Power: Theories in Subjection* (Stanford, Calif.: Stanford University Press, 1997); Lauren Berlant, *The Queen of America Goes to Washington City: Essays on Sex and Citizenship* (Durham, N.C.: Duke University Press, 1997); Michael Warner, ed., *Fear of a Queer Planet: Queer Politics and Social Theory* (Minneapolis: University of Minnesota Press, 1993); Lee Edelman, *No Future: Queer Theory and the Death Drive* (Durham, N.C.: Duke University Press, 2004).

10. Wendy Brown and Janet Halley, introduction, in *Left Legalism/Left Critique*, 7.

11. Butler, "Kinship," 231.

12. Jane Addams, *The Second Twenty Years at Hull-House, September 1909 to September 1929, With a Record of Growing World Consciousness* (New York: Macmillan Company, 1930), 23.

13. Julia Lathrop, "Letter of Transmission," in H. Harris, *Maternity Benefits Systems in Certain Foreign Countries, U.S. Children's Bureau Bulletin* 57 (Washington, D.C., 1919), 2.

14. Brown and Halley, 13–14.

15. Addams, *Democracy and Social Ethics*, 14, 16, 17–18.

16. Beatrice Webb, *Beatrice Webb's American Diary, 1898*, reprint (Madison: University of Wisconsin Press, 1963), 107.

17. Butler, "Kinship," 235.

18. Jackson, *Lines of Activity*, 37–94, 147–202.

19. Ibid., 186.

20. Ibid., 164–87.

21. Ibid., 187. See also Louise W. Knight's account of how Addams was influenced by and participated in the cooperation movement, in "Jane Addams's Theory of Cooperation," in this volume.

22. Elshtain, *Private Man, Public Woman*, 305.

23. Elshtain, *Jane Addams*, 160.

24. Jackson, *Lines of Activity*, 147–202.

25. Elshtain, *Public Man, Private Woman*, 325.

26. Ibid., 330.

27. Ibid., 331.

28. Ibid., 327.

29. Jackson, *Lines of Activity*, 163, 170.

30. Kath Weston, *Families We Choose: Lesbians, Gays, Kinship*, rev. ed. (New York: Columbia University Press, 1997).

SECTION III

Democratic Cosmopolitanism and Peace

8

The Conceptual Scaffolding of *Newer Ideals of Peace*

MARILYN FISCHER

How can we make sense of *Newer Ideals of Peace*? Even a number of Addams's closest associates questioned the extent to which her 1907 book was in fact a book about peace. Florence Kelley, Addams's longtime colleague at Hull-House, wrote in her review, "The title of Miss Addams's volume is not altogether a happy one. The book is . . . 'a curious commentary on the fact that we have not yet attained self-government.'" Allen Davis, in his 1973 biography of Addams, advanced the same critique. "Much of the book was not about war and peace, but about the plight of the cities—the immigrants, the working women and children." In an otherwise appreciative review, George Herbert Mead wrote, "One does not feel, in reading Miss Addams, the advance of an argument with measured tread. I think in logical organization this book suffers more than her earlier writing."[1]

In contrast to such critics, I will argue that the book is fundamentally and throughout a book about peace, and that the chapters on domestic reform function as essential parts of Addams's argument. The underlying structure of the book and the role of these chapters become clear when we approach the book as Addams's response to the dominant peace advocates of the time. I will argue that although Addams and these peace advocates shared the conceptual paradigm and vocabulary of nineteenth-century social evolutionary thought, particularly that of Herbert Spencer, in *Newer Ideals* Addams uses these conceptual tools to argue against the conclusions of Spencer and the peace advocates.

This task is less straightforward than it may appear. To her editor's request to include more citations in *Newer Ideals*, Addams replied she had assumed "that the book was to be kept popular and colloquial in style rather than exact and scholarly."[2] She does not name Spencer or many of the theorists or theories with which she works; she refers to the advocates of peace fleetingly and rarely. In proposing the following construction of her argument, I interpret what she says in light of contemporary historical events and the people and texts with which she was acquainted. This approach will enable us to read *Newer Ideals of Peace* as giving a sustained, unified argument regarding peace.

The Practical Peace Advocates

Addams sets the terms of the debate in the book's first sentence: "The following pages present the claims of the newer, more aggressive ideals of peace, as over against the older dovelike ideal."[3] The book is an analysis of the deficiencies of older ideals that peace advocates had advanced in a number of ways, along with Addams's own proposal of "newer, more aggressive ideals." Although she rarely names them in the book, Addams met many of these peace advocates at the Thirteenth Universal Peace Congress, held in Boston in October 1904.[4] A number of these peace advocates, members of the Universal Peace Union and the Peace Association of Friends, emphasized nonresistance. However, the dominant voices at the congress offered more "practical" approaches to peace. These were elite representatives of international law and commerce to whom international peace was fully consistent with political, economic, and social conservatism and with full national sovereignty.[5]

The international lawyers, led by men such as Nicholas Murray Butler, president of Columbia University, and Elihu Root, secretary of war under William McKinley and secretary of state under Theodore Roosevelt, focused their practical activity on developing international legal institutions, ranging from arbitration treaties to a formal, permanent world court.[6] They claimed they wanted to "convert international conflicts into cases,"[7] and thus defined international conflicts as legal disputes, rather than as embedded in social, economic, or political contexts. At the Universal Peace Congress, a number of the speakers described their efforts with rhetorical flourish. Pointing at the Permanent Court of International Arbitration recently established at The Hague, Oscar Straus, a member of the court from the United States, called it "the most enduring humanitarian achievement of the ages," the "Magna Charta of International Law," and "an International Covenant on the Mount."[8] Business leaders such as industrialist and philanthropist Andrew Carnegie, publisher Edwin Ginn, and banker George Foster Peabody stressed how wasteful and disruptive war was to international commerce and how international commerce created and sustained fruitful interdependence among nations.[9] At the congress John Lund of Norway likened international trade routes to blood circulating in the body, and just as vital to keep open. Economist Edward Atkinson envisioned the trajectory of world progress moving toward "the day . . . when the ships that pass between this land and that shall be like the shuttle of the loom, weaving the web of concord among the nations."[10]

The majority of these "practical" peace advocates assumed Herbert Spencer's evolutionary framework for social change. It is difficult to remember today how enormously influential Spencer was in nineteenth-century Britain and the United States. In *Social Darwinism in American Thought,* Richard Hofstadter pointed out, "Although its influence far outstripped its merits, the Spencerian system serves students of the American mind as a fossil specimen from which the intellectual body of the period may be reconstructed."[11] Spencer coined the phrase, "survival of the fittest," and was the founder of social Darwinism.[12] To understand Addams's critique of these peace advocates, we need to review Spencer's definitions of militarism and industrialism.

In *Principles of Sociology* Spencer uses the terms "militarism" and "industrialism" to designate pure theoretical types of social organization. Few purely industrial societies ever existed; most societies have been a mixture of both militant and industrial social organization. A "militant" society is one that is organized principally around meeting external threats. The primary characteristic of both military and civilian organization is centralized, hierarchical control. Spencer writes that in the military, in religion, in civic governing structures, and in the household, "all are slaves to those above and despots to those below."[13] People whose traits or activities are not warlike are treated with contempt. Economic self-sufficiency of the group is important, as dependence on trade with outside groups could weaken the society's ability to survive during times of war.[14] Spencer observes that under militarism, indications of civil society, such as private associations in commerce, culture, or philanthropy are rare and individual initiative is suppressed, as these break the power of the central controlling hierarchy. He defines social interaction as based on "compulsory cooperation." The industrial part of a militant society, that is, that part concerned with perpetuating the life of the group, he calls "a permanent commissariat." Women have low status because they do not fight. As noncombatants, women's function is to supply the needs of the military for food, equipment, and new recruits.[15]

For Spencer, an industrial society is one principally structured to sustain its members.[16] Rather than hierarchy and status determining people's roles, relations are voluntary and based on exchange and contract. Such societies tend toward democratic governance via elections and representation, with government's role in society being highly restricted. Individual freedoms and rights, humane sentiments, and respect for others, including women and children, characterize the society. The society is flexible and adaptable; it is likely to engage in peaceful trade with other groups.[17]

Spencer was a pacifist. He thought that in the past, militarism had contributed to civilization's advance through creating complex systems of governance and production. But he believed that civilization had reached the point where continued militaristic social organization was counterproductive, particularly as it hindered liberty and the development of altruistic sentiments. Further social evolution depended on peace, and the cessation of war.[18]

Many of the practical peace advocates Addams addresses in *Newer Ideals* agreed with Spencer's evolutionary trajectory of the progress of civilization from militarism to industrialism. They worked to create an industrialism characterized by laissez-faire economics in industry and international commerce. In their view, international legal institutions would settle international disputes, while international commerce would help to foster peaceful interdependence.[19]

Survivals of Militarism under Industrialism

Addams argues that the efforts of these peace advocates were of limited value. They had failed to recognize the then-current stage of industrialism was not peaceful because survivals of militarism continued to function in institutions of government, industry, and international commerce.

Addams frames *Newer Ideals* with Spencer's vocabulary and evolutionary perspective. Throughout the book Addams gives many references to evolutionary theory, stating that we should adopt "the modern evolutionary standpoint" and heed the lessons of "evolutionary science."[20] Early in the book she expresses this evolutionary paradigm by quoting British philosopher and journalist L. T. Hobhouse, who wrote, "Universal and permanent peace may be a vision; but the gradual change whereby war, as a normal state of international relations, has given place to peace as the normal state, is no vision, but an actual process of history."[21] She agrees that we are in the stage of industrialism, locates the origins of industrialism with the rise of the middle class, and identifies the modern city as "a stronghold of industrialism."[22]

One reviewer of *Newer Ideals* wrote, "This antithesis between militancy and industrialism will be recognized by students as having been borrowed from Herbert Spencer's works, but it is given an application which would have astonished that philosopher."[23] Addams uses Spencer and the practical peace advocates' vocabulary and concepts against their own conclusions by adopting a different methodology. She claims that they hold their positions as creeds, employing "the a priori method of the schoolmen." For this she will substitute "the scientific method of research."[24] As a sociologist and a pragmatist, Addams insisted on testing theories in light of observation and concrete experience. She gave particular attention to those at the bottom of society, specifically immigrants and the urban poor, with special focus on women and children. Addams's operative question was: as a matter of daily, lived experience, do those at the bottom experience industrialism as a time of peace?[25]

In making her critique Addams employed the notion of "survivals," a term from British evolutionary anthropologist E. B. Tylor. Trying to understand why cultures exhibit customs and beliefs that have no or even maladaptive evolutionary value, Tylor hypothesized that such practices provided clues to previous stages in social evolution. In the past these practices had served an evolutionary function, and then continued to persist as "survivals" of an earlier age.[26] In *Newer Ideals* Addams argues that basic social institutions of the day were laced through with survivals of militarism. Exhibiting the characteristics of hierarchical control and contempt for those in inferior positions, these institutions cannot lead to peace. These institutions are the principal arenas of industrialism that Spencer and the peace advocates claimed would lead to peace: limited government and laissez-faire economics in industry and international commerce.

Survivals of Militarism in Government

Addams argues that in spite of the rhetoric of liberty and natural rights, municipal and national governments in the United States contain survivals of militarism and thus function militaristically.[27] Noting how central militarism is to the United States' sense of identity, Addams observes, "Having looked to the sword for independence from oppressive governmental control, they came to regard the sword as an essential part of the government they had succeeded in establishing." While Jefferson proclaimed that "all men are created free and equal," Addams argues that the founders in fact adapted the Anglo-Saxon aristocratic pattern of developing governmental laws and structures that primarily protected the property and privilege of the rich against the poor.[28]

The ideals of the founders were doctrinaire and nonempirical; their language of liberty and rights merely served to mask the people's lived reality. Jefferson's "natural man" with "in-born rights," Addams claims, is a phantom.[29] In Addams's time, 75 percent of Chicago's population were immigrants or children of immigrants.[30] Though a number had immigrated for political freedom, the majority came primarily for economic reasons. Promised a land of freedom and equality, their new lives were better characterized by continual industrial exploitation. Addams argues that those in power continue to cling to cramped governmental ideals, assuming that the franchise and constitutionally defined rights would meet all the immigrants' needs. The immigrants experienced government and law as essentially repressive and punitive rather than as expressions of their own voices as public participants.[31]

To show how this militaristic strain manifests itself, Addams analyzes city and police corruption and corresponding reform efforts, identifying survivals of militarism in both. She draws one example from New York saloons, which were closed by law on Sunday. Community members knew that for many immigrants, the saloon was as much a social gathering place as a site of temptation. Local entrepreneurs kept the saloons open during forbidden hours, paying off the local police and aldermen. These local officials understood the issue from the neighborhood's point of view. Out of both kindness and personal weakness they participated in the corruption. Crusading reformers came along, with grand rhetorical flourishes about eliminating vice and the vicious. After all, in the military mentality, lawbreakers are enemies. As Addams points out, these reformers most often belonged to the business class and were more attuned to safeguarding property than to seeing how the law cramps the normal life impulses of the people. She writes that it is contemptuous for those with political power to make decisions on behalf of people they do not know. Echoing Spencer, she writes that such contempt is a "survival of the spirit of the conqueror toward an inferior people."[32]

Addams takes a second example from women's lack of the franchise in municipal elections, which she interprets as a manifestation of militarism. She responds to the claim, commonly given at that time, that the original function of the feudal city was to protect people from external threats, so the franchise was given to male soldiers as the ones responsible for defense.[33]

Addams points out that the modern city, by contrast, is industrial in Spencer's sense of the word. It is organized as a vast, interdependent whole, functioning for the "sustentation of the group" and at the time, largely independent of government regulation. Its problems are industrial problems: Addams lists them as "insanitary housing, poisonous sewage, contaminated water, infant mortality, the spread of contagion, adulterated food, impure milk, smoke-laden air, ill-ventilated factories, dangerous occupations, juvenile crime, unwholesome crowding, prostitution, and drunkenness." The maladjustment here is that these problems concern everyone, yet the mechanism for addressing them, the franchise, is assigned based on militaristic assumptions, even though military prowess is irrelevant to solving the city's problems.[34]

To build her argument that in order to address these problems, women need the franchise, Addams gives an account of women's traditional labors, using anthropological theories current at the time.[35] From early days of tribal life when almost all economic activity was domestic, women were responsible for health, sanitation, textile and food production, and so on. Modern industry takes these traditional responsibilities away from women and the domestic sphere and moves them into the modern factory. This change creates new hierarchies of wealth and power and reduces women to a state of dependency. To continue to deny women the franchise on the grounds that they do not defend the city militarily perpetuates militarism's hierarchy and its contempt. In this context, gaining the municipal franchise would give women the tools and opportunities they need to resume their historic responsibilities and regain control over the conditions of their labor.[36]

Survivals of Militarism in Industry

Here Addams goes right to the heart of industrialism. She argues that private property in the means of production, which Spencer envisioned as the foundation of laissez-faire capitalism, is itself a survival of militarism. Addams sees a direct, clear analogy between the powers of control private property gives factory owners over workers' lives and militarism's hierarchical control. She writes, "The possessor of the machine, like the possessor of arms who preceded him, regards it as a legitimate weapon for exploitation, as the former held his sword." Addams suggests that had industrial machinery been considered social rather than private property, many of the widespread industrial abuses of her day might have been avoided, such as inadequate wages, child labor, monotonous work, and dangerous workplaces.[37]

In spite of advances in industrial relations made through negotiation and arbitration, Addams saw employers and unions at times exhibiting "group morality," a survival from tribal times. Each side defined morality in terms of loyalty to its own group, viewing those outside as threats. The militaristic survivals embedded in these opposing moral stances were particularly destructive during times of labor tension and strikes. At these times, racial animosity was enflamed as strike breakers were brought in and the public itself became polarized, greatly increasing the probability that violence rather than fair-minded negotiations would end the disputes. Addams characterized the 1905 Chicago teamsters' strike as "street warfare," with employers and the unions "engaged like feudal chiefs with their recalcitrant retainers."[38]

Addams also finds militarism in government and industry's repressive stance toward children. She gives many specific examples of how police, ignoring children's developmental needs for education and recreation, interpret children's vitality as something to repress rather than something to foster. Addams points out the irony: both government and industry show their contempt by their tolerance for child labor, not recognizing how this practice stunts physical growth and health and denies education and development of abilities to their own future citizens and workers.[39]

Militarism in International Commerce

In May 1903 Addams wrote to her publisher, Richard Ely, "The book moves slowly, but I hope to get at it a little later. Hobson has really said it all in his 'Imperialism' which seems to me to be a very masterly presentation of moral and economic claim."[40] Addams uses British economist and journalist John Hobson's analysis of imperialism in identifying militaristic aspects of international commerce. With Hobson she argues that much of international commerce at the time was not free trade "weaving a web of concord among nations"; rather, it provided the justification for and the impetus behind imperialism.

The historical context for Hobson and Addams was late-nineteenth-century European and American imperialism. The rate and success of European imperialism was staggering. Between 1876 and 1914 a handful of European nations gained colonial control of one-fourth of the world's landmass, primarily in Africa and Asia. Britain added four million square miles; France added 3.5 million.[41] The acquisition methods were often unspeakably cruel, made unspeakably efficient by the machine gun. Justifications for imperialism were heavily tinged with social Darwinism, and ranged from nationalism to economic viability to the duty to civilize and Christianize nonwhite populations, and as a method for maintaining masculine vigor.[42] The United States got into the act, annexing Hawaii and acquiring Puerto Rico, Guam, and the Philippines in 1898 following the Spanish-American War, and maintaining military and economic control over an ostensibly independent Cuba.[43]

In his highly influential analysis of late-nineteenth-century European and American imperialism, Hobson interpreted imperialism as a deviation from the evolutionary path toward peaceful progress. Hobson entered the debate regarding the economic value of imperialism by arguing that imperialism is extremely advantageous to just one sector of the business community, but harmful to other interests in the home country. The taproot of imperialism, he claims, is the search for foreign investment. Capital accumulates faster than the nation can reinvest it, so financiers look for foreign opportunities. Once investments are made, investments need to be protected. Using their political clout at home, financiers bring the power of government to protect their investments, to further their investments, and to find new locations for investment.[44]

Hobson argued that this explanation applied equally well to the United States, observing, "The adventurous enthusiasm of President Roosevelt and his 'manifest destiny' and 'mission of civilisation' party must not deceive us. It is Messrs. Rockefeller, Pierpont Morgan, Hanna, Schwab, and their associates who need Imperialism. . . . (T)hey desire to use the public resources of their country to find profitable employment for the capital which otherwise would be superfluous."[45]

This expansion of investment proceeds by wars abroad, and has devastating effects on the home country's domestic agenda. Hobson explains that as expenditures for armaments and the military dominate the budget, social reforms in education, housing, and labor conditions are neglected. The mystique of militarism infiltrates people's patterns of thought and action. Patriotic myths are taught as history in the schools. Religion turns imperial and sends its missionaries to civilize and Christianize the heathens. The press is owned by or dependent upon the very financial interests that fuel imperial expansion. Representative government becomes increasingly irrelevant as foreign policy rests in the hands of an unelected few. The institutions so vital to democracy become masks in the service of imperial domination.[46]

Addams builds on Hobson's account in her analysis of international trade. With the Spanish-American War a fresh memory, Addams did not need to search for survivals of militarism in international commerce. Here, militarism, "the philosophy of force," was fresh and explicit. This explanation and defense of militarism was advocated by Germans such as Bismarck, von Moltke, and Treischke, and by British theorists such as Karl Pearson.[47] Theodore Roosevelt's "manifest destiny" was an American version of the same vision. In a speech to the Naval War College, Roosevelt told his audience, "All the great masterful races have been fighting races. . . . No triumph of peace is quite so great as the supreme triumph of war."[48] Addams responds to those who claim this "war spirit" is "interwoven with every fibre of human growth and is at the root of all that is noble and courageous in human life." She agrees that courage and energetic response are admirable qualities, but argues that war as a method of social change is "clumsy and barbaric" and will not advance social justice. International commerce, she writes, "has been the result of business aggression and constantly appeals for military defense and for the forcing of new markets." Addams identifies such commerce as "the modern representative of conquest."[49]

Her comments could have been directed at fellow anti-imperialists such as Jordan, Carnegie, and Atkinson, as well as at explicit imperialists such as Theodore Roosevelt. At that time the dominant debate regarding the Spanish-American War and imperialism was more a debate over whether the Philippines should be made a United States colony than over the morality of expansionist foreign policy and commerce. The majority of the dominant peace advocates were blind to the connection between economics and imperialism. Jordan, for example, had praised the American capitalists' "peaceful conquest of Mexico." He had opposed colonizing the Philippines, thinking that its inhabitants could not become civilized and were incapable of self-government.[50]

Addams brought the question squarely back to morality and democracy, claiming that commercial imperialism had a devastating impact on both. She had argued in a speech to the Central Anti-Imperialist League in April 1899 that militarism "can never be made a democratic instrument."[51] When such militaristic international commerce contributes to national prosperity, people are apt to "take the commercial view of life" and define national success in terms of business profits. As evidence for how the moral basis of democracy is lost, Addams points to the contempt businesses show for the workers at home, particularly immigrants, when they are unconcerned with their workers' low standard of life.[52]

Pairing international commerce with governmental military aggression also damages the possibility of democracy in the invaded country. Addams responds to the argument, frequently made at the time, that Europe and the United States were bringing the blessings of civilization to the unenlightened. To do this with military force, Addams argues, is counterproductive. "Militarism enforces law and order and insists upon obedience and discipline, assuming that it will ultimately establish righteousness and foster progress. In order to carry out this good intention, it first of all clears the decks of impedimenta, although in the process it may extinguish the most precious beginnings of self-government and the nucleus of self-help, which the wise of the native community have long been anxiously hoarding."[53]

At the end of *Newer Ideals* Addams defines peace not as "an absence of war, but the unfolding of world-wide processes making for the nurture of human life."[54] That is, for Addams, peace is defined in terms of structures of social justice. By pointing out survivals of militarism under industrialism, with their hierarchical control and contempt, she has identified structures of social injustice that even in the absence of war hinder the nurturing of human life.

Toward Humanitarianism and Peace

Newer Ideals is a hopeful book. While Addams identifies survivals of militarism in the society, she also identifies dynamic, transnational social forces at work. These could provide a moral substitute for war and thus help society progress from the stage of industrialism to a further stage of humanitarianism, which would be an era of international peace.

There are several points of continuity between Addams's 1902 book *Democracy and Social Ethics* and *Newer Ideals of Peace.* Both books deal with social reform, arguing that communities and civic and national governments should be engaged in ensuring standards of decent well-being for all inhabitants. The books put forward the same conception of social democracy as a form of associated living, extending to communities and industry as well as to political institutions. Responding to needs, developing capabilities and powers, and fostering cooperative methods of addressing concerns with affection and respect for all its varied members are the hallmarks of social democracy.[55]

Both books also employ a parallel form of argument, a parallel that in *Newer Ideals* further confirms that it is fundamentally a book about peace. In *Democracy and Social Ethics* Addams argues that because society has evolved into an era of urban industrialization, a corresponding evolution in morality is needed. People need to move from individual morality, characterized by individual virtues, to social morality, or social democracy, in which the social point of view is paramount. Throughout the book Addams gives evidence that the poor and oppressed, and particularly recent immigrants, are already making this adjustment. In *Newer Ideals of Peace* Addams presents a parallel argument: that we need to move from nation-centered patriotism and nationalism to a cosmopolitan humanitarianism and internationalism. Throughout *Newer Ideals* Addams claims that such a humanitarian stage is beginning to emerge out of industrialism and she gives evidence that the poor and oppressed, particularly recent immigrants, have moved quite a ways along this trajectory.[56]

The Newer Ideals: from Industrialism to Humanitarianism

At the 1904 Universal Peace Congress in Boston, Addams and William James both spoke at the closing banquet. In *Newer Ideals* Addams refers to James's speech there, writing, "An American philosopher has lately reminded us of the need to 'discover in the social realm the moral equivalent for war—something heroic that will speak to men as universally as war has done, and yet will be as compatible with their spiritual natures as war has proved itself to be incompatible.'"[57] These emerging humanitarian ideals, Addams claims, meet James's criteria. These ideals are indicative of forces that are "strenuous" and "aggressive." For the heroism of war, they will substitute the heroism "which pertains to labor and the nourishing of human life," evolving toward a time when "virile good-will will be substituted for the spirit of warfare."[58]

Addams refers to this new, emerging stage of humanitarianism variably as "an enlightened industrialism," an "enlarged industrialism," "a rising tide of humanitarianism," and even "cosmopolitan humanitarianism."[59] This is a stage that seeks "that which will secure the health, the peace of mind, and the opportunity for normal occupation and spiritual growth to the humblest industrial worker, as the foundation for a rational conduct of life adapted to an industrial and cosmopolitan era."[60]

Addams claims that these newer ideals of peace are emerging in several different international arenas. She sees manifestations of these ideals based on "a new vital relation—that of the individual to the race."[61] Though *Democracy and Social Ethics* stresses social morality among members of a local or national community, *Newer Ideals* explicitly extends the scope of community to the international arena, encompassing all of humanity. For twenty-first-century readers, the term "transnational" is more appropriate than "international." For Addams, the nation-state was not the primary unit of analysis; "international" to her did not refer only to a collection of separate, sovereign states. She saw many sorts of community groupings forming cosmopolitan, transnational ties and acting upon humanitarian ideals.[62]

In *Newer Ideals* Addams gives particular attention to how these ideals were emerging among immigrants in urban communities, such as the one where Hull-House was located. Addams gives several reasons why immigrants are likely to recast their ideals and sensibilities toward internationalism and humanitarianism. Immigrants from disparate nations, stripped of the contexts of traditional village life, gather into tightly congested urban settings. They are "reduced to fundamental equalities and universal necessities of human life." Using the vocabulary of social evolutionary theory, Addams writes that they need, simultaneously, to reconstitute tribal bonds of compassion and to break through tribal bonds to attain cosmopolitan relations. Because they are in the midst of dealing with such a cultural transition, they have "an unusual mental alertness and power of perception." Addams sees among the immigrants countless acts of kindness toward each other, repeatedly exhibiting "an unquenchable desire that charity and simple justice shall regulate men's relations." In such neighborhoods, Addams finds evidence that nationalistic patriotism is being reconfigured into internationalism. "They are really attaining cosmopolitan relations through daily experience," Addams notes, and forecasts the implications for international peace. "We may then give up war, because we shall find it as difficult to make war upon a nation at the other side of the globe as upon our next-door neighbor."[63]

It was not only among immigrants to the United States that Addams saw evidence of the newer ideals. Addams was in contact with social justice reformers in other nations, and points to protective legislation from many nations as evidence that the newer ideals were emerging internationally. She cites the international effort to eliminate tuberculosis; efforts in Germany, Australia, and elsewhere to respond to the needs of the elderly; and efforts in England and on the European continent to regulate dangerous occupations.[64]

Addams also sees evidence of new humanitarian ideals guiding the labor movement, in spite of or alongside the survivals of militarism she finds there. Unions at the time were working toward fair wages and decent, safe working conditions, the sorts of provisions for humane life with which government ought to be concerned. Through union activity, workers had many more opportunities for democratic discussion and decision making than they had in political arenas. This was particularly true for working women, who at the time could not vote in federal elections and only spottily in municipal affairs. Also, unions were quite conscious of the burdens war imposes upon the working classes. Addams notes the resolution of the International Association of Workingmen to call for a universal strike among workers in the event of war.[65]

In all the examples given above, these humanitarian ideals give Addams a way to articulate the clear link she sees between social justice and peace. This realization marks a clear difference between Addams's newer ideals of peace and the ideals of the practical advocates of peace. As members of business and legal elites, they benefited from and in some cases actively perpetuated institutions and practices of social injustice. The practical peace advocates understood "international" as the arena in which separate, independent, sovereign nations met to work through differences either through war or through diplomacy. Their advocacy of international legal institutions was meant to strengthen the alternatives to war available to these states without threatening their independence or sovereignty. They did not regard unjust practices within sovereign states or by nonstate actors as germane to questions of peace.[66] Addams projects that if these newer, humanitarian ideals are deepened and made more active throughout the world, the strictures of nationalism will be transformed into a peaceful internationalism. Like James, Addams admires the patriotic virtues of self-surrender and high enthusiasm. However, these virtues need to be detached from a militaristic nationalism, with its tribal attachment to arbitrary borders, and attached to humanitarian commitments on an international scale. Admitting the term sounds absurd, Addams offers "cosmic patriotism" as one way of articulating this transformation.[67]

At the end of the book, Addams brings in a Bible passage, one very familiar to peace advocates, to underscore the relation between peace and social justice. She interprets the prophet Isaiah's call to turn swords into plowshares, writing, "He founded the cause of peace upon the cause of righteousness, not only as expressed in political relations, but also in industrial relations."[68] This underscores just how radical her peace proposal was and how deeply she believed that social justice and peace must go hand in hand if we are to have either. *Newer Ideals of Peace* is an extended argument to make exactly that point.

Notes

1. Kelley's review (1907) can be found at *The Jane Addams Papers, 1860–1960,* ed. Mary Lynn McCree Bryan (Ann Arbor, Mich.: University Microfilms International, 1984), addendum 11:201. The microfilm collection is referred to as JAPM, the Jane Addams Papers, microfilm; Allen F. Davis, *American Heroine: The Life and Legend of Jane Addams* (Chicago: Ivan R. Dee, 2000), 146; George Herbert Mead, "Review of Newer Ideals of Peace," *American Journal of Sociology* 13 (July 1907): 128.

2. JAPM 4:1478, October 15, 1906.

3. Addams, *Newer Ideals of Peace* (Urbana: University of Illinois Press, 1907/2007), 5.

4. Her three speeches can be found in *Jane Addams's Writings on Peace,* vol. 4, *Addams's Essays and Speeches on Peace,* ed. Marilyn Fischer and Judy D. Whipps (Bristol, U.K.: Thoemmes Press, 2003), 31–37; and in the *Official Report of the Thirteenth Universal Peace Congress* (Boston: The Peace Congress Committee, 1904), 120–23, 145–47, 261–62.

5. For a discussion of peace societies advocating nonresistance, see David S. Patterson, *Toward a Warless World* (Bloomington: Indiana University Press, 1976), 3–5; For discussions of "practical" advocates of peace, see Sondra R. Herman, *Eleven Against War* (Stanford, Calif.: Hoover Institution Press, 1969), 16–19; Merle Curti, *Peace or War: The American Struggle, 1636–1936* (Boston: J.S. Canner & Company,

1959), 206–7; C. Roland Marchand, *The American Peace Movement and Social Reform, 1898–1918* (Princeton, N.J.: Princeton University Press, 1972), chapters 2–3.

6. Marchand, *The American Peace Movement,* chapter 2; Herman, *Eleven Against War,* chapter 2.

7. Herman, *Eleven Against War,* 24.

8. Oscar Straus, "Address," *Thirteenth Universal Peace Congress,* 62, 63.

9. Marchand, *The American Peace Movement,* 86; See the address by Samuel B. Capen, *Thirteenth Universal Peace Congress,* 84–87.

10. John Lund, "Address," *Thirteenth Universal Peace Congress,* 104; Edward Atkinson, "Address," *Thirteenth Universal Peace Congress,* 109.

11. Richard Hofstadter, *Social Darwinism in American Thought* (Boston: Beacon Press, 1983), 32; Addams makes three references to Spencer in *Twenty Years at Hull-House* (Urbana: University of Illinois Press, 1990), 200, 231, 236, none of them complimentary.

12. For an extensive discussion of the development of Spencer's social Darwinism, see Robert C. Bannister, *Social Darwinism: Science and Myth in Anglo-American Social Thought* (Philadelphia: Temple University Press, 1979), especially chapter 2.

13. Herbert Spencer, *The Principles of Sociology,* vol. 1, part 2 (New York: D. Appleton and Co., 1896), 546.

14. Ibid., 596, 577.

15. Ibid., 552, 549; vol. 2, part 2, 578.

16. Spencer, *The Principles of Sociology,* vol. 1, part 2, 552.

17. Spencer did not consider socialist or communist societies to be industrial, because they are structured on the basis of "compulsory cooperation." *The Principles of Sociology,* vol. 2, part 2, 604, 607–9.

18. Ibid., 663–65.

19. For extended discussions of Spencer's influence in the United States, see Bannister, *Social Darwinism;* and Hofstadter, *Social Darwinism,* chapter 2. For discussions of Spencer's influence on the practical peace advocates, see Marchand, *The American Peace Movement,* 83; Curti, *Peace or War,* 119–20, 127.

20. Addams, *Newer Ideals,* 65, 36.

21. Ibid., 7; the quotation is from L. T. Hobhouse, *Democracy and Reaction* (London: T. Fisher Unwin, 1904), 199.

22. Addams, *Newer Ideals,* 114, 101.

23. The review was published in Baltimore, February 16, 1907. It is hostile to Addams, and very hostile to sociology. JAPM Addendum 11:0217.

24. Addams, *Newer Ideals,* 18.

25. For an excellent discussion of Addams's pragmatism, see Charlene Haddock Seigfried's introduction to *Addams, Democracy and Social Ethics* (Urbana: University of Illinois Press, 1902/2002). For a discussion of Addams's involvement with Chicago sociologists of the time, see Mary Jo Deegan, *Jane Addams and the Men of the Chicago School, 1892–1918* (New Brunswick, N.J.: Transaction Press, 1990).

26. Edward Burnett Tylor, *The Origins of Culture* (New York: Harper & Row, 1958), 16. (Part I was originally published as *Primitive Culture* in 1871.)

27. See Camilla Stivers's discussion of similar material in "A Civic Machinery for Democratic Expression: Jane Addams on Public Administration," in this volume.

28. Addams, *Newer Ideals,* 22, 20, 32.

29. Ibid., 19, 35.

30. Victoria Bissell Brown, *The Education of Jane Addams* (Philadelphia: University of Pennsylvania Press, 2004), 212.

31. Addams, *Newer Ideals,* chapter 2.

32. Ibid., 33–35, 29.

33. Ibid., 100–101. This argument was commonly used at the time. See Marchand, *The American Peace Movement,* 200–201. Spencer held this position: see *The Principles of Sociology,* vol. 1, part 2, 757.

34. Addams, *Newer Ideals,* 101.

35. This account can be found in Otis Tufton Mason, *Woman's Share in Primitive Culture* (New York: D. Appleton and Co., 1898).

36. Addams, *Newer Ideals,* 113–15. Addams was vice president of the National American Woman Suffrage Association for five years. Unlike many of her colleagues at the time, she does not base her argument for women's suffrage on equal rights, nor on the separate spheres' assumption that women will be able to purify politics. Instead, Addams argues that women should have the franchise because they have the experience and the expertise to attend to the city's industrial problems. It is a matter of being given the tools that dealing with these industrial problems requires.

37. Addams, *Newer Ideals,* 82.

38. Ibid., 67, 78–79, 73.

39. Ibid., 91–93.

40. May 3, 1903, JAPM 4:600. For further discussion of Addams's analyses of internationalism and imperialism, see Wendy Sarvasy, "A Global 'Common Table': Jane Addams's Theory of Democratic Cosmopolitanism and World Social Citizenship," in this volume.

41. Eric Hobsbawm, *The Age of Empire: 1875–1914* (New York: Vintage Books, 1987), 59.

42. Hobsbawm, *Empire,* chapter 3.

43. Howard Zinn, *A People's History of the United States* (New York: HarperCollins, 1995), 303–4.

44. Hobson, *Imperialism,* 10–11, 51, 60.

45. Ibid., 82–83.

46. Ibid., 228–34.

47. See Barbara W. Tuchman, *The Proud Tower* (New York: Ballantine Books, 1994), 243, 249–50, and Niall Ferguson, *Empire* (New York: Basic Books, 2003), 261.

48. Quoted in Zinn, *A People's History,* 293. Roosevelt criticized Addams's argument in Newer Ideals, stating, "Militarism is a real factor for good or for evil in

most European countries. In America it has not the smallest effect one way or the other; it is a negligible quantity." See Theodore Roosevelt, "Tolstoy," *Outlook* (May 15, 1909): 104.

49. Addams, *Newer Ideals,* 116–17, 118, 64.

50. Quoted in Patterson, *Toward a Warless World,* 76–77. See David Starr Jordan, *Imperial Democracy* (Boston: Women's Educational and Industrial Union Leaflet #8, 1898), 3–4.

51. Addams, *Essays and Speeches,* 3.

52. Addams, *Newer Ideals,* 123, 64–65.

53. Ibid., 121–22.

54. Ibid., 131.

55. See, for example, ibid., 28–29, 41, 52.

56. Addams, *Newer Ideals,* 11–12. Others used this same vocabulary. On page 12 of *Newer Ideals,* Addams cites Adna Ferrin Weber, who used the same vocabulary in *The Growth of Cities in the Nineteenth Century* (New York: Macmillan, 1899), 434. Weber cites British philosopher John S. Mackenzie, who also identifies the age of humanitarianism with legislation for personal welfare, and identifies industrialism with laissez-faire capitalism. See John S. Mackenzie, *An Introduction to Social Philosophy* (Glasgow: James Maclehose & Sons, 1890), 78–81.

57. Quoted in Addams, *Newer Ideals,* 16. James's original speech is in "Address," *Thirteenth Universal Peace Congress,* 266–69. Though Addams speaks here appreciatively of James's speech, her own position differs significantly from his. For a comparison, see Marilyn Fischer, "Jane Addams's Pragmatist Pacifism," in *Peacemaking: Lessons from the Past, Visions for the Future,* eds. Judith Presler and Sally J. Scholz (Atlanta: Rodopi, 2000), 209–10.

58. Addams, *Newer Ideals,* 8, 16, 17. Thomas Carlyle, whom Addams studied extensively, articulated this vision of peace. See *Thirteenth Universal Peace Congress,* 83.

59. Addams, *Newer Ideals,* 131, 82, 55, 43.

60. Ibid., 14.

61. Ibid., 14.

62. Herman refers to Addams's sense of internationalism as "community internationalism." Herman, *Eleven Against War,* 7–10 and chapter 5. Hansen classifies Addams as a "cosmopolitan patriot," along with James, Dewey, Debs, Du Bois, and others. See Jonathan M. Hansen, *The Lost Promise of Patriotism: Debating American Identity, 1890–1920* (Chicago: University of Chicago Press, 2003), xiv.

63. Addams, *Newer Ideals,* 11, 10, 13.

64. Ibid., 16–17; 105. For documentation of Addams's long association with social justice feminists in Europe, see Kathryn Kish Sklar, Anja Schüler, and Susan Strasser, eds., *Social Justice Feminists in the United States and Germany: A Dialogue in Documents, 1885–1933* (Ithaca, N.Y.: Cornell University Press, 1998).

65. Addams, *Newer Ideals,* 63.

66. Herman, *Eleven Against War,* 40–41.

67. Addams, *Newer Ideals,* 120, 130–31. James used the term "cosmic patriotism" in another context in *The Varieties of Religious Experience* (1902) (New York: Modern Library, 1994), 52.

68. Addams, *Newer Ideals,* 131. Addams mentions in the text that Isaiah's prophesy was referred to at the *Thirteenth Universal Peace Congress.* The irony is that the practical peace advocates used Isaiah's words to support their proposals for international arbitration and not, as Addams did, to support social justice reforms in industry.

9

A Global "Common Table"

Jane Addams's Theory of Democratic Cosmopolitanism and World Social Citizenship

WENDY SARVASY

The purpose of this essay is to recover Jane Addams's overlooked contribution to thinking beyond the nation-state, so that her insights can be incorporated into contemporary theorizing about how to take democracy to a transnational level. This new problem emerged in a period of hopefulness at the end of the cold war. The effectiveness of nonstate human rights activists in campaigns, such as the one to end the use of land mines, and the evolution of the European Union created new relations across borders that challenged the old boundaries of state-centric notions of democracy. Needing a new expansive language, theorists revived and proposed ways to democratize the cosmopolitan tradition of thought with its vision of multi-leveled governance and world citizenship.[1] In a very different time, Addams also turned to this tradition and proposed answers to questions that are once again being raised: What are the sources of cosmopolitan ethics? How are diversity and transnationalism interconnected? Is a democratic version of world social citizenship viable? Addams's explicit and implicit answers came out of her opposition to the U.S.–forced annexation of the Philippines in 1899 and to the United States' entry into World War I. Formulated as a substitute for imperialism and militarized nationalism, her theory of democratic transnationalism has become even more relevant in the post-911 context, which has put on the defensive those who hold contemporary cosmopolitan commitments to multilateral governance and human rights.

Addams's originality as a theorist rested on her application of a pragmatist method of analysis that set up a tension between experience and theoretical or ideological concepts.[2] She used the method to show that the concepts no longer fit the experience and that the experience, properly understood, pointed to new concepts and understandings. Addams viewed experience through the eyes of a theorist who "ascend[s] to a more enveloping point of view."[3] She also uncovered how the proper interpretation of the memory of experience could provide "a selective agency in social reorganization."[4] Yet she assumed that old concepts would not be abandoned unless "substitutes" were presented. So she articulated those substitutes, although she declared that "it is hard to formulate" them.[5]

Specifically, to challenge the late-nineteenth-century justifications of U.S. imperialism based on a hierarchy of civilizations and a paternalistic understanding of the United States' role in the world, Addams pointed to migrant workers, transnational families, and acts of solidarity among immigrant working-class men and women, and she theorized the significance of these cross-border relations of mutual aid for a democratic rethinking of cosmopolitan ethics and international relations. To flesh out how to demilitarize nationalism, Addams connected two experiences: the Allied governmental coordination of food provision during World War I and women's subconscious memory of their primitive role as bread laborers. She theorized a new feminized transnational food politics that could be coordinated by the League of Nations (LON) and supported by cross-class alliances of women, who would respond to global food needs through their daily habits. Exposing the contradictions between "genuine" experience and understandings, and pointing to the potential for new cross-border relationships to generate new understandings, Addams argued, did not guarantee results. As a theorist, she aimed to create alternative ways of thinking to open up a space for "hope" that a new internationalism was possible.[6]

By grounding her vision of transnational democracy in the *potential* of these new relations across borders, Addams's theory provides a missing component in current thinking. In answer to the first question about the sources of cosmopolitan ethics, Held advocates the promulgation of a new cosmopolitan public law by expanding Kant's universal right to hospitality. Held's legalistic answer rests on a distinction between international law that applies to nation-states and cosmopolitan or human rights law to which individuals can appeal outside the authority of nation-states.[7] Drawing on the Stoics and Kant's moral theory, Nussbaum's answer is to embrace rationally derived universal humanistic values, such as the equal moral worth of each individual.[8] Rejecting abstract universals, Rorty proposes sentiments as the source of cosmopolitan ethics. Though he claims he would "prefer a bottom-up way of achieving utopia," he does not believe it likely; therefore he argues for using stories to manipulate the sentiments of elites to support a "human rights culture."[9] Addams's answer was closer to Rorty's, because she also used stories to create empathy across differences and she was critical of an abstract, disembodied rights approach. Yet, unlike Rorty, her focus was always on how to nourish global ethics in the soil of helping and feeding relations with and among the less powerful. Therefore, only Addams's approach offered a way to think about how to democratize cosmopolitan ethics by bringing into the project the less powerful.

In response to the second question of how to integrate ethnic, racial, and cultural pluralism within notions of transnationalism, Habermas proposes one solution: "constitutional patriotism" or agreement on basic constitutional principles, rights, and procedures as the glue that holds together transnational civic identity. To justify this formulation, he rejects European notions of citizenship that use ethnic identity as the basis for civic identity. In making his case for depoliticizing and privatizing ethnicity, Habermas assumes that Western liberal/democratic principles would define the content of transnational "constitutional patriotism."[10] In contrast to Habermas, Addams applied a relational method to discover how new principles and forms of government would come out of the acts of solidarity among peoples in cosmopolitan cities. She pointed to how her neighbors were refounding American democracy as they shifted the relational basis of government from negative protection to positive provision for human welfare. Addams was also very open to learning from different political traditions; in her writings against imperialism, she welcomed the possibility that non-Western peoples could devise new forms and principles of democracy to accompany the evolution of multileveled governance.

With the third question about how to infuse world social citizenship with "democratic processes," Held and Linklater deemphasize the need for a world government, and they point to the participatory possibilities of formal assemblies and transnational civil society.[11] Addams actively supported both. She called for the democratization of the LON and she helped found the Women's International League for Peace and Freedom (WILPF), a player in transnational civil society. Yet because civil society, defined as associational life, is used to demarcate a space antagonistic to formal government, it is an inadequate notion to capture her theoretical contribution. As her feminist-bread politics showed, her theory of transnational democracy rested on interconnecting relations of daily mutual aid to multileveled governmental programs. To support this theory, Addams deepened the meaning of democracy to include a "rule of living."[12] According to this definition, migrant workers and transnational families with their allies were democratizing world social citizenship as they engaged in reciprocal relations of helping across borders. Alliances of women bread providers democratized world social citizenship by turning the management of global food needs into a daily social ecological practice. Starting from participation in daily life, Addams aimed to enlarge the democratic imagination and to empower the less powerful by privileging their experiences in order to bring them in as agents of change.

Thus I will argue that Addams, through the application of her pragmatist method, exposed the necessary relational foundations for a democratic vision of multileveled governance. To demonstrate this argument, I will construct her two-part vision, which illustrates her relational insight, and I will draw out the implications of the vision for a notion of democratic world social citizenship. The first part of the vision revealed the potential of global cities with immigrant communities and migrant workers to generate new democratic cosmopolitan ethics, and to initiate new principles and forms of democratic social politics, locally and globally. I prefer the term democratic social politics to social democracy, because I want to emphasize the participatory aspect of the partnership of democracy and the social, or the provision of social welfare. While the first part of the vision pointed to the need for new transnational institutions, the second part evolved within the context of an actual experience of transnational governmental provision of food. The second part of the vision outlined how cross-class alliances of women could support new global democratic social ethics through feminist bread politics. Both parts of Addams's vision suggested a notion of global social citizens as active synthesizers of local, national, and international relations directed at sustaining life.

Vision Part I: Local Genesis of a New Internationalism

In presenting the first part of Addams's vision, I challenge Elshtain's characterization of Addams's method of theorizing about the genesis of transnationalism as the presentation of an untenable analogy between immigrant neighbors and nation-states. Elshtain argues that Addams assumed that if neighbors in a cosmopolitan city could get along, then nation-states could also enjoy peaceful relations. Elshtain dismisses this reasoning by analogy as naïve, because she argues that relations between neighbors in the United States are peaceful because of law enforcement. At the international level, there is no world government capable of enforcing international law; therefore the analogy falls apart.[13] In presenting this interpretation, Elshtain ignores completely how Addams's political opposition to U.S. imperialism in the Philippines led her to apply her pragmatist relational method of theorizing. Instead of resting her theorizing on an analogy, I argue, Addams pointed to how immigrants in cosmopolitan cities were creating a web of relations across borders that could inoculate them against the appeal of militarized nationalism carried out through expansionism.

For example, Addams presented a discussion of patriotism and how her immigrant neighbors were "developing the only sort of patriotism consistent with the intermingling of the nations."[14] Why was this? They did not want to be forced to choose between two allegiances: to their country of birth or to their adopted country. In modern terms, Addams supported dual citizenship[15] and "the hope" of creating a larger patriotism she called "cosmic patriotism," because it would "overcome arbitrary boundaries and soak up the notion of nationalism." Once "the citizens of a cosmopolitan quarter" evolved to this extent, she envisioned the following: "We may then give up war, because we shall find it as difficult to make war upon a nation at the other side of the globe as upon our next-door neighbor."[16] None of her analysis rested on the role of the law, local or international; instead it rested on immigrants maintaining and deepening the significance of cross-border relations and allegiances. Residents in global cities would learn to resist the demonization of foreign peoples as the pretext for imperialism, because they would have ties to those peoples.

To speak out against U.S. imperialism in the Philippines, Addams, as theorist, sought to articulate "substitutes" for the Anglo-Saxon "ethics of dominion, the political and industrial control of one nation by another."[17] She argued that this ethical stance did not fit the growing relations of mutual respect and economic interdependence generated by the movement of peoples around the world.[18] Drawing on the democratic potential of the cross-border relations of her immigrant neighbors, Addams called on the United States "to trust" democracy at home and abroad.[19] To clarify what she meant, I develop two themes: the democratization of cosmopolitan ethics and the beginnings of a multileveled development of democratic social politics. Both themes offered a vision of how to refound international relations, not because neighbors are like states but because neighbors in global cities are linked through transnational families to people in other parts of the world. Through these themes, Addams created a vision of multileveled democratic governance that was moored to cross-border relations of daily life, defined as a democratic practice of providing for the global human welfare.

DEMOCRATIC COSMOPOLITAN ETHICS

When Addams characterized her working-class immigrant neighbors as "cosmopolitan," she was pointing to how they were democratizing a concept previously defined in reference only to scholars and international congresses.[20] Addams did not assume her neighbors were consciously trying to create new cosmopolitan relations of interdependence or that as individuals they were embracing a universal ethic of helping. As she observed, "It is not that they are shouting for peace—on the contrary, if they shout at all, they will continue to shout for war—but that they are really attaining cosmopolitan relations through daily experience. . . . [B]elow their shouting, they are living in the kingdom of human kindness."[21] As a theorist, Addams was constructing a notion of democratic cosmopolitanism based on the potential of the relations among her neighbors.

Addams argued that when her diverse neighbors confronted the "universal necessities of human life itself" they did not turn to a survival of the fittest ethic.[22] Instead they helped each other as they "inevitably develop[ed] the power of association which comes from daily contact with those who are unlike each other . . ." The workplace was one setting where, for example, "a Southern Italian Catholic" might be "forced by the very exigencies of the situation to make friends with an Austrian Jew representing another nationality and another religion."[23] Addams used this example to show how common economic interest could be the basis for building relations across differences.

She was also struck by the willingness to help that was so characteristic in her working-class neighborhood. For example, a man might volunteer to spend seven nights on a park bench, so his wife's pregnant friend would have a bed.[24] "When looked at too closely," Addams acknowledged, "this nascent morality disappears, and one can count over only a thousand kindly acts and neighborly offices." Yet her pragmatist method did not limit her to enumerating individual acts of kindness. As a theorist, she insisted, "when meditated upon in the whole," she found "suggestions" of a new ethic that could radiate out from the neighborhood to the global context. Thus she argued that through their helping relations, her neighbors were "laying the simple and inevitable foundations for an international order as the foundations of tribal and national morality have already been laid."[25]

Addams's notion of democratic cosmopolitan ethics went far beyond Kant's formulation of "universal hospitality" as the core rationally derived "cosmopolitan right" that he distinguished from philanthropy. Kant derived "the right of the stranger not to be treated with hostility when he arrives on someone else's territory" from "our right to communal possession of the earth's surface." Though Kant's "cosmopolitan right" was quite limited, because it did not include "the right of the guest," or a right to citizenship, it supported Addams's theme of the significance of international travel for generating the relational foundations for the new cosmopolitanism. Yet Addams challenged Kant's antidemocratic hierarchy of host and stranger. According to Kant, the stranger "can indeed be turned away, if this can be done without causing his death."[26] Addams stressed reciprocal relations of helping among strangers as a key cosmopolitan relationship. Instead of hospitality as a negative and presumably temporary relationship, Addams was proposing a positive embracing of social interdependence that required breaking with a disembodied, individualistic approach to cosmopolitanism.

Nussbaum presents one version of the individualistic argument when she asserts that the embracing of a cosmopolitan outlook "is often a lonely business. . . . [I]t offers only reason and the love of humanity, which may seem at times less colorful than other sources of belonging."[27] In contrast, Addams rejected the appeal to an abstract "love of humanity" because it resulted in loving "the people without really knowing them." She aimed "to dissolve 'humanity' into its component parts of men, women, and children." Her cosmopolitanism emerged out of addressing specific "needs with an enthusiasm which . . . can be sustained only by daily knowledge and constant companionship."[28] For Addams, cosmopolitanism was fundamentally about forging new interdependent relationships, including cross-class alliances, between individuals in all their complexity and specificity.

Addams's concept was also quite different from Pogge's disembodied, individualistic version. According to him, one essential ingredient of "all cosmopolitan positions . . . is individualism . . . rather than, say, family lines, tribes, ethnic, cultural, or religious communities, nations, or states."[29] Addams rejected the opposition between cosmopolitanism and collective identities. She did not believe that a new ethic of "cosmopolitan humanitarianism" could or should ignore "national differences." So she used interchangeably the concepts of "new cosmopolitanism" and "new internationalism" as she set out a dual project: to maintain the integrity of nationalities to provide "compassion and kindliness" and to forge new humane relations between nationalities. In her cosmopolitan neighborhood, Addams found "the condition for breaking into this double development; for making a fresh start . . . toward a synthesis upon a higher moral line which shall include both."[30] For this new synthesis to flourish, it required the constant support of new governmental forms of institutionalization.

COSMOPOLITAN RELATIONS AS A DEMOCRATIZING FORCE

Through her interactions with her cosmopolitan neighbors, Addams discovered "the newer manifestations of government, in which personal welfare is considered a legitimate object." She argued that her neighbors would not be satisfied with privatized helping alone; rather, they "persistently expected that [their kindheartedness] shall be given some form of governmental expression," including at the transnational level. To show how the new cosmopolitan relations were generating a new model of democracy, Addams posited "a new history of government" that "begins with an attempt to make life possible and human in large cities."[31] Thus Addams's analysis uncovered how cosmopolitan relations provided a motor for the evolution of democratic social politics in the United States and beyond.

Addams presented her new evolution of government as a response to "[t]he constant cry that American institutions are in danger"[32] because of immigrants. She argued that the institutions, not the immigrants, were inadequate. Designed according to an outdated eighteenth-century framework, the institutions combined an "unbending theory of individualism" with "an inherited belief in America that government is of necessity oppressive, and its functions not to be lightly extended."[33] By holding on to the ideas of the Founders, Addams pointed out, "We ignore the fact that world-wide problems can no longer be solved by a political constitution assuring us against opposition." Addams held out the possibility that an ethnically diverse working class, not "stranded on the rock of Anglo-Saxon individualistic ownership,"[34] could bring the needed changes by undoing a laissez-faire structuring of democracy.

To achieve this end, the experiences, needs, and agency of the immigrants would have to drive the new evolution of government. Addams criticized her audience for failing to consider the "political ideals" of different immigrant groups. As she explained, "[I]n our overwhelming ambition to remain Anglo-Saxon, we have fallen into the Anglo-Saxon temptation of governing all peoples by one standard. We have failed to work out a democratic government which should include the experiences and hopes of all the varied people among us."[35] Clearly, she did not support a process of simply combining a privatized ethnicity with the existing constitutional principles. She looked to the immigrants to redesign the principles as they helped to create a democratic social cosmopolitan conception of government.

This defense of non–Anglo-Saxon contributions to the evolution of democracy grew from her engagement with the debate over Philippine annexation. Pro-imperialists, like Theodore Roosevelt, asserted the superiority of Anglo-Saxons, with their traditions of the town meeting. He argued that democracy could not be spread around the world without military occupation.[36] In response, Addams counterposed self-government and empire. She argued that self-government could not be exported, for "all progress must come from the native soil."[37] Military occupation in the name of bringing civilization, Addams argued, would "kill the most precious germs of some exotic contribution to the science of human government," because "it may extinguish the most precious beginnings of self-government and the nucleus of self-help which the wise of the native community have long been anxiously hoarding."[38] This combination of self-government and self-help pointed to new forms of democratic social politics. She advocated trusting "the people although they are a different color, although they are of a different tradition from ours." Through trust, the United States could "nourish them into another type of government, not Anglo-Saxon even."[39] Addams did not spell out her notion of nourish here, except to state that "old and possibly worn out ideas" should not be imposed. Instead she called for experimentation with "the most wonderful thing in the world, a new combination of people coming together in the line of self-government."[40] In this call, she could not rely on the existence of transnational institutions; however they played a crucial role in her theorizing the second part of the vision.

Vision Part II: Feminist Multileveled Bread Politics

In presenting the second part of the vision, I offer a critique of and an alternative formulation to Elshtain's presentation of what I call feminist multileveled bread or food politics. When she asserts that Addams could not explain the overwhelming support of women for World War I, Elshtain attributes to Addams an essentialist, maternalist view of woman's nature.[41] In her explication of Addams's assertion of "an unalterable cleavage between Militarism and Feminism,"[42] Elshtain also assumes that Addams equated feminism and maternalism. This interpretation leads Elshtain to emphasize that maternalism was the sole basis for Addams's critique of militarized nationalism.[43] Finally, Elshtain argues that Addams hoped to generate a transnational ethic of food provision as emergency humanitarian aid by extending to the global level the bread labor of primitive mothers, who developed agriculture to secure a stable food supply for their children.[44] Elshtain is less pointedly critical of this second type of local/global stretch, perhaps because she depoliticizes it.[45]

In contrast to Elshtain, I honor Addams's pragmatist method that would be violated by an essentialist notion of woman's nature. Addams certainly made rhetorical appeals to women as mothers, especially in the period before the United States entered World War I. Yet she did not assume that women were inherently opposed to war. The most she could write about the relationship between maternal practice and antimilitarism was to conjecture that mothers who nurture future soldiers "must experience a peculiar revulsion when they see them destroyed, irrespective of the country in which these men may have been born."[46] This "revulsion" was certainly not strong enough to inoculate women against the pull of militarized nationalism. For Addams the theorist, maternal nurturing was only one type of experience that she utilized in thinking about how to demilitarize nationalism. Moreover, Addams assumed that there were two instincts that comprised men and women's human nature: bread labor and fighting in self-defense.[47] Both instincts were "founded upon repeated and unrecorded experiences."[48] Based on this framework, Addams was easily able to explain women's support for war: their self-defense motives overrode or redirected their maternal urges.

I also contextualize Addams's use of the term feminism, because in the pre-1920s period, the combination of gender difference and gender equality was unproblematic. When Addams analyzed the opposition between militarism and feminism, she put the discussion in the mouth of a composite European woman, who in 1915 declared that she had "never been a Feminist." She asserted that feminists "talk of the peculiar contribution women might make to the State," and "It would be absurd for women even to suggest equal rights in a world governed solely by physical force. . . ." While Elshtain overlooks the equal rights statement to make her maternalist interpretation of feminism, by including both statements I show how Addams was seeking a new synthesis of difference and equality. This new synthesis would be possible only by demilitarizing nationalism, because a politics based on force and physical strength blocked women's inclusion in "the consent of the governed."[49]

Addams envisioned women citizens helping to fold a humane nationalism into a multileveled regulation of the world's crucial resources, starting with food. As with her vision of the settlement house, Addams sought not to create a transnationalism based on the unequal charity relationship. Her aim was to eradicate the economic causes of war; therefore emergency humanitarian aid was only one aspect of the vision. To flesh out the second part of her vision, I will analyze how she drew on two experiences: memories of primitive feminine bread labor and the coordination of food production by the Allied nations during the war. She used the former to feminize the latter. She argued that the feminization of transnational democratic social politics opened up spaces for women's political agency, but only if they were prepared to alter radically the domestic/global line.

FEMINIZATION OF TRANSNATIONAL DEMOCRATIC SOCIAL POLITICS

Drawing on anthropology, Addams "uncovered" what she called "sub-conscious memories,"[50] including those of primitive feminine bread labor. As a pragmatist theorist, she viewed memories as "hoarding woman's genuine experiences."[51] To expose the tension between her interpretation of the "genuine" primitive experience and current modes of acting, Addams theorized a distinction between feminine and masculine approaches to food provision. She pointed out that "women were the first agriculturalists" and that primitive women "supplied all cereals and roots eaten by the tribe." The worldwide myths of the "feminine" Corn or Rice Spirit reflected the gendered nature of the primitive division of labor. When women controlled tribal bread production, according to Addams, their only aim was to provide enough food to feed the tribe. As soon as bread production became profitable, men took over. Therefore, the feminine approach stressed "human use," while the masculine approach pursued exchange or "money-making" value. When the Allied governments "suppressed" market forces in order to get food to the hungry, according to Addams, they feminized modern bread politics. Their actions demonstrated that the masculine market approach "could not be trusted to feed the feeble and helpless."[52]

As part of her feminization of bread politics, Addams suggested that cross-border relations created to provide food for use could generate a new transnational democratic social ethic. To bolster her case for the connection between food and ethics, she pointed to how primitive tribal women's aim to grow food for use created the foundations for "our domestic morality and customs." In a parallel fashion, she hoped that new socialized habits of global food provision forged during the war were generating "a new international ethic."[53] In making the comparison, Addams was not arguing that maternalism alone was a sufficient basis for the new transnational ethic. Instead, she emphasized how transnational governmental relations that practiced the feminized food-for-use approach were a necessary condition.

Addams as theorist could feminize transnational bread politics and democratic social ethics, only because she had an actual cross-border experiment from which she could draw out an emancipatory potential. She pointed to the lessons nations were learning in how to make "concessions to the common good that the threat of famine for all might be averted." In the midst of war,

Addams argued "[a] new internationalism was being established day by day. . . ." These new "human relations in world politics" made women's subconscious memory relevant to constructing multileveled bread politics. Prior to this experiment, according to Addams, social democratic projects were located only at local and nation-state levels, not at the international level. After the war, as president of WILPF, she supported the proposals of the British Labor Party to democratize and to extend to all peoples the Allied efforts through the newly created LON. She and the organization completely opposed the use of food as a tool of war and militarism, as in the form of a blockade.[54]

To encourage women to take a leadership role in the new feminized transnational context, so that they could shape policy and provide one relational foundation for the new transnational ethics, Addams drew a feminist lesson from the memory of primitive bread labor. The women of her day should imitate the primitive women, because they succeeded in getting the men to accept a reshaping of tribalism in a more socially humane direction. To build a movement to support the demilitarization of nationalism, Addams understood that women would have to make a deliberate decision to create a new synthesis of domestic and global regulation of food. She called on women to "so enlarge their conception of duty that the consciousness of the world's needs for food should become the actual impulse of their daily activities." She acknowledged that this aim amounted to taking up "the most compelling challenge which has been made upon woman's constructive powers for centuries."[55] Her argument for why women might be receptive to this challenge was that in the early twentieth century, they were both focused on world affairs and engaged in movements to achieve equal rights.[56] The 1915 Hague Congress illustrated how women, not framed as mothers, could engage in cross-border exchanges and could work to insert the centrality of gender democracy into the creation of multileveled governance.[57]

FEMINIST REDESIGNING OF THE DOMESTIC/GLOBAL LINE

To create cross-class alliances of women to expand the relational underpinnings of multileveled governance, Addams called for a feminist redesigning of the household/global line, so that "a synthesis" between "household requirements" and the global need for food could emerge.[58] She assumed most women would require such a synthesis. Because of this aim, her radical critique of the privatized household in her prewar writings and in the way she lived at Hull-House took on a new transnational significance. Central to her critique was an argument against "separate preparation and serving of food" for the isolated home.[59]

As an early twentieth-century feminist, Addams did not call for identical tasks for men and women within the household. Instead she advocated socialized forms of providing food as the means for improving the status of all women and for increasing their ability to be agents of change.[60] At Hull-House there was a dining room where the residents could eat together, and the food was prepared by a unionized, professional staff. Hull-House also experimented with different ways of making prepared meals available to working-class neighbors. Addams believed that the household had to be integrated into the larger industrial and political contexts so that it would not block processes of democratization, locally and globally. In this democratic spirit, she objected to the undemocratic mistress/servant relationship and she supported the trend to professionalize and organize domestic workers.[61]

In calling for the socializing and democratizing of women's domestic duty, Addams emphasized the possibilities for creating new participatory spaces for global bread politics. During the war, she urged women's groups to organize their local communities for concerted action.[62] She suggested that the food supply could be increased "if intelligent women not only worked themselves but organized other women to work with them." She gave the inspiring example of "a city garden plot" that was cultivated by immigrant women.[63] Once women were willing to leave their isolated households to reorganize food production, Addams believed they could develop new cross-class and cross-ethnic democratic relations directed at providing for a global "common table."[64]

The new bread politics certainly involved conflict and negotiation. Addams learned from the failure of Hull-House when it tried to impose standards of a nutritional diet on immigrant communities with their own culinary traditions.[65] As she explained, "To make radical changes in our food habits . . . implies a struggle, none the less real, because it is concerned with domestic adjustments." Through these struggles, Addams envisioned women, in particular, expanding from "the blindness of individuality to the consciousness of common ends . . ."[66] Addams hoped that a feminist redesigning of the domestic/global line would turn women into practitioners of new global democratic social ethics. Thus through her pragmatist method, she showed how cross-class alliances of women in the United States could support democratic social cosmopolitan ethics and a new participatory version of world social citizenship.

WORLD SOCIAL CITIZENSHIP

Although Addams never used the term "world social citizenship," I want to show how her two-part vision suggested a formulation of the concept. My justification for assuming that such a notion does not violate Addams's sensibility or method of theorizing is that in a number of places, she pointed in this direction. She actually used the phrase "citizen of the world" to characterize her immigrant neighbors.[67] She also presented *The Second Twenty Years at Hull-House* as what she called "a record of a growing world consciousness." Because consciousness for Addams was always about new experiences and practices, I assume that the new world consciousness rested on practices of cross-border relations that could be called world social citizenship.

Emphasizing the social dimension of world citizenship puts Addams's theory within the context of discussions of social citizenship and how to take it beyond the nation-state. A Marshallian notion, the predominant one today, is limited to the nation-state. It focuses on the achievement of citizen rights in the area of social welfare, such as health care and education.[68] Addams explicitly called for redesigning international relations according to "motives of humanitarian action" that were shaping nation-state "ameliorative legislation."[69] That this call was compatible with a notion of world social citizenship is supported by the line of thought that led her to posit the need for a concept of "cosmic patriotism." Such a need reflected the growing desire of people to join with the worldwide movement toward social justice that emphasized "the abolition of degrading poverty, disease, and intellectual weakness."[70] Heater uses world social citizenship to capture an unequal philanthropic relationship in which the affluent nations have a duty to aid the less affluent, as in the case of a famine.[71] Through her leadership of WILPF, Addams aimed to seek global structural economic changes, so that charity would not be necessary.

Key to understanding her implicit notion of world social citizenship was her use of the metaphor of concentric circles. Echoing Mazzini, she insisted "the duties of family, nation, and humanity are but concentric circles of one obligation"[72] and that each circle "surrounds and completes" the inner circle(s).[73] As political actors, world social citizens would engage in relationships that synthesize these circles. This extrapolation is justified by Addams's own language. Immigrant neighbors synthesized tribal and intertribal relations; feminist bread providers synthesized the domestic and the global.

Unlike other theorists of world citizenship who use the metaphor of levels or circles to justify the trumping role of the highest level of law[74] or the outer circle of humanity,[75] Addams clearly looked to the crucial humanizing and democratizing relations within the common center to synthesize the circles. While Addams used Mazzini's formulation, which puts the family at the center, I reframe the inner circle to reflect Addams's critique of the privatized family and her broad understanding of nurturing relationships, no longer contained solely within the privatized family. Accordingly I place, in the center, relations of nurturing and helping in the community, the workplace, and the household. Once these relations are put at the center, the practice of world social citizenship has the potential to strengthen the nurturing side of human nature, lessen the destructive gap between "them" and "us," and ultimately forge an actively engaged democratic will on the ground to support transnational institutions.

The metaphor of concentric circles allowed Addams to depict how a private activity could be transformed into a public obligation and a new form of democratic participation, by placing it as the defining core of national and international relations. Addams hoped the politicization and socialization of nurture, practiced in diverse neighborhoods and through bread provision, would enhance its ability to counter and ultimately to replace the aggressive urges as they played out in international affairs. To achieve this end, nurture would have to be attached to the new transnational mechanisms of governance. Here Addams's example was turning the LON into a regulatory body of the world's resources, including food.

According to Addams, the inner circle provided the LON with "a human motive," such as feeding the hungry, that was capable of "transcending and yet embracing all particularist nationalisms." In fact, she argued the focus on food could actually resolve "the more sophisticated questions of national grouping and territorial control."[76] Like most current thinking about going beyond the nation-state,[77] Addams did not call for ending this formation. Instead she proposed the strengthening of ties between transnational institutions and local world social citizenship to pressure nations to join the globalizing of the second stage of democracy.

Addams's focus on the inner circle of relations of helping also offered one way to construct world social citizenship, so that it produced a very inclusive "us" instead of the polarizing superior, helping "us" versus the inferior, needy "them."[78] After the war, in a period of extreme anti-immigrant sentiment, Addams urged native-born Americans to align with the efforts of immigrants, especially within eastern European communities, to provide bread to starving people in their countries of origin. Such new relations with transnational families, according to Addams, would result in "finding a new center and perspective."[79] Both sides would learn a new tolerance as they participated together in a transnational network of interdependence. Such a vision clearly suggested that transnational families and their allies could play a crucial role as synthesizers of local, national, and transnational relations.

In the inner circle of daily relations of providing for human needs, Addams found the forging of a democratic will to support international institutions.

The example she developed was the linking of migrant agricultural workers to the International Labor Organization (ILO), a transnational institution established by the 1919 peace process. To illustrate her aim, Addams reported on conversations with migrant workers in her neighborhood, who followed the discussions on migrant labor at the ILO. They hoped that transnational regulation of the working conditions of migrant workers would follow.[80] Addams argued that a just response from the ILO would result in migrant workers providing a forceful democratic relational foundation to support the strengthening of the ILO and the LON.

Conclusion

I have situated Jane Addams within a late-twentieth-century revival of the cosmopolitan tradition of thought, because it provides a theoretical language that allows me to recover the originality of her contribution to thinking about transnational democracy. I showed that she built her vision from the vantage point of the less powerful: working-class immigrant men and women, and women as a diverse group. She brought them into the cosmopolitan project by showing how relations in daily life could anchor multileveled democratic social ethics and politics, could combine diversity and transnationalism, and could deepen the participatory aspects of world social citizenship.

By looking at both parts of her transnational vision, I showed that her notion of nurture as a driving force for shaping the new transnational democracy was not limited to the mother/child relationship. She applied the notion to relations of helping in her working-class immigrant neighborhood and at Hull-House. She characterized both men and women as capable of participating in nurturing activities. In the end, she crafted an intersectional notion of nurture, because it was shaped by class, gender, race, and ethnicity. Addams analyzed the notion of nurture in a similar fashion to the way Tronto defines care, as an activity engaged in by those in a subordinate position.[81] Addams added to this formulation that a condition of common economic need encouraged practices of helping in daily life.[82] In a multileveled context, a common economic need could be created by a recognition of global interdependence. Her approach could be called a global social ecological understanding of how a range of issues from infectious diseases to climate change could not be addressed successfully without a multileveled response.

To fully incorporate Addams into our twenty-first-century discussions, we have to acknowledge that she presented a romanticized portrait of cosmopolitan neighborhoods. Ethnic cleansing in Bosnia and genocide in Rwanda would appear to discredit Addams's theorizing about the potential of neighbors to further the development of transnational democratic social politics. Of course, she assumed that U.S. cosmopolitan cities could play a unique prefigurative role, because the immigrant neighbors had left behind in their countries of origin the long-festering animosities between various groups. Even if this assumption were accurate for some immigrants, it is not a completely satisfactory response. Addams's participation in the organizing of WILPF congresses, which brought together women from a variety of hostile contexts, suggested another answer: the need for truth and reconciliation processes,[83] so that neighbors could heal from past atrocities and hatreds. This healing process could possibly inoculate neighbors against the appeals of militarized nationalism.

Finally, I want to suggest how Addams's theory of transnational democracy, as a substitute for imperialism and militarized nationalism, has become even more relevant in the post-9/11 climate. By placing transnational families and bread politics at the center of multileveled democratic social politics, Addams's vision challenges each of us to organize our daily lives to further alternatives to the expansionist and militarized approaches to combating terrorism. We can become allies with those Muslim communities in which transnational families are discrediting, through their daily cross-border relations, the "clash of civilizations" justification of imperialism. Through a reorganization of our daily use of food and other basic resources, such as oil, we can help to build a multileveled politics of addressing the underlying economic causes of terrorism. Because Addams integrated theorizing with practice, her vision of democratic cosmopolitanism and world social citizenship provides a timely, hopeful, and compelling participatory method for how to construct, from the bottom up, a global "common table."

Notes

1. Yasemin Nuhoglu Soysal, *Limits of Citizenship: Migrants and Postnational Membership in Europe* (Chicago: University of Chicago Press, 1994); David Held, *Democracy and the Global Order: From Modern State to Cosmopolitan Governance* (Stanford, Calif.: Stanford University Press, 1995); Daniele Archibugi, David Held, and Martin Kohler, eds., *Re-imagining Political Community* (Stanford, Calif.: Stanford University Press, 1998); Jurgen Habermas, *The Inclusion of the Other: Studies in Political Theory* (Cambridge, Mass.: MIT Press, 1998); Bruce Robbins, "Introduction Part I: Actually Existing Cosmopolitanism," in *Cosmopolitics,* ed. Pheng Cheah and Bruce Robbins (Minneapolis: University of Minnesota Press, 1998).

2. Charlene Haddock Seigfried, *Pragmatism and Feminism* (Chicago: University

of Chicago Press, 1996); Charlene Haddock Seigfried, "Socializing Democracy: Jane Addams and John Dewey," *Philosophy of Social Sciences* 29 (June 1999): 207–30; Charlene Haddock Seigfried, introduction to Jane Addams, *The Long Road of Woman's Memory* (Urbana: University of Illinois Press, 2002).

3. Jane Addams, *Newer Ideals of Peace* (London: Macmillan Company, 1907), 19.

4. Addams, *The Long Road of Woman's Memory,* 4–5.

5. Jane Addams, "The New Internationalism," in *Jane Addams on Peace, War, and International Understanding 1899–1932,* ed. Allen Davis (New York: Garland Publishing, 1976), 58–59.

6. Ibid.

7. Held, *Democracy and the Global Order.*

8. Martha Nussbaum, "Patriotism and Cosmopolitanism" and "Reply," in *For Love of Country: Debating the Limits of Patriotism,* ed. Joshua Cohen (Boston: Beacon Press, 1996), 2–17; 131–44.

9. Richard Rorty, "Human Rights, Rationality, and Sentimentality," in *On Human Rights,* ed. Stephen Shute and Susan Hurley (New York: Basic Books, 1993), 130, 117.

10. Habermas, *The Inclusion of the Other.*

11. Held, *Democracy and the Global Order*; Andrew Linklater, "Citizenship and Sovereignty in the Post-Westphalian European State," in *Re-imagining Political Community,* ed. Daniele Archibugi, David Held, and Martin Kohler (Stanford, Calif.: Stanford University Press, 1998), 126.

12. Jane Addams, *Democracy and Social Ethics* (Urbana: University of Illinois Press, 2002), 7.

13. Jean Bethke Elshtain, *Jane Addams and the Dream of American Democracy* (New York: Basic Books, 2002), 220–21.

14. Addams, *Newer Ideals of Peace,* 18.

15. Rivka Lissak, *Pluralism and Progressives: Hull House and The New Immigrants, 1890–1919* (Chicago: University of Chicago Press, 1989), 32.

16. Addams, *Newer Ideals of Peace,* 237, 18–19.

17. Addams, "The New Internationalism," 58; Jane Addams, "Commercialism Disguised as Patriotism and Duty," in *Jane Addams on Peace, War, and International Understanding 1899–1932,* 16.

18. Addams, *Newer Ideals of Peace,* 221–22.

19. Jane Addams, "Democracy or Militarism," in *Jane Addams's Writings on Peace,* ed. Marilyn Fischer and Judy D. Whipps (Bristol, U.K.: Thoemmes Press, 2003), 1.

20. Addams, "The New Internationalism," 56.

21. Addams, *Newer Ideals of Peace,* 18.

22. Ibid., 14.

23. Jane Addams, *Twenty Years at Hull-House* (New York: New American Library, 1961), 217.

24. Addams, *Democracy and Social Ethics,* 14.

25. Addams, *Newer Ideals of Peace,* 14, 18.

26. Immanuel Kant, "Perpetual Peace," in *Kant's Political Writings,* ed. Hans Reiss (New York: Cambridge University Press, 1991), 105–6.

27. Nussbaum, "Patriotism and Cosmopolitanism," 15.

28. Addams, *Newer Ideals of Peace,* 29–30.

29. Thomas W. Pogge, "Cosmopolitanism and Sovereignty," *Ethics* 103 (October 1992): 48.

30. Addams, *Newer Ideals of Peace,* 76, 11–12.

31. Ibid., 15, 13, 236, 15.

32. Ibid., 40.

33. Ibid., 68, 151.

34. Ibid., 42, 68.

35. Ibid., 47–48.

36. Matthew Frye Jacobson, *Barbarian Virtues: The United States Encounters Foreign Peoples at Home and Abroad, 1876–1917* (New York: Hill and Wang, 2000), 226; Jonathan M. Hansen, *The Lost Promise of Patriotism: Debating American Identity, 1890–1920* (Chicago: University of Chicago Press, 2003), 22–23.

37. Jane Addams, "Address of Miss Jane Addams," in *Jane Addams on Peace, War, and International Understanding 1899–1932,* 45.

38. Ibid.; Addams, *Newer Ideals of Peace,* 220.

39. Jane Addams, "Address of Miss Jane Addams," 46.

40. Ibid., 45.

41. Jean Bethke Elshtain, ed., *The Jane Addams Reader* (New York: Basic Books, 2002), 249.

42. Addams, *The Long Road of Woman's Memory,* 63.

43. Jean Bethke Elshtain, *Women and War* (New York: Basic Books, 1987), 234; Elshtain, *Jane Addams and the Dream of American Democracy,* 237.

44. Ibid., 240–44; Elshtain, ed., *The Jane Addams Reader,* 250.

45. Elshtain, *Jane Addams and the Dream of American Democracy,* 244.

46. Jane Addams, "Women and Internationalism," in *Women at The Hague* (New York: Macmillan Company, 1915), 127–28.

47. Jane Addams, *Peace and Bread in Time of War* (New York: King's Crown Press, 1945), 75–76.

48. Addams, *The Long Road of Woman's Memory,* 61.

49. Ibid., 63.

50. Addams, *Peace and Bread in Time of War,* 77, 205.

51. Addams, *The Long Road of Woman's Memory,* 56.

52. Addams, *Peace and Bread in Time of War,* 78, 77, 82, 87.

53. Ibid., 80, 85.

54. Ibid., 84, 209–10.

55. Addams, *The Long Road of Woman's Memory,* 62; Addams, *Peace and Bread in Time of War,* 79–80, 81.

56. Jane Addams, "The Corn Mother," in *Jane Addams on Peace, War, and International Understanding 1899–1932,* 158.

57. Jane Addams, Emily Balch, and Alice Hamilton, *Women at The Hague,* 154, 157.

58. Addams, *Peace and Bread in Time of War,* 80.

59. Addams, *Democracy and Social Ethics,* 50.

60. Dolores Hayden, *The Grand Domestic Revolution: A History of Feminist Designs for American Homes, Neighborhoods, and Cities* (Cambridge, Mass.: MIT Press, 1981), 5.

61. Addams, *Democracy and Social Ethics,* chapters 2, 3; Hayden, *The Grand Domestic Revolution,* 170–71.

62. Addams, *Peace and Bread in Time of War,* 81–82.

63. Addams, "The Corn Mother," 157.

64. Addams, *Peace and Bread in Time of War,* 205.

65. Addams, *Twenty Years at Hull-House,* 102–3.

66. Addams, "The Corn Mother," 157–58.

67. Addams, *Newer Ideals of Peace,* 18.

68. T. H. Marshall, "Citizenship and Social Class," in *Class, Citizenship, and Social Development: Essays by T.H. Marshall* (New York: Doubleday & Co, 1965).

69. Addams, *Peace and Bread in Time of War,* 83.

70. Addams, *Newer Ideals of Peace,* 236.

71. Derek Heater, *Citizenship: The Civic Ideal in World History, Politics, and Education* (London: Longmans, 1990), 272–76.

72. Jane Addams, *The Second Twenty Years at Hull-House: With a Record of a Growing World Consciousness* (New York: Macmillan Company, 1930), 174.

73. Addams, "Women and Internationalism," 126.

74. Held, *Democracy and the Global Order,* 234; Pogge, "Cosmopolitanism and Sovereignty"; Jana Thompson, "Community Identity and World Citizenship," in *Re-imagining Political Community,* 179–97.

75. Nussbaum, "Patriotism and Cosmopolitanism," 9.

76. Addams, *Peace and Bread in Time of War,* 201, 89.

77. Held, *Democracy and the Global Order,* 22–23.

78. Andrew Linklater, "Citizenship and Sovereignty in the Post-Westphalian European State," in *Re-imagining Political Community,* 124–29.

79. Jane Addams, "Nationalism, a Dogma?" *The Survey* 43 (February 7, 1920): 526.

80. Addams, *Peace and Bread in Time of War,* 217.

81. Joan C. Tronto, "Beyond Gender Difference to a Theory of Care," *Signs: Journal of Women in Culture and Society* 12 (1987): 649.

82. Addams, *Democracy and Social Ethics,* 14.

83. Leila J. Rupp, *Worlds of Women: The Making of an International Women's Movement* (Princeton, N.J.: Princeton University Press, 1997), 119.

10

Can Jane Addams Serve as a Role Model for Us Today?

HARRIET HYMAN ALONSO

In January 2002, I began a quest to see if I could find in Jane Addams a role model for peace-minded people (including myself) in these confusing times following the attacks on the World Trade Center and the unleashing of the U.S. military on the Middle East. I was particularly interested in finding a historical voice that could help me bring hope to my distressed students. My journey began when I was asked to present a paper on Addams and peace at the February 2002 Jane Addams symposium held at Swarthmore College. Because of the close proximity of my workplace to the World Trade Center and the trauma that ensued, I felt a deep need to connect September 11 to that paper, which I did by discussing the "Reverberations of the 1915 Hague Conference on 2002." That exercise led me to intensive reading.

From January 2002 to May 2003, I read almost every one of Addams's books (in print or not), four biographies, and innumerable speeches and articles on peace.[1] Yet, less than two weeks before presenting a second paper on the topic at another Jane Addams symposium (this time at the University of Dayton, Ohio), I could not formulate any thoughts on the relevancy of her ideas to today's world. My problem was that I was trying to fit Addams into the pigeonhole of heroism rather than really evaluating her thoughts objectively—if that is possible for a women's peace historian who has been studying Addams for more than twenty years and who considers her one of the most radical feminist pacifists of all time. Eventually, I wrote that paper—and then this article. However, I still find myself thinking about Addams each time U.S. foreign policy takes a new twist or turn.

My first task in trying to evaluate Addams's credentials as a twenty-first-century role model was to look at her road to pacifism. Was it an exemplary journey with no contradictions or did Addams have to do a great deal of soul searching? For example, much has been written about Addams's father and her close identification with him. At first, biographers presented him as Addams did in her writings—as a Quaker; more recently, biographers have discovered that he was not a Quaker at all but more of a Quaker-sympathizer.[2] This seemingly minor fact has confused many a historian regarding Jane Addams's own identity. How important did she consider having a Quaker heritage (no matter how quasi) to her pacifist image? Apparently, it was quite important, but even more so was the fact that John Addams was a good humanitarian, a man who was passionately against slavery (and therefore a social-justice man). However, much to many a peace activist's chagrin, he funded a regiment to fight in the Civil War, an action his daughter later related in the most admirable terms. As a young woman, she also enjoyed the military parades and exercises she witnessed during her two European jaunts and appeared to have great interest in visiting U.S. battlefields and war memorials.

At first, this portrayal of John and Jane Addams's interest in the physical symbols of war seems puzzling and even disconcerting when seeking out a role model for peace. Does this mean that neither of them had a true pacifist bent, but rather that Jane used that image later in life in some way to explain and legitimize her pacifist actions? Not necessarily. Because of my ten years spent working on the family history of the abolitionist leader and war resister William Lloyd Garrison, I have a different, and I believe more complex, reading of this fascination with militarism, one that I think points in a positive direction.[3] Jane Addams (like many children born somewhere between the mid-1830s and 1865 who had antislavery activist parents) can be categorized as an "abolitionist child." What this means is that, even though she was born in 1860 and obviously not able to actually recollect the war, her father most likely explained the necessity of this particular "just" war to end slavery. Many abolitionist children found themselves either joining the Union army or refusing to do so on the moral ground of being nonresisters or conscientious objectors, but even these folk supported those who resorted to military violence. (In the Garrison family, for example, son George fought with a Massachusetts regiment, while two of his brothers, William and Wendell, took a nonresister position. The family as a whole, however, stood by George.)

In general, those abolitionist children who did not join the fighting had no qualms about donating money for uniforms or cheering as the troops drilled in such places as the Boston Common or marched through the streets on their way to the South. For the rest of their lives, the Garrisons (and others, including

Jane Addams) who were in on the founding of the Anti-Imperialist League in 1898 and innumerable other peace efforts also enjoyed watching public displays of militarism, that is, until the outbreak of World War I, the same conflict that turned Jane Addams into a radical pacifist. I feel comfortable slotting Addams into this category of being an abolitionist child, although I am still perplexed and somewhat troubled by that group's seemingly contradictory behavior vis-à-vis nonviolence versus the military establishment.

With this knowledge of the mindset of that generation, I could at least put aside my own desire for a pure role model created from a nonviolent gene pool and consider, instead, Addams's growth as a pacifist. Because she was not a Quaker and she was affected by the contradictions of the abolitionists, I came to understand that the greatest influences upon her growth into a pacifist rested with her education and her life and work experiences. Addams's creation and leadership of Hull-House, of course, defined her entire adult life.[4] Once ensconced at the settlement, however, she began to shape her beliefs concerning peaceful coexistence, conflict resolution, and the possibilities of using the lessons the Hull-House neighborhood and residents taught her in developing methods for educating people for peace—whether through actions, public programs, lectures, writing, or by example. Let us look at just a few of the peace ideas that came out of Hull-House and reflect on their progress over the past century and their possible relevance today. My comments come primarily from Addams's *Newer Ideals of Peace* (1907), *Women at The Hague: The International Congress of Women and Its Results* (1915), and *The Second Twenty Years at Hull-House* (1930).[5]

Most important was that Addams saw firsthand that people of different backgrounds could live and work together in relative peace—at least outwardly. (With all of her exposure to folks in the Hull-House neighborhood, Addams still could not have witnessed the more private forms of racism that pervaded their and our lives—the snide remarks made among friends about other coworkers, the off-hand racial slurs passed along with the salt at the dinner table, the rules set down at home against cross-cultural or interracial dating, and the great fear of a marriage or children resulting from that union.) Why, she wondered, could not this great example of coexistence serve as a lesson to those men who held power over foreign policy? In an effort to help the world reach the same stage as she perceived the Hull-House community to be in, she began her own search for what she termed "a moral substitute for war."

Newer Ideals of Peace, written in 1907, came on the heels of Addams's involvement in the Anti-Imperialist League founded in 1898 in response to the

Spanish-American War. One of the concerns of the more conservative members of the league was that the colonization of the Philippines, Guam, Puerto Rico, and, in effect, Cuba, would lead to massive immigration of people of color into the United States. Addams, whose Hull-House work revolved around an immigrant population (largely Italian, Irish, Greek, and Mexican), was acutely aware of the fears of racist labor, business, and political leaders.

The book reflects Addams's thoughts on the relationship between a multi-ethnic urban industrial workforce and peaceful coexistence. It consists of "studies in the gradual development of the moral substitutes for war [that] have been made in the industrial quarter of a cosmopolitan city where the morality exhibits marked social and international aspects."[6] Workers who lived and labored in close proximity apparently learned to depend upon each other—even to like and understand each other. This intimacy broke down the barriers of nationalism, language isolation, religion, and cultural differences that were so strong outside the city or the U.S. border. Once the city dwellers overcame their hostility and shyness, they formed a mini-nationless state, if you will, almost a utopia of foreign relations. As Addams stated, this would lead to a natural abhorrence of war, "because we shall find it as difficult to make war upon a nation at the other side of the globe as upon our next-door neighbor."[7] So, if nations could establish Hull-House type centers or ensure that all workplaces represented a cross-section of the world, war would disappear.

In addition, *Newer Ideals of Peace* proposes that the military-like structures in society be altered so that police, for instance, would need to be trained in conflict resolution and be rid of their punitive style of behavior as well as their guns. Indeed, local governments in general should be made to address the needs of the people so that poverty could be eliminated and democracy be put into practice. Peace depended upon the elimination of repression, a condition that could only be reached when all people had the education and material needs to be able to participate. For Addams, the immigrants in the Hull-House neighborhood most needed the government to address their social and economic needs, not to act as a bullying big brother.

Before continuing, because I am trying to see if Addams can serve as our guide through these troubling times, I would like to reflect a bit on my own neighborhood in mid-2008. I live in an area of Brooklyn, New York, that attracts new immigrant populations every time foreign affairs result in the need for people to leave their native lands for a more just, richer place. When I first moved here more than thirty years ago, there was a mixture of Jewish, Italian, African American, and Puerto Rican people who had been in the country (and the neighborhood) for years, even generations. Soon came Koreans, then Haitians, then Russians, then Iranians (mostly Jewish), then Hasidic Jews (a number of them from Canada), then Pakistanis, then Mexicans and Central Americans, and, very recently, white yuppies seeking affordable housing. As new groups moved in, a number, but not all, of the others left, so that now the neighborhood is a wonderful hodgepodge of people. We all walk the same streets, frequent the same supermarkets, and the majority send our children to the same public schools.

Yet, for the most part, we have all remained separate. The neighborhood is peaceful, yet contradictory. I have seen Hasidic young men in friendly conversation with their Pakistani neighbors, and I have also seen pro-Israeli, anti-Palestinian posters alongside notices for events at the local mosque. After September 11, the police (or perhaps the feds) put up surveillance cameras on many of the local streets, and a Hasidic vigilante group attempted to form armed patrols, an effort the police (thankfully) squashed. In November 2002, there were protests on nearby Coney Island Avenue (which I affectionately call the CIA) because Pakistanis in the area were being systematically arrested and deported. The following summer, several newspapers reported a decline in the number of Pakistani businesses in the area because of these deportations. Left behind are women, many with children, abruptly thrown on welfare or dependence on family members who are themselves financially strapped. On occasional days, when the federal government fuels rumors of terrorism, I fear that the neighborhood will experience some expression of violence.

So, I ask myself, what of Jane Addams's vision is present or missing from this picture? My neighborhood is not an industrial area where people work side-by-side in factories, but is instead a very mixed residential area with many small businesses. Yet, people generally have stuck "to their own kind." Did that happen in the Hull-House neighborhood as well? Like today, did people tend to frequent the smaller shops owned by landsmen? Did they perhaps smile at their "different" neighbors but not engage them? Although idealistic, Addams was also very cognizant of the issue I just raised. As she noted in *Newer Ideals,* "Chicago is preëminently a city of mixed nationalities. It is our problem to learn to live together in forbearance and understanding and to fuse all the nations of men into the newest and, perhaps, the highest type of citizenship. To accept this responsibility may constitute our finest contribution to the problems of American life but we may also wantonly and easily throw away such an opportunity by the stirring up of race and national animosity which is so easily aroused and so reluctantly subsides."[8]

How, I ask myself, do you "fuse" people who simply do not want to be fused? One possible route is through education. Hull-House created many educational experiences—reading groups, the labor museum, English classes, craft and homemaking classes, cultural and social events, lectures, and a kindergarten. My neighborhood has one main center for true intermingling, and that is P.S. 217, a local elementary school that until the war in Iraq began had named itself the "peace" school and sported a peace symbol above its main entrance. Even though the visible sign of its mission of global peace has been removed, the school still features multicultural activities and fosters the principles of conflict resolution.

Perhaps the most idealistic message to emerge from *Newer Ideals of Peace* is that war is old hat, that even militarists of the day could only justify it by "reminding us of its ancient origin."[9] Although Addams remained acutely aware of the growth of U.S. imperialism during this period, she also wrote in 1907 that war "is gradually becoming impossible . . . because great constructive plans and humanized interests have captured our hopes and we are finding that war is an implement too clumsy and barbaric to subserve our purpose. We have come to realize that the great task of pushing forward social justice could be enormously accelerated if primitive methods as well as primitive weapons were once and for all abolished."[10]

Addams's hope was that "human constructive labor" would make militarism extinct in colonized nations and "give the newly invaded country a sense of its place in the life of the civilized world."[11] If one substituted the newer ideals of peace and constructive work for those of warfare and military occupation, colonized people would respond positively to their situation and develop their nations into "civilized" places. Only "the unrestricted commercial spirit" could put a damper on this movement away from war.[12] Otherwise, the world would see that "under an enlightened industrialism peace would no longer be an absence of war, but the unfolding of worldwide processes making for the nurture of human life."[13] Industry plus progress plus working for the public good equals the end of the need for war. Greed was the only obstacle, and time and again, greed has won out. Today we see this all too clearly, especially in our nation's involvement in the Middle East.

Thinking about the Middle East takes me back to thoughts about September 11, for it was the events on this day that unleashed the furor of current U.S. greed mongers who have used the tragedy for personal gain. At 8:45 A.M. on that morning, I was preparing to leave Brooklyn for my job as dean of the Center for Worker Education of the City College of New York, which at that time was located just eight blocks from the twin towers. In my role, I became responsible for pulling together more than one thousand students, faculty, and staff members and reopening an educational center that was closed for two weeks. The innumerable ways in which our educational community was affected made me feel that, in some small sense, I had experienced something close to war. Hearing the traumatic stories from students who were in the area that morning, advising students who were afraid to return to the area or even to leave their homes, working in the neighborhood of "missing" posters, smelling the burning plastic and steel, and, most of all, seeing the vacant space in the sky and, ironically, the presence of more sunlight, filled my days for close to a year, the traditional period of mourning. During that time, I reread the 1915 publication of *Women at The Hague: The International Congress of Women and its Results* by Jane Addams, Emily Greene Balch, and Alice Hamilton and was surprised by the new lens through which the material appeared.[14]

For those readers not familiar with the Hague conference, let me provide just a bit of background. In the years previous to the 1914 outbreak of war in Europe, suffragists from several nations met yearly to discuss the strategies and tactics of organizing for the vote and to build their feminist networks. Hence, when war erupted, the women reached out to each other for ideas about possible action to bring the warring parties to the mediation table. In April 1915, these suffragists decided to hold their meeting in The Hague and to set the agenda for a discussion of peace rather than only on the vote. The meeting, organized chiefly by Aletta Jacobs, a physician and president of the Dutch suffrage organization, and Chrystal Macmillan, a Scottish lawyer and secretary of the International Woman Suffrage Alliance, was attended by 1,136 delegates from twelve nations.

The conference combined the issues of peace and women's rights and resulted in the formation of two delegations assigned to visit European leaders in an effort to promote mediation. Jane Addams, with Alice Hamilton as an unofficial delegate, joined Aletta Jacobs and Rosa Genoni of Italy to meet with leaders of England, Germany, Austria-Hungary, Italy, France, Belgium, the Netherlands, and Switzerland. Emily Greene Balch joined Chrystal Macmillan, Rosika Schwimmer of Austria-Hungary, and Cor Ramondt-Hirsch of the Netherlands to visit Denmark, Norway, Sweden, Russia, and the Netherlands. From May to August, the two groups paid a total of thirty-five visits to leaders in both neutral and belligerent nations, asking each directly if he would like to see the war mediated, ended, or both.

As a result of the congress and the visits, Addams, Balch, and Hamilton wrote various journalistic articles that were later put together as the book *Women at The Hague.* Sensitive about the "slight material" in the volume, the three women justified their approach by pointing out that "widespread interest" in the articles seemed to demand such a publication, one that was "a report of European conditions from the point of view of that peace sentiment which survives in the midst of every war, but which is not easily uncovered."[15] A small-sized book of approximately 170 pages, the text consists of seven chapters (three by Addams, three by Balch, and one by Hamilton) and three appendices including the resolutions adopted by the congress and Julia Grace Wales's now well-known proposal on "Continuous Mediation without Armistice." A quick and entertaining read, the book presents ideas and examples of life during war that resonate today.

Addams's first chapter was entitled "The Revolt Against War." Just as today we search for people's true feelings about the major powers' wars in Afghanistan and Iraq in the name of ending terrorism, so did Addams try to give the events of 1914 and 1915 "some human interpretation" of the "overevolved and much-talked-of situation in which so much of the world finds itself in dire confusion and bloodshed."[16] To do so, she sought out the voices of "certain young men" and "groups of civilians."[17] In her search, Addams came across a number of people and organizations that believed resolving conflicts violently was not the answer. In her description, she addressed a question with which we are currently confronted. If your nation is attacked and your country goes to war, do you, as a citizen, blindly accept the government's policy? If you do not fly a flag from every car and house window and do not have a "United We Stand" button pinned to your shirt, are you unpatriotic or, worse, a traitor? What happens if you disdain yellow ribbons or wear a "No War in Iraq" button? How many people feel compelled to say, "I support the troops," when, in fact, they abhor the military and its barbaric behavior in the Middle East?

Addams felt hopeful in her discovery that in every country she visited, there were people "quite as eager for the retention and development of their national ideals and quite as patriotic as the militarists, but believing with all their hearts that militarism cannot establish those causes which are most dear to them."[18] However, she also found well-meaning people in each country who felt that their nation was reacting in self-defense, and not just in defense of land but in defense of "its traditions and ideals from those who would come in to disturb and destroy them."[19] These people would not normally seek a violent resolution to problems, but in 1915, they felt they had no choice but to support their governmental leaders.

Addams met many young men who saw their world as much more international than that of their fathers. As a result, they questioned the use of war, just as many young people here protested and questioned the Bush administration's haste to punish two legitimate nations for the actions of a nonnational group. Although there were numbers of older peace activists then and now, the reins of power have rested in the older generation's hands. As one Cambridge University student wrote in 1914, "The greatest trial that this war has brought is that it has released the old men from all restraining influences, and has let them loose upon the world. The city editors, the retired majors, the amazons, and last, but I fear, not least, the venerable archdeacons, have never been so free from contradiction."[20]

For those of us who protested the Vietnam War, the use of the contras against Nicaragua, the continuing blockade against Cuba, and then moved on to Panama, Bosnia, Somalia, and Iraq, it is clear that many of the younger generation do not wish to run off to join the military. To try to avoid instituting a draft, our government at first resorted to "hit and run" types of warfare, where ground troops were unnecessary, at least for long periods of time. In today's Iraq, the U.S. government has resorted to calling in the National Guard, the majority of whose members never seriously considered the possibility of being sent overseas and are not happy about their situation. Jane Addams recognized that by 1914 "there has grown up a generation in Europe, as there has doubtless grown up a generation in America, who have revolted against war. It is a god they know not of, whom they are not willing to serve; because all of their sensibilities and their training upon which their highest ideas depend, revolt against it."[21] In Addams's time, this generation ended up fighting in two major global conflagrations. We do not yet know what will happen to our youth, but it is clear that the government still wishes to avoid reinstituting the draft.

One of our main concerns has been the effects of the terrorist attacks on our own way of life. Freedom of speech has certainly been curtailed. At City College, where I work, a teach-in held soon after the events of September 11 was blasted in the New York newspapers. Faculty and students were misquoted and misrepresented, and the chancellor of the City University made a statement (which he later retracted) that such members of the CUNY community who spoke out against revenge were ignorant and shameful and should be disciplined. I was asked by another dean to cancel a planned teach-in at our downtown location, which I refused to do, but our faculty and staff were intimidated enough to remove advertising from the Tribeca community and encouraged only our own students and faculty to attend. Addams had these same worries. "War itself destroys democracy wherever it thrives and tends to entrench militarism," she stated.[22] In addition, as she addressed in her chapter, "Factors in Continuing the War," the press deserved major blame for allowing democracy to deteriorate. As many of us have felt since September 11 when newspaper headlines screamed out for retaliation, so Addams felt about the irresponsibility of the press during World War I. "At moments," she wrote, "I found myself filled with a conviction that the next revolution against tyranny would have to be a revolution against the unscrupulous power of the press."[23]

Addams formed two conclusions about the press. First, by selecting to print only that information it chose, rather than to provide varying points of view, the press prevented people of the fighting nations from getting a true picture of what was going on and therefore from making an informed opinion about it. She compared this power of the press to "the power once exercised by the church" in bygone days.[24] Second, Addams felt that "leading minds" themselves were prohibited from thinking creatively about possible solutions to the war because they, too, relied upon the press for information, and much of it was confused and limited.[25] As we too know, even an all-news station such as CNN has consistently presented limited information. After September 11, with the government's allowance of reporting only certain details about military actions in Afghanistan and Iraq, we frequently had to depend upon what appeared to be computer graphics out of a space film to try to see what actions the military took. During the current occupation of Iraq, we see either insane- and angry-looking Iraqis or friendly, children-loving U.S. soldiers—usually men. (Images of women in combat often involve torture as in Abu Ghraib or injuries hinting at female vulnerability. But that is another issue.)

As Addams claimed, the withholding of information by the press inhibits the formation of an honest, well-informed, collective public opinion and acts to prolong violence. Furthermore, the more that the public sees or hears about possible violent threats from a so-called enemy, the less likely it is to seek nonviolent solutions to a conflict. The media's constant stories on bio-terrorism, possible attacks on various holidays, and never-ending stories about airport security have kept in our minds the frightening possibilities of another terrorist attack. Their stories of young children attending fundamentalist Muslim schools that supposedly train them to hate all Americans, their pictures of scrappy-looking Afghanis and Iraqis, their continued use of Osama bin Laden and references to Saddam Hussein as the models for Satan, and their insincere outrage for the treatment of women under Taliban rule fueled the hatred so necessary to carry out a foreign policy not necessarily related to the September 11 attacks.

Concern for women, especially during a time of war, inspired the participants of the congress at The Hague to combine their call for peace with a demand for equal citizenship for women. Citizenship did not mean only the right to vote; it meant equal participation of women in all political life, including the peace settlement to be made after the war ended. In the resolutions issued, the women also protested "vehemently against the odious wrongs of which women are the victims in time of war, and especially against the horrible violation of women which attends all war."[26] The violations Addams and the other women referred to included rape, economic distress when breadwinners were killed, displacement from homes and jobs, the loss of children either as soldiers or collateral damage of war, psychological trauma, and physical harm. We all can identify with these concerns. Certainly, rape was highlighted as a crime against the women of Bosnia, as was the terrible repression of the women of Afghanistan and the displacement of women and children from their homes into refugee camps in numerous war-torn countries.

In her chapter "Women and Internationalism," Addams echoes the feelings of many women peace activists today. For example, of the women who traveled through war-torn Europe, sometimes against the wishes of their nations and their families, Addams stated that they "must have been impelled by some profound and spiritual forces. During a year when the spirit of internationalism had apparently broken down, they came together to declare the validity of the internationalism which surrounds and completes national life, even as national life itself surrounds and completes family life; to insist that internationalism does not conflict with patriotism on one side any more than family devotion conflicts with it upon the other."[27]

World War I was the war that sharpened Addams's ideas about peace and also solidified her developing view that women experience war differently than men and have a unique contribution to make to the discussion. In *The Second Twenty Years at Hull-House*, published in 1930, Addams relates her transformation into a global feminist pacifist, and it is here that I found some of her more profound and relevant ideas about peace. Most timely is her acknowledgment that she (and we) cannot ignore the globalization of the world, a phenomenon as exciting as it is challenging. "But whether we care for it or not," she wrote, "our own experiences are more and more influenced by the experiences of widely scattered people; the modern world is developing an almost mystic consciousness of the continuity and inter-dependence of mankind. There is a lively sense of the unexpected and yet inevitable action and reaction between ourselves and all the others who happen to be living upon the planet at the same moment."[28] This sense of connectedness was not really expressed until after Addams had attended several international congresses of the Women's International League for Peace and Freedom (WILPF—the global organization created in 1919 by the women peace activists who met in The Hague in 1915) and traveled around the world on WILPF's behalf. Before that, her connectedness basically included the United States and Europe.

As before, after World War I Addams maintained her position that "peace was not merely an absence of war, but the nurture of human life."[29] Only the elimination of poverty, disease, hunger, and ignorance can provide the environment in which peace will survive, and women, predominantly, can foster this agenda—particularly younger women. Addams observed that in China in the 1920s, older women still encouraged foot binding and in India, purdah and veils. Younger women fought against these practices because they saw them as cruel and repressive, not as representing some great traditional cultural values. Many young women then and today as well bridge both worlds—a return to traditional cultural values while still embracing women's rights.

Certainly, Addams's work in fostering WILPF has had a positive effect on our world. Today, WILPF carries its ideas to the United Nations as an NGO (and Addams certainly supported the creation of the League of Nations and the World Court, hoping that more and more nations would form "the habit," as she put it, of using those institutions to mediate conflict).[30] Indeed, after sixty-two nations signed the Kellogg-Briand Pact in 1928, which pledged that they would negotiate before turning to violence, Addams and many others proclaimed that it was the most important measure to date to outlaw war and make it illegal as an international tool. "I firmly believe," she claimed, "that nothing else will prevail but this gradual moralization of our international relations. Quite as the truculent citizen no longer settles a quarrel with his neighbor by means of his fists but takes his case into court for logical adjustment, so the nations must learn gradually to substitute law for war."[31]

In her desire to see the success of some sort of peaceful international organization such as the League of Nations, Addams also supported an international police force. (The great suffrage leader, Carrie Chapman Catt, also supported this idea, especially after World War II.) I do not think that either of these women would have expected this to take the form of the U.N. peacekeeping force, which has little or no specific training in conflict resolution, or the U.N.-sanctioned forces we see more frequently these days, made up of the U.S. military and a few allies. I think Addams would have approved of a nonmilitary police force that used the skills of conflict resolution and negotiation, but I am not absolutely certain of this.

Before Addams died in 1935, the world was already heading into its next war, and the next, and the next. My darker side looks around glumly and says that peace will never exist in any form. Things are only getting worse and one day, we human beings will finally succeed in destroying ourselves. Then, my more positive voice kicks in. Look around you, it says, all these people in the world who are on the move, all these global travelers who leave one destination to seek a better life in another—they are making the world so much more heterogeneous. Although the people with power and greed in their hearts have embarked on a dangerous style of globalization, these traveling folk may become the bearers of a more peaceful, humane globalization.

As of the writing of this article, my neighborhood has not erupted into violence. In fact, recently I saw a Russian family in the Chinese restaurant and a Mexican neighbor in the corner Hasidic grocery store. The Greek coffee shop now has a Pakistani manager and the older Italian waitresses are still on the job. Most interesting is that the Pakistani-owned Dunkin Donuts, with its African American and Central American staff, has gone "kosher." Are people beginning to "fuse"?[32] Are we on our way to building a global neighborhood even if the initial steps all involve food, that great unifier of people? As Addams concluded in 1915, "Out of the present situation, which certainly presents the spectacle of the breakdown of the whole philosophy of nationalism, political, racial, and cultural, may conceivably issue a new birth of internationalism, founded not so much upon arbitration treaties, to be used in time of disturbance, as upon governmental devices designed to protect and enhance the fruitful processes of cooperation in the great experiment of living together in a world become conscious of itself."[33] I think Jane Addams was on to something—and I, for one, plan to use her as a role model for myself and my students.

Acknowledgments

This work was supported (in part) by a grant from the City University of New York PSC-CUNY Research Award Program. I would also like to thank the participants of both the Swarthmore and Dayton conferences and Anne Marie Pois for their helpful and insightful comments.

Notes

1. That reading resulted in an extensive book review of thirteen new or reprinted volumes and one out-of-print book by and about Jane Addams. See Harriet Hyman Alonso, "Jane Addams: Thinking and Acting Locally and Globally," *Journal of Women's History* 16, no. 1 (Spring 2004): 147–63.

2. The four biographies I relied upon were: Victoria Bissell Brown, *The Education of Jane Addams: From Heroine to Democrat in the Gilded Age* (Philadelphia: University of Pennsylvania Press, 2003); Allen F. Davis, *American Heroine: The Life and Legend of Jane Addams* (1973; reprint, Chicago: Ivan R. Dee, 2000); Jean Bethke Elshtain, *Jane Addams and the Dream of American Democracy: A Life* (New York: Basic Books, 2002), and James Weber Linn, *Jane Addams: A Biography* (1935; reprint, Urbana: University of Illinois Press, 2000).

3. See Harriet Hyman Alonso, *Growing Up Abolitionist: The Story of the Garrison Children* (Amherst: University of Massachusetts Press, 2002).

4. I always like to hyphenate Hull-House as this is true to the way Jane Addams referred to it.

5. See Jane Addams, *Newer Ideals of Peace* (Chautauqua, N.Y.: The Chautauqua Press, 1907); Jane Addams, Emily Greene Balch, and Alice Hamilton, *Women at The Hague: The International Congress of Women and Its Results* (New York: Macmillan Company, 1915); and *Jane Addams, The Second Twenty Years at Hull-House, September 1909 to September 1929,* (New York: Macmillan Company, 1930).

6. *Newer Ideals of Peace,* vii. For an extended analysis of *Newer Ideals of Peace,* see Marilyn Fischer, "The Conceptual Scaffolding of *Newer Ideals of Peace,*" in this volume, and Berenice A. Carroll and Clinton F. Fink's excellent introduction in the 2007 reprint from the University of Illinois Press.

7. *Newer Ideals of Peace,* 19.

8. Ibid., 141.

9. Ibid., 210.

10. Ibid., 212.

11. Ibid., 220.

12. Ibid., 229.

13. Ibid., 238.

14. In 2003, this book was reprinted by the University of Illinois Press. I wrote the new introduction for the reprint, which is why I happened to be reading it at the time.

15. Addams, Balch, and Hamilton, *Women at The Hague,* v.

16. Ibid., 56.

17. Ibid., 55.

18. Ibid., 57.

19. Ibid., 58.

20. Ibid., 67.

21. Ibid., 69.

22. Ibid., 77.

23. Ibid., 91.

24. Ibid., 92.

25. Ibid.

26. Ibid., 150.

27. Ibid., 125–26.

28. Addams, *The Second Twenty Years at Hull-House*, 7.

29. Ibid., 35.

30. Ibid., 117.

31. Davis, *American Heroine*, 217.

32. For discussions of Addams, food, peace, and transnational connections, see Wendy Sarvasy, "A Global 'Common Table': Jane Addams's Theory of Democratic Cosmopolitanism and World Social Citizenship" in this volume.

33. Addams, Balch, and Hamilton, *Women at The Hague*, 141.

Contributors

HARRIET HYMAN ALONSO is professor of history at the City College of New York and the CUNY Graduate Center. She is the author of *Peace as a Women's Issue: A History of the U.S. Movement for World Peace and Women's Rights* (1993); *Growing Up Abolitionist: The Story of the Garrison Children* (2002); and *Robert E. Sherwood: The Playwright in Peace and War* (2007). She wrote the introduction for the new reprint edition of *Women at The Hague* (2003), published by the University of Illinois Press.

VICTORIA BISSELL BROWN is L. F. Parker Professor of History at Grinnell College, Iowa, where she teaches U.S. women's history and U.S. immigration history. She is the author of *The Education of Jane Addams* (2004) and *Going to the Source: The Bedford Reader in American History* (2004). She edited and wrote the introduction for the Bedford Books edition of *Twenty Years at Hull-House: With Autobiographical Notes,* by Jane Addams (1999). Brown has served as book review editor for the *Journal of the Gilded Age and Progressive Era* and the Women and Social Movements Web site.

WENDY CHMIELEWSKI is a historian and the George Cooley Curator of the Swarthmore College Peace Collection. The Peace Collection holds the largest collection of Jane Addams's papers and other material related to Addams and her work for peace. Chmielewski has published several scholarly articles on women and peace in the nineteenth and twentieth centuries.

MARILYN FISCHER is professor of philosophy at the University of Dayton. She is the author of *Ethical Decision-Making in Fund Raising* (2000), *On Addams*

(2004), and coeditor of the four-volume set *Jane Addams's Writings on Peace* (2003). She is currently writing a book on Addams's internationalism.

SHANNON JACKSON is professor of rhetoric and professor and chair of theater, dance, and performance studies at the University of California, Berkeley. She is the author of *Lines of Activity: Performance, Historiography, Hull-House Domesticity* (2000) and *Professing Performance: Theatre in the Academy from Philology to Performativity* (2004). She is currently at work on a new book entitled *Social Works: The Infrastructural Politics of Performance.*

LOUISE W. KNIGHT is an independent scholar and adjunct professor of communication studies at Northwestern University. She is the author of *Citizen: Jane Addams and the Struggle for Democracy* (2005).

CAROL NACKENOFF is Richter Professor of Political Science at Swarthmore College, where she teaches American politics and constitutional law. She is the author of *The Fictional Republic: Horatio Alger and American Political Discourse* (1994). She is working on a book examining the contested meaning of citizenship in the U.S. Progressive Era.

KAREN PASTORELLO is associate professor of history and chair of the Women and Gender Studies Program at Tompkins Cortland Community College in Dryden, New York. She is the author of *A Power among Them: Bessie Abramowitz Hillman and the Making of the Amalgamated Clothing Workers of America* (2008).

WENDY SARVASY is a member of the Political Science Department at California State University, East Bay. Her publications include articles on John Stuart Mill's political thought, the feminization of poverty, post-suffrage feminism, and social and global citizenship. She is finishing a book on democratic social politics and feminist theorizing from activism.

CHARLENE HADDOCK SEIGFRIED is professor of philosophy and American studies at Purdue University. She is the author of *Pragmatism and Feminism* (1996), editor of *Feminist Interpretations of John Dewey* (2002), and author of two books on William James. She also wrote the introductions to the reprint editions of *Democracy and Social Ethics* and *The Long Road of Woman's Memory* (2002). She is currently working on a book on Jane Addams's social philosophy.

CAMILLA STIVERS is professor and distinguished scholar of public administration emerita at Levin College of Urban Affairs, Cleveland State University. She is the author of *Bureau Men, Settlement Women: Constructing Public Administration in the Progressive Era* (2000); *Gender Images in Public Administration* (2002); and *Governance in Dark Times: Practical Philosophy for Public Service* (2008).

Index

The University of Illinois Press
is a founding member of the
Association of American University Presses.

University of Illinois Press
1325 South Oak Street
Champaign, IL 61820-6903
www.press.uillinois.edu